D0629545

BOOKS ON BUDDHISM:

An Annotated Subject Guide

by

YUSHIN YOO

With a Foreword by
Edwin C. Strohecker

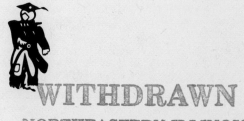

The Scarecrow Press, Inc.

Metuchen, N.J.   1976

Yoo is also the author of Buddhism: A Subject Index to Periodical Articles in English,
1728-1971 (The Scarecrow Press, 1973)

Library of Congress Cataloging in Publication Data

Yoo, Yushin.
    Books on Buddhism.

    Includes index.
    1. Buddhism--Bibliography. I. Title.
Z7860.Y64 [BQ4012]   016.2943   76-2706
ISBN 0-8108-0913-3

To Maura
and Virginia Strohecker

FOREWORD

Whenever one develops an interest in a specific phase of a subject but finds it difficult to trace because of its lack of control there is need for a bibliography. Of course, the need for such a published work is not always combined with the factor of urgency, but when this need-urgency syndrome is evident, the desired publication occurs.

One of the great religions of the world, Buddhism is an integral part of the history, life and philosophy of Asian countries. Through the centuries, this living culture has had an influential appeal among the intellectuals of the Western World. Today, it has been not only the emigration of Asians to Europe and America that has increased the popularity of the study of Buddhism: it is the Buddhistic teaching of a sense of security and a feeling of hope--obfuscated by our technological age--that has attracted the general reader. The reaching out toward humanity, the developing of bonds of brotherhood and the searching for the simplicity of life, which are expressed in Buddhism, help in cultivating the character of a responsible being.

During the past fifty years the library researcher has had the use of the Bibliographie bouddhique and the Bibliography of Buddhism (which emphasizes the Oriental publications). But, not until 1973 did there appear a reference tool of English language sources which provided an up-to-date supplement to these earlier bibliographies. This was Yushin Yoo's Buddhism: A Subject Index to Periodical Articles in English, 1728-1971 (Scarecrow Press, 1973). His present compilation, Books on Buddhism, provides a complement to his former work. A conveniently organized book, it is arranged in the same manner as his former bibliography, with additional headings that include Fiction, Juvenile Literature, and Parables.

According to Kenko, the 14th-century Japanese Buddhist:

"Too many books in a bookcase there can never be." Dr.
Yoo has provided the researcher with a much needed bibliographical tool.

Edwin C. Strohecker
Professor and Director of
Libraries

Murray State University
Murray, Kentucky
June, 1975

TABLE OF CONTENTS

PREFACE

Items cited in this bibliography are in the English language. In an attempt at complete representation of available English literature, some non-recommended titles have been included. The works listed herein are the earliest available through those published in 1973.

All the area and country studies were listed under Missions by the specific country name (see Table of Contents).

The "General References" section includes extensive and comprehensive bibliographies with further study information, condensed bibliographies, and bibliographies arranged on some special plan to facilitate the ready and accurate finding of information. The "General Surveys" section lists titles that present basically introductory notes on Buddhism.

Under the "Sermons" section most titles are related to Buddha's preaching or seem to serve as good preaching aids. The section on "Study and Teaching" tries to list all the titles intended to supply teaching ideas or hints on how to study Buddhism.

I wish to express my appreciation to Professor Stewart E. Fraser, Professor Jack Conrad Willers, and Professor Edwin Gleaves for their guidance and encouragement.

I am especially grateful to Professor Frances Neel Cheney who reviewed this work word by word and gave me so many valuable suggestions and corrections, even though at a hardship to herself.

I would also like to thank Dr. Edwin Strohecker, Director of the Libraries and Chairman of the Library Science Department, Murray State University, for giving me special leave as well as for all the other privileges granted to encourage my study.

Finally, I am grateful to my wife for her typing and support.

Yushin Yoo, Ph. D.
Assistant Professor

Murray State University
Murray, Kentucky
May, 1975

INTRODUCTION

Buddhism is a religion as well as a philosophy. It grew out of the teaching of Gautama Buddha that suffering is inherent in life and that one can be liberated from it by spiritual enlightenment. As it spread around the world as such, it began to influence humans' philosophies of life, the social structure, and their whole culture.

Gautama Buddha, who was a self-perfected man, one who had achieved the mind's enlightenment, is the historic founder of Buddhism. Details of his life were not written down earlier than 236 years after his death. Since then they are preserved variously in the Pali, Sanskrit, Chinese, and Tibetan writings of Buddha's philosophy and life.

Buddhism is a 3000-year-old religion and one of the most comprehensive and profound spiritual achievements in human history. In its earliest form it included the finest moral philosophy known to mankind, and concerned itself with mind development and pioneer philosophy, psychology, mysticism, metaphysics, magic, ritual, morality and culture. In every country it exalted the indigenous culture, and it produced the greatest culture of China, Japan, Tibet, Thailand, and Korea, i.e., the art of the Tang Dynasty of China, the greatest art of the Saiko period in Japan, the period of King Asoka in India, and the Silla Dynasty of Korea. Throughout the East it has set a standard of tolerance and love of nature. These cultures are altogether beautiful; Buddhism is an integral part of their libraries, gardens, anecdotes, tales and romances of various sorts. The construction of Buddhist temples and pagodas and the publication of scriptures came to be regarded as a symbol of protection for the state against enemy powers. Some countries absorbed the mythological elements while containing its philosophical and scientific dissertations. As a result, it became not merely a religion nor a system of philosophy, but also a culminating form of their countries' culture, embracing all fields of mythology, religion, literature, and the arts.

1

Buddhists show themselves to be profound humanists. Buddha said, "Under my teachings, brothers should respect each other and refrain from disputes; they should not repel each other like water and oil, but should mingle together like milk and water...." Buddhism is called the religion of peace because there has never been a Buddhist war, nor has any man at any time been persecuted by a Buddhist organization for his beliefs or the expression of them. Maha-Sudassana Sutta described the Buddhist by saying, "And he lets his mind pervade one quarter of the world with thoughts of love, with thoughts of compassion, with thoughts of understanding, joy and with thoughts of equanimity; and so the second quarter, and so the third, and so the fourth. And thus the whole wide world, above, below, around, and everywhere, does he continue to pervade with heart of love, compassion, joy, understanding, and equanimity, far-reaching, great, beyond measure, free from the least trace of anger or ill will."

Buddha taught humanity, brotherhood, gentleness, and the simple way of life. His task involved making a good person of a man or woman, developing their human nature, and cultivating their character. Later, cultivating one's character became one of the most important points of educational philosophy throughout Asian countries. Teaching good personality is seen to be as important as teaching language, art, literature, arithmetic, etc.

Buddhism always places emphasis on human affairs and the central idea of Buddha's teaching is humanism. All the other world religions are God-centered religions: we are subjects of God, we are created by Him, we are living according to His order, not by our will. Buddhism, however, is a human-centered religion, teaching that it is up to man to make himself better or worse.

There are two doctrines of cultivating human nature in Buddhism. One is a priori virtue, which assumes original good in the human character. The other one is a posteriori virtue, which refers to good acquired by cultivating one's character.

The principle of aprioristic virtue is the so-called "Buddha's character," or the august virtues that are within every human being (as well as every other living thing). The "becoming Buddha," or enlightened one, in Buddhism means one who has attained this Buddha's character.

The principle of a posteriori virtue is called "attained Buddha's character," which means the august virtues have been attained through cultivating one's character. In other words, in order to rediscover or to regain one's original Buddha's character, one must work hard to practice virtue. This could be illustrated as the gold within the mountain. Here the gold is the human's original august virtue, which is the Buddha's character, and the mountain is the human being or any living thing. In order to mine the gold so much hard work is required. After digging, not only on the surface, but also very deep into the mountain, finally one can see the real light of the gold.

This parable explains very well the meaning of the Buddhist philosophy of education. In order to find the inner gold of man which is the Buddha's character, it requires many processes and much hard work.

One may say that this theory of the inborn Buddha's character is a dogma. But Buddha himself went through many hardships before he finally attained the enlightenment and practiced virtue in his life. And later many of his followers also attained this Buddha's character through Buddha's teaching. Therefore this is not merely one man's prescription, or dogma, but it became the belief of many. The Buddha himself said, "Alas, why can man not see the most august wisdom which is in his mind. I must teach those, who can not see in their mind, to see the august wisdom which is Buddha's character." Also he said, "Those who have 'will' shall build up 'Anuttora, Samyak, and Sambodhi' which is Supreme Righteousness and Enlightenment. Therefore, I said unto you all living things are born with Buddha's character."

Everyone will doubt the gold in the mountain says the Buddhist tradition, until they go through the work to get to it. Therefore, the processes of a posteriori virtue (cultivating one's character) are very important as educational activities in most Asian countries.

Through self-discipline one can achieve the original aprioristic virtue or august virtue. Buddha's six years of discipline were to cultivate his character and then his works of the last 45 years were to cultivate other people's minds. This was his educational career. Everyone is born with august virtues, according to Buddha, but we see so many different classes of humans because they cultivate their characters to differing degrees.

Nothingness, selflessness, and self-denial are fundamental principles for the Buddhist. As a Buddhist one should
learn, in self-effacement or humility, that he is nothing.
This is the first requirement for all the Buddhists.

Buddha also mentioned that, as a follower of his, one
should not expect any kind of honor for his services. True
learning must be self-learning and the Buddhist as an enlightened one should overcome his individuality or should
achieve emancipation from ego. It might seem helpful to
give rewards for good services to the followers as morale
boosters. But for a Buddhist this kind of reward is second-
ary--or not necessary at all. The true rewards should come
from an inner desire to help other human beings to claim the
Buddha's character. Buddha gave us good examples in this
matter. After he taught his followers about the Buddha's
character, he used to disappear from the crowd. He did not
want a monument to his achievement, not even the honor of
having his way named for him, Buddhism.

Many teachings of Buddhism suggest strongly that a
Buddhist has great responsibility in social service. The individual Buddhist student should be concerned, of course, with
the fullest possible development of the whole person. But
from the social point of view, he is involved in the promo-
tion of understandings regarding the social relations in which
the growing person is found, in other words, his moral training, his attitude of cooperation, etc.

Buddha's emphasis on moral and social responsibility
within his philosophy of education was concerned with the development of a certain quality of person whose attitudes and
behaviors are inspired and controlled by moral and spiritual
ideas, and with a society in which are united justice and
brotherhood, right and responsibilities. Since personality is
primarily a social product, and society is composed of individual persons whose character collectively determines the
integrity of the group, these two important elements of Buddhist doctrine can not be separated. Neither exists without
the other.

According to Buddha, all the Buddhist teaching theory
must be based upon the Four Noble Truths and the Eightfold
Path, which lead ultimately to Buddha's character. By Buddha's character he meant "freedom from all kinds of suffering." It also meant freedom from self. If we analyze the
Four Noble Truths, we can see more clearly the method of
the Buddha's teaching.

(1) All men are suffering. According to Buddha it is
     our main problem or our aim to free men from
     suffering.
(2) It is Buddha's hypothesis that desire is the cause
     of all sufferings, and therefore various means
     might be tried to eliminate our desires, such as
     fasting, practicing right conduct, concentration, etc.
(3) Buddha tried out himself those various ways in the
     attempt to eliminate his desire.
(4) From the results of the various attempts, Buddha
     concluded the Eightfold Path is the only way that
     leads to elimination of desire and thus of suffering.
     This method can be applied to most areas of teach-
     ing.

"Do goodness and stop wickedness. Those who are
poor in their mind will be blessed" are Buddha's teachings.
By following these teachings one can cultivate his virtues.
But first what is goodness and what is wickedness? According to Buddha, "The goodness is following the true and anything against the truth is wickedness." And there are the
famous teachings of the Ten Commandments of Goodness and
the Ten Rules against Wickedness.

Regarding cultivation of virtues, there are four virtues
of expression. These are (1) the virtue of care, (2) of loving language, (3) of sacrifice, and (4) of helping. These four
virtues are required for making friendship with other people.

There are seven virtues of attitudes for the Buddhist
student. They are (1) the virtue of interest in others, (2) of
obeying law, (3) of compassion, (4) of perseverance, (5) of
progressiveness, (6) of concentration, and (7) of wisdom.

Most people understand that Buddhism emphasizes spiritual activities like any other religion. But this idea is a
widely held misunderstanding among many people, because
there are several sports which are very popular these days
developed by Buddhists for the purpose of disciplining mind
and body. Judo, karate, and yoga are a science because
each implies mastery of various laws of nature such as gravity, friction, momentum, velocity, and unison of forces. In
its most important phase, this science constitutes a kind of
higher logic developed through practice and the ascension of
the true personality, which requires realization of the spiritual self, in the philosophic rather than the religious sense
of the word "spiritual." The study of true judo, karate, and

yoga are symbolic of mental attitudes and behavior. The sub-
conscious mind is where our behavior patterns are collected
in a vast reservoir of many years' experience. These sports
are part of daily exercise in a Buddhist monastery as a means
of achieving greater powers of the mind through concentration.

And Buddha mentioned several times to his followers
that eating and drinking should be only in the proper quanti-
ties. Proper quantity is one of the best means to good health.
Buddha emphasized proper quantity, because he spent most of
his lifetime in the tropical area of India. In his days there
were many sicknesses resulting from over-indulgence, much
as in our own day in the Western world. Another teaching
related to physical education was that of hygiene. This matter was also related to social living in his day. There were
no bath accommodations in the house in those days and there
was always a shortage of clean water in the tropics area.
Some anthropologists have said that most people had a bath
only once a year, say for New Year's Day, in those days.

When Buddha taught for long hours, he used to ask
his followers to take a walk for a while. He thought sitting
several hours at one place was not good for the health.
Walking was to refresh one's mind and body. He suggested
that when many were walking together they should walk in a
straight line as he felt it would help them to have a straight
mind and be better able to concentrate on one thing.

There can be no doubt that the Buddha was a great
educator. Numerous records about him in the Pali, Sutra,
and Pitaka illustrate his teaching principles and practices.
For example, in the Digha-Nikaya is found the Lohicca-Sutta,
which concerns the ethics of teaching, and the Pasadika-Sutra,
which concerns the perfect and imperfect teacher. These
Sutras, in particular, describe in detail the philosophy of
Buddha's teaching.

BIOGRAPHICAL SKETCH OF BUDDHA

Since Buddha is the central figure of Buddhism some
historical background of his life should be presented. He
was born of the Aryan race, Sakya clan, south of present-
day Nepal in the Southern Himalayas, the first son of King
Suddhodava Gotama and Queen Maya in the year 563 B.C.
The account of his birth is a very interesting one. His parents had been childless for twenty years. One night Queen

Maya dreamt of a white elephant entering her womb. After that she found herself with child. As was the custom of her country, she started on the journey to her parents' home to be delivered of the child. On the way, however, at a place called Lumbini Park, she gave birth to a son. He was given the name Siddhartha, which means "every wish fulfilled."

His birth was attended by wise men, interpreted in his land as a good omen; they told of this child, "If he remains in the palace, he will become a great king to rule over the Four Seas. But if he leaves, he will become a Buddha, a self-enlightened one, and the world's savior."

When Buddha was 12 years old, only then was he first allowed out of the palace, where he encountered for the first time old people, sickness, suffering and misery. Upon returning to the palace Buddha could not regain any peace of mind.

For the first time in his life he began to meditate seriously about life and death. He perceived clearly the evils of disease, old age, wretchedness, sickness and suffering in general. He wondered what life was, who he was, from where he came, to where he was destined, and how human beings could be liberated from all this suffering.

Buddha continued to wonder and to meditate and he asked about these wonderings to his father and his teachers, receiving satisfactory answers from none. His father, the King Suddhodava Gotama, remembered the wise men's predictions and tried every way to induce his son to remain at the palace. But at the age of 30, Buddha reached a desperate climax in his years of mental struggles and meditations. He decided to leave the palace and to seek the solutions elsewhere, to try to save himself and the rest of mankind.

Buddha set out to visit the wisest scholar of his day. First he visited Alara Kalama to study for awhile under him. But he could find no satisfactory answers to the wonderings of his heart. So he went to another teacher, Uddaka, to seek the answers. Again the seeking was in vain. He wandered in search of still another teacher who could give him his answers.

Finally he settled in the town of Uruvilva, where he began his meditations for enlightenment. Buddha, for about six years, concentrated in his deep thoughts about how to

control his mind, practicing asceticism as the main method
for his meditations. He gave up the asceticism one day by
accepting a bowl of food from a village maiden. His immediate followers became disillusioned and deserted him. However, Buddha stayed under a jambu tree, called the tree of
wisdom, until he had found enlightenment.

On December 8, at the age of 35, Gotama found the
path to enlightenment and became Buddha, an enlightened one.
Some called him Shakyamuni, or the world-honored, blessed
one.

Then he arose from the jambu tree with the decision
to preach his idea of enlightenment to mankind. First he
went to those followers who had so recently deserted him,
meeting them at the Deer Garden of Isipatana where he started his first sermon about the Four Noble Truths of Suffering
and its Cause, the Removal of that Cause, and the Eightfold
Path, which is the path of liberation from suffering. The
Four Noble Truths are:

(1) The Noble Truth of Pain or Suffering: birth is
      pain, sickness is pain, death is pain. Union with
      the unpleasant is pain, separation from the pleas-
      ant is pain, not obtaining what one wishes is pain.
      In short, even a person living finely, in clinging to
      existence suffers pain.

(2) The Noble Truth of the Cause of Pain: the craving
      that leads to rebirth, accompanied by delight and
      passion, rejoicing at finding delight here and there,
      namely the craving for lust, for existence, for non-
      existence.

(3) The Noble Truth of the Cessation of Pain: the com-
      plete cessation of that craving--its forsaking, re-
      linquishment, release and detachment from it.

(4) The Noble Truth of the Path that leads to the Ces-
      sation of Pain: this is the Noble Eightfold Path,
      which is:

      1. The right view is understanding the Four Truths.
      2. The right thought is free from lust, ill will,
           cruelty and untruthfulness.
      3. The right speech is abstaining from lying, tale-
           bearing, harsh language and vain talk.

4. The right action is abstaining from killing, stealing, and sexual misconduct.
5. The right livelihood is earning a living in a way not harmful to any living thing.
6. The right effort is to avoid evil thoughts and overcome them, to arouse good thoughts and maintain them.
7. The right mindfulness is to pay vigilant attention to every state of the body, feeling, and mind.
8. The right concentration is concentration on a single object so as to induce certain special states of consciousness in deep meditation.

By following the path a disciple aims at complete purification of mind, hopes to become enlightened, to be one free from the necessity of rebirth, ready for Nirvana.

Buddha went on a journey preaching to the people for 45 years. The most important of his teachings concerned the power of thought. He showed how men could control their minds through concentration and meditation. In the first verse of the Dhammapada he said, "All that we are is the result of what we have thought; it is founded on our thoughts, it is made up of our thoughts." When he arrived at the border of the Kusinagava Castle, he was stricken seriously ill, and there he died at the age of 80 in 483 B.C.

Today there are about four schools of Buddhism, each proclaiming its own view. The oldest school, a very traditional and conservative group that holds strictly to doctrine, is the Theravada, known at first to the West as the Hinayana, which today is the faith of Sri Lanka, Burma, Thailand, Cambodia and Vietnam.

The others together, the liberal tendency, interpret doctrine and practice, calling themselves Mahayana or Great Vehicle; they include the rest of the world. The peculiarities of Tibetan Buddhism, which cover Tibet and its neighbors, Bhutan, Sikkim, and Nepal, are so marked that though it is part of the Mahayana, some people consider it a school of its own. The same applies to the Zen school of Japan, which is very different from any other school of Buddhism.

Each country has preserved many volumes of Buddhist scriptures. The Tripitaka Koreana was printed in A.D. 313. This monumental work, with well-arranged contents and wood-

en type, has been preserved. It was an epochal event in the
whole history of printing. Actually metal printing types were
invented and used for the first time in the world at Buddhist
temples in Korea more than two hundred years before Guten-
berg's time in Germany. The earliest book presently known
to have been printed with metal types is the Sangjongyem Buddhist scripture, published sometime between 1232 and 1242.
Twenty-eight copies of the 50 volumes of this book were re-
printed with metal types.

The following are some of the basic truths of 12 principles of Buddhism. These principles, drafted for the use
of Western Buddhists, have been translated into seventeen languages. In Japan, the 17 major sects approved them; the
late Venerable Tai Hsu approved them on behalf of millions
of Chinese Buddhists; the Supreme Patriarch of Siam, after
consulting the Buddhist Order, approved them; responsible
lay Buddhists have approved them in Burma and Ceylon.
They are in process of adoption by Buddhist organizations in
various European countries and in the U. S. A. They may become the common platform for a world Buddhism.

(1)   Self-salvation is for any man the immediate task.
      If a man lay wounded by a poisoned arrow he would
      not delay extraction by demanding details of the man
      who shot it, or the length and make of the arrow.
      There will be time for ever-increasing understanding
      of the Teaching during the Treading of the Way.
      Meanwhile, begin now by facing life as it is, learn-
      ing always by direct and personal experience.

(2)   The first fact of existence is the law of change or
      impermanence. All that exists, from a mole to a
      mountain, from a thought to an empire, passes
      through the same cycle of existence--i. e. , birth,
      growth, decay, and death. Life alone is continuous,
      ever seeking self-expression in new forms. "Life
      is a bridge; therefore build no house on it. " Life
      is a process of flow, and he who clings to any form,
      however splendid, will suffer by resisting the flow.

(3)   The law of change applies equally to the "soul. "
      There is no principle in an individual which is im-
      mortal and unchanging. Only the "Namelessness, "
      the ultimate Reality, is beyond change, and all forms
      of life, including man, are manifestations of this
      Reality. No one owns the life which flows in him

any more than the electric light bulb owns the current which gives it light.

(4) The universe is the expression of law. All effects have causes, and man's soul or character is the sum total of his previous thoughts and acts. Karma, meaning action-reaction, governs all existence, and man is the sole creator of his circumstances and his reaction to them, his future condition, and his final destiny. By right thought and action he can gradually purify his inner nature, and so by self-realization attain in time liberation from rebirth. The process covers great periods of time, involving life after life on earth, but ultimately every form of life will reach enlightenment.

(5) Life is one and indivisible, though its everchanging forms are innumerable and perishable. There is, in truth, no death, though every form must die. From an understanding of life's unity arises compassion, a sense of identity with the life in other forms. Compassion is described as "the Law of laws--eternal harmony," and he who breaks this harmony of life will suffer accordingly and delay his own Enlightenment.

(6) Life being One, the interests of the part should be be those of the whole. In his ignorance man thinks he can successfully strive for his own interests, and this wrongly-directed energy of selfishness produces suffering. He learns from his suffering to reduce and finally eliminate its cause. The Buddha taught Four Noble Truths: the omnipresence of suffering; its cause, wrongly directed desire; its cure, the removal of the cause; and the Noble Eightfold Path of self-development which leads to the end of suffering.

(7) The Eightfold Path consists in Right (or perfect) Views or preliminary understanding, Right Aims or Motives, Right Speech, Right Acts, Right Livelihood, Right Effort, Right Concentration or mind-development, and, finally, Right Samadhi, leading to full Enlightenment. As Buddhism is a way of living, not merely a theory of life, the treading of this Path is essential to self-deliverance. "Cease to do evil, learn to do good, cleanse your heart." This is the teaching of the Buddha.

(8) Reality is indescribable, and a God with attributes is
     the final Reality. But the Buddha, a human being,
     became the All-Enlightened One, and the purpose of
     life is the attainment of Enlightenment. This state
     of Consciousness, Nirvana, the extinction of the limi-
     tations of self-hood, is attainable on earth. All men
     and all other forms of life contain the potentiality of
     Enlightenment, and the process therefore consists in
     becoming what you are. "Look within; thou art Bud-
     dha. "

(9) From potential to actual Enlightenment there lies the
     Middle Way, the Eightfold Path "from desire to
     peace, " a process of self-development between the
     "opposites, " avoiding all extremes. The Buddha trod
     this Way to the end, and the only faith required in
     Buddhism is the reasonable belief that where a Guide
     has trod it is worth our while to tread. The Way
     must be trodden by the whole man, not merely the
     best of him, and heart and mind must be developed
     equally. The Buddha was the All-Compassionate as
     well as the All-Enlightened One.

(10) Buddhism lays great stress on the need of inward
     concentration and meditation, which leads in time to
     the development of the inner spiritual faculties. The
     subjective life is as important as the daily round,
     and periods of quietude for inner activity are essen-
     tial for a balanced life. The Buddhist should at all
     times be "mindful and self-possessed, " refraining
     from mental and emotional attachment to the "passing
     show. " This increasingly watchful attitude to cir-
     cumstance, which he knows to be his own creation,
     helps him to keep his reaction to it always under
     control.

(11) The Buddha said: "Work out your own salvation with
     diligence. " Buddhism knows no authority for truth
     save the intuition of the individual, and that is au-
     thority for himself alone. Each man suffers the con-
     sequences of his own acts, and learns thereby, while
     helping his fellow men to the same deliverance; nor
     will prayer to the Buddha or to any God prevent an
     effect from following its cause. Buddhist monks are
     teachers and exemplars, and in no sense intermedi-
     aries between Reality and the individual. The utmost
     tolerance is practiced towards all other religions and

philosophies, for no man has the right to interfere
in his neighbor's journey to the Goal.

(12) Buddhism is neither pessimistic nor "escapist," nor
does it deny the existence of God or soul, though it
places its own meaning on these terms. It is, on
the contrary, a system of thought, a religion, a spiritual science and a way of life, which is reasonable,
practical and all-embracing. For over two thousand
years it has satisfied the spiritual desires of nearly
one-third of mankind. It appeals to the West because
it has no dogmas, satisfies the reason and the heart
alike, insists on self-reliance coupled with tolerance
for other points of view, embraces science, religion,
philosophy, psychology, ethics, and art, and it points
to man alone as the creator of his present life and
sole designer of his destiny.

The secret of Buddhism's success was that it gave human beings what they lacked--a sense of security and a feeling of hope. The contribution of Buddhism to human beings
is to protect against sterile abstractions and pure logic, sub-
stituting instead an emphasis upon the concrete and individual.
Life is much larger than logic; human existence can not be
measured merely by a concept of human existence. The
strength of Buddhism lies therefore in its recognition that
man is a striving, aspiring and responsible being.

REFERENCE WORKS

GENERAL

1 Adams, C. J.   A Reader's Guide to the Great Religions.
New York: Free Press, 1965. 364 p.
This work contains eight bibliographical essays by
specialists of professional rank in American or Canadian universities on primitive religion, religions of China, Hinduism,
Buddhism, religions of Japan, Judaism, Christianity, and Islam. Each essay provides a sectionalized survey of the literature with a running commentary, often evaluative; some
have appendices listing reference works with comments and
relevant periodicals. Works in English predominate, although
many European languages are included.

2 Archer, J. C.   Faiths Men Live By. 2nd ed. Revised
by Carl E. Purinton. New York: Ronald, 1958.
553 p.
A useful general outline for Asian religion, each religion is viewed both in its cultural setting and in itself, with
regard for interactions when meeting other faiths. A list of
references arranged mostly by topics, a list of questions for
discussion, and a full bibliographic aid make this an important book.

3 Bahm, A. J.   The World's Living Religions. New York:
Dell, 1964. 384 p.
This book brings a new dimension and outlook to the
traditional study of comparative religion. In addition to a
thorough analysis and explanation of the basic elements common to all religions, it also offers an especially detailed
treatment of the Eastern religions.

4 Ballou, R. C.   The Bible of the World. New York: Viking, 1939. 1514 p.
This work contains the scriptural essence of eight
great religions for the use of the modern English reader.

The main purpose of the author is to bring together in this
book the more thoughtful and philosophic scriptures of all
these religions, so the reader may easily compare them and
discover their differences himself.

5 Bouquet, A. C.   Comparative Religion; A Short Outline.
       5th ed.   Baltimore: Penguin Books, 1956.   320 p.
       This is a handy outline with a list of books for further
study.   The author discusses a brief history of Zoroastrian
literature, the Upanishads, the Buddhist texts, the Analects
of Confucius, and the Bhagavad Gita, and gives extracts from
the Old and the New Testaments.

6 _____ . Sacred Books of the World.   New Orleans:
       Pelican Books, 1953.   343 p.
       Intending this book for the students of religion, the
author has shown how the various religions have evolved from
primitive ritual chants, hymns and prayers, as well as the
sacred books; but his own love of his subject has made his
presentation acceptable to the lay as well as to the student
public.   The author divides his work into four parts.   The
first contains the chants and hymns; the second part is devoted to the Khannurabi Circle, stories of Babylon, and much
of the Egyptian literature.   The third part ranges over the
period from 800 B.C. to A.D. 300, and the last part is concerned with post-Biblical literature, including Rabbinical writings.

7 Braden, C. S.   The World's Religions: A Short History.
       Nashville: Abingdon, 1954.   256 p.
       This work gives a brief, readable, comprehensive,
reliable account of the development of the world's religions,
past and present.   It is not in any sense a book for technical
scholars or advanced students, but it does aim to present the
most important features of the great faiths of the world.

8 Bradley, D. G.   A Guide to the World's Religions.   Engle-
       wood Cliffs, N.J.: Prentice-Hall, 1963.   182 p.
       The author analyzes the 12 main faiths from the stand-
point of their underlying concepts, philosophy, history and
current influence.   The religions of the Biblical lands, religions of India, and the religions of East Asia are treated
as groups.   Since Dr. Bradley believes that the greatest understanding among men rests in the knowledge of differences,
he describes not only basic similarities but also the distinc-
tive features of the religions.

9   A Buddhist Bible. 2nd ed.   Edited by D. Goddard.   Lon-
        don: Harrap, 1938.   677 p.
     The work represents a collection of translations of
texts from Pali, Sanskrit, Chinese and Tibetan sources and
from Japanese modern collections.   The appendix contains
bibliographical and other notes.

10   Clemen, C.   Religions of the World: Their Nature and
        their History. New York: Harcourt, 1931.   482 p.
     This work provides the general reader with an account
of the history of the various religions of the world.   The contributors emphasize chiefly those aspects of the religions
which are really important for their adherents.   There are
135 illustrations throughout the text.

11   Cranston, R.   World Faith: The Story of the Religions
        of the United Nations.   New York: Harper, 1949.
        194 p.
     The work presents an account of the great world re-
ligions in simple form for the general reader of any faith or
race.   The author tries to clarify the importance of understanding another's philosophy of life and basic ideas.   It
gives an outline of seven great faiths: Hinduism, Buddhism,
Taoism, Confucianism, Judaism, Christianity, and Moham-
medanism.

12   De Bary, W. T.   Source of Chinese Tradition.   New
        York: Columbia University Press, 1960.   976 p.   3
        vol.
     This three volume series deals with the literary
sources material of India, Japan and China.   The interest
of the Buddhist reader will be focused on Chapters XV to
XVII which deal with the arrival of Buddhism in China and
the genesis and scriptures of Chinese Buddhism.

13   Eitel, E. J.   Handbook of Chinese Buddhism, Being a
        Buddhist Sanskrit Chinese Dictionary.   Hong Kong:
        Lane Crawford, 1888.
     The work is especially useful for its brief descrip-
tions of principal Buddhist dictionaries.

14   Farquhar, J. N.   An Outline of the Religious Literature
        of India.   London: Oxford University, 1920.   451 p.
     This work is a survey of the religious history of In-
dia as an individual whole through a long process of development.   Attention is restricted to the literature as a chief
source of knowledge of the religions.   The extensive bibli-

ography covers the important religious works, their translations into European languages, and pertinent modern critical
works published in book form and as articles in journals.

15 Finegan, J. The Archeology of World Religions: the
       Background of Primitivism, Zoroastrianism, Hinduism,
       Jainism, Buddhism, Confucianism, Taoism, Shinto and
       Islam. Princeton, N.J.: Princeton University Press,
       1952. 599 p.
     The study being primarily archaeological, attention is
focused upon the ancient monuments and documents of the
various religions. Thus it is mainly concerned with the
early history of the religions rather than with their recent
and contemporary aspects. It contains bibliographic footnotes, 260 plates, and nine maps.

16 Gaer, J. How the Great Religions Began. New York:
       Dodd, 1956. 424 p.
     What the faiths of the world are and how their many
forms came to be is the subject of this book. It attempts
to give to the reader a glimpse of how the living religions
of the world arose, how they differ, and what they have
basically in common one with another.

17 Hocking, W. E. Living Religions and a World Faith.
       New York: Macmillan, 1940. 291 p.
     How should the world religions treat each other? In
what way is mankind moving toward a world faith? To what
extent is Christianity prepared to assume the role of world
faith? The author presents his answer to these vital questions based upon his Hibbert lectures.

18 Hume, R. E. Treasure House of the Living Religions:
       Selections from their Sacred Scriptures. New York:
       Scribner's, 1932. 493 p.
     This is a classified anthology of 3074 selected quota-
tions from the sacred books of the 11 great historical religions. Its bibliography gives the canonical order of con-
stituent documents of the several sacred scriptures together
with the English translations of each document, pp. 405-443.

19 Humphreys, C. A Buddhist Student's Manual. London:
       The Buddhist Society, 1956. 279 p.
     Edited by the founder-president of the Buddhist Society,
this work includes a brief glossary of Buddhist terms, by
A. C. March, amended and enlarged by C. Humphreys, and
also an analyzed bibliography of books on Buddhism in English.

Too, there are the scholarly catalogues of the Tibetan, Chinese, and Japanese Canon.

20 _____. A Popular Dictionary of Buddhism. London: Arco Publications, 1962. 224 p.
    This is designed to assist those interested in Buddhism who are troubled by numerous foreign terms they meet in Buddhist literature.

21 James, E. O. Comparative Religion: An Introductory and Historical Study. New York: Barnes and Noble, 1961. 334 p. London: Methuen, 1962. 334 p.
    This work is a comparative study of the history of religion intended primarily as a textbook for students with references and a full bibliography of relative literature. It is also designed to give the general reader an account of religious thought and practice in the light of recent research from rudimentary beginnings.

22 Lyon, Q. M. The Great Religions. New York: Odyssey, 1957. 732 p.
    The author discusses some tentative criteria with which to compare and judge the religions of mankind. He also presents, with a casual informality, the religions of man from prehistoric times to the present. He seeks to make clear, by example, the basic techniques of obtaining historical facts, and he has applied them to religious traditions. Finally in the concluding chapter he sketches a philosophy of religion.

23 McCasland, S. V., Cairns, G. E., and Yu, D. C. Religions of the World. New York: Random House, 1969. 760 p.
    This work presents the major living religions of the world, the faiths by which most peoples of the world live at the present time. The authors are compelled by geography to consider Buddhism as one of the great religions of East Asia. They give foundations of Buddhism by discussing its Indian legacy and some of its main schools like Theravada and Mahayana.

24 Noss, J. B. Man's Religions. New York: Macmillan, 1956. 784 p.
    This serves as an introduction to the world's religions, containing adequate amounts of descriptive or interpretative details from the original source materials. It also presents man's most noteworthy faiths in a time-setting

that does justice to their development as well as to their
origins.

25 Nyanaponika, V. Pathways of Buddhist Thought. Lon-
       don: Allen and Unwin, 1971. 245 p.
    This brilliant book is a series of essays from the
Wheel series of publications which have been issued by the
Buddhist Publication Society of Kandy, Ceylon, during the
past ten years. The series selected by M. O. Walshe provides a rational sequence on Buddhist thought, knowledge,
conduct and ethics, science, mindfulness, Anatta and Nibbana,
Nirvana, Nihilism and Satori. They are all well written by
practicing Buddhists.

26 Parrinder, G. Dictionary of Non-Christian Religions.
       Philadelphia: Westminster Press, 1973. 320 p.
    This work is a dictionary of terms associated with
non-Christian religions throughout world civilization. The
author seems to emphasize Buddhism, Hinduism, and Islam.
The dictionary is designed for the layman so that the entries
tend to be simple and easy to understand.

27 Sacred Books of the East, with critical and biographical
       sketches by E. Wilson, translated by various Oriental
       scholars and edited by F. M. Muller. Rev. ed.
    New York: Colonial Press, 1900. 457 p.
    This work includes all the most important works of
the seven Asian religions that have influenced the civilization
of Asia. Its index can be used for both general and narrow
topics.

28 Stroup, H. Four Religions of Asia. New York: Harper
       & Row, 1968. 212 p.
    This is an excellent introduction to Indian religions
for the general reader: Hinduism, Buddhism, Jainism and
Sikhism. It presents the history, founder, geographic spread,
school of thought, teachings and sacred scriptures of each.

29 Thera, H. S. Handbook of Buddhists. New Delhi:
       Sarnath, Benaras, 1957. 158 p.
    This little book of pocket size, though not well pro-
duced, may be of great worth in the field of Indian Buddhism.
In Pali and English on opposite pages, it contains detailed
precepts, the Mahamangalla and other short Suttas, and some
excellent material for meditation.

30 Tiele, C. P. Outlines of the History of Religion.

Translated from the Dutch by J. E. Carpenter.
London: Trubner, 1878. 249 p.

A unique work indicative of able and laborious study,
it will enable the reader to gain a better view of the results
of investigations into the religious history of nations. It
consists of the condensed statements on what is certainly
known of all the chief religions of the world up to the rise
of Buddhism.

31 Winternitz, M. A Concise Dictionary of Eastern Re-
    ligion. Oxford: Clarendon Press, 1910. 683 p.

Forming volume 50 of The Sacred Books of the East,
it is a remarkably detailed, analytical index with many cross-
references. It is designed on the basis of a "scientific
classification of religious phenomena."

BIBLIOGRAPHIES

32 Bando, S. and others. A Bibliography on Japanese
    Buddhism. Tokyo: CIIB Pr., 1958.

This is a classified bibliography listing books and
periodical articles (1660 numbered items) written mainly in
European languages up to July 1958.

33 Barrow, J. G. A Bibliography of Bibliographies in
    Religion. Ann Arbor, Mich.: Edwards Brothers,
    1955. 489 p.

This is a comprehensive work attempting to bring together all separately published bibliographies in the field of
religion, from the 15th century to the present. It is primarily Christian, but it has a brief section on Buddhism.

34 Beal, S. A Catena of Buddhist Scripture from the
    Chinese. London: Trubner, 1878. 436 p.

This work is a collection of Chinese versions of
Buddhist scriptures, some translated in full and others in
part, arranged in chronological order, showing the origins
of the Buddhist system in China and its expansion, fully
annotated.

35 Bibliographie Bouddhique, 1928/29-1954. Paris: Li-
    brairie d'Amérique et d'Orient, 1930-1961. Annual
    [in French].

This is an important annotated (in French) bibliography

which includes both books and the indexing of some 200
periodicals in many languages.

36 Ch'en, K. K. S. Buddhism in China: A Historical
        Survey. Princeton, N. J. : Princeton University
        Press, 1964. 560 p.
    This work is comprised of the Virginia and Richard
Stewart memorial lectures in the Princeton studies on the
history of religions. "The professor of religion and Oriental
studies at Princeton ... traces in a lucid and authoritative
fashion the vicissitudes of Buddhism in China from its arrival during the Han dynasty 2000 years ago to present
times ... [it] will be standard reading on the subject for many
years to come." Giving a comprehensive bibliography of
Chinese Buddhism and its historical background, this book
is written primarily for those people who already have a
general acquaintance with the history and religions of China.
It will serve as a useful source of collateral readings for
courses dealing with history and culture of China.

37 Hamilton, C. H. Buddhism in India, Ceylon, China,
        and Japan: A Reading Guide. Chicago: University
        of Chicago Press, 1931. 107 p.
    This work presents the subject for four of the great
Buddhist countries in a form compact enough to maintain the
large outlines of its development and at the same time make
clear its vast range and depth. Special references are given
and also outlines are added simply to afford general orienta-
tion in adjacent topics. Especially full bibliographic information is beneficial for further studies.

38 Hanayama, S. Bibliography on Buddhism. Tokyo:
        Hokuseido Press, 1961; New York: Perkins Oriental,
        1962. 869 p.
    This is an extensive bibliography of 15, 073 numbered
entries, arranged alphabetically with subject index. It lists
books and articles in Western languages primarily of the
19th and 20th centuries.

39 Holzman, D. et al. Japanese Religion and Philosophy:
        A Guide to Japanese References and Research Ma-
        terial. Ann Arbor: University of Michigan Press,
        1959. 102 p.
    Containing 992 numbered, briefly annotated items,
giving authors and titles in Japanese with English translation,
this work is limited to Japanese books dealing with the

doctrines and histories of the religions and philosophies of
Japan published since the Meiji era.

40   International Bibliography of the History of Religions.
        UNESCO, 1952- . Annual.
        Under the supervision of C. J. Bleeker Company,
published in connection with the periodical Numen, with the
support of UNESCO, this work lists books and articles published during the year on the history of the various religions
of the world.

41   Morgan, K. W. Asian Religions. New York: Mac-
        millan, 1964. 30 p.
        An introduction to the study of Hinduism, Buddhism,
Islam, Confucianism, and Taoism, the work gives a very
useful thirty-page bibliographical essay evaluating relevant
books suitable for laymen.

42   Nanjio, B. A Catalogue of the Chinese Translation of
        Buddhist Tripitaka. Oxford: Clarendon Press, 1883.
        480 p.
        This book lists 1662 different works, arranged and
classified as in the original Chinese catalogue. It is based
on a copy of the Japanese edition in the India Office Library,
London. Three appendices systematically list authors' and
famous translators' works, indexes of the original Sanskrit
titles and of Indian and Chinese authors and translators.

43   Newark Museum Association, Newark, N. J. Catalogue
        of the Tibetan Collection and other Lamaist Material
        in the Newark Museum. Newark: The Association,
        1961.
        This work concerns textiles, rugs, needlework, cos-
tumes, and jewelry. It gives an introductory bibliography
at the end of the book (pp. 70-76) about Tibetan Buddhist art.

44   no entry

45   Rowland, B. The Harvard Outline and Reading Lists for
        Oriental Art. Cambridge, Mass.: Harvard University
        Press, 1958. 74 p.
        The work concerns Oriental art divided into artistic-
historical periods in each region. There are helpful reading
lists for the general reader with a bibliography, not annotated. It was first published in 1938 under the title, Outline
and Bibliographies of Oriental Art.

46 Yoo, Y. Buddhism: A Subject Index to Periodical
        Articles in English, 1728-1971. Metuchen, N.J.:
        Scarecrow, 1973. 162 p.
    A classified unannotated bibliography, including such
topics as art (subdivided into architecture, dance, paintings,
music, and sculpture), doctrine, Gantama Buddha, missions
(subdivided by country), Nirvana, Pali Canon, etc.; appended
are a directory of Buddhist associations around the world, a
list of periodicals indexed, a title index, and an author/sub-
ject index.

ENCYCLOPEDIAS and DICTIONARIES

47 Brandon, S. G. F. A Dictionary of Comparative Re-
        ligion. London: Weidenfeld and Nicolson, 1970.
        704 p.
    This dictionary, produced by a first-class team of
British scholars, is an excellent piece of work. There are
four sections, the one on Buddhism by Trevor Ling, regarding which the amount of accurate information succinctly
provided in the various articles is enormous.

48 Conze, E. Materials for a Dictionary of the Prajnapara-
        mita Literature. Tokyo: Suzuki Research Foundation,
        1967. 447 p.
    This is a useful reference tool, practically amounting
to a concise Buddhist Sanskrit-English dictionary, with all
the uncompounded words followed by their Tibetan equiva-
lents, and romanized throughout. Although not a complete
dictionary, it contains most words necessary for reading the
Sutras of the Perfection of Wisdom.

49 Encyclopedia of Buddhism edited by T. P. Malalasekera.
        Colombo, Ceylon: Government Press, 1961-1972.
        I-III.
    Designed as a scholarly and definitive work and pro-
duced under the aegis of the Government of Ceylon, this
encyclopedia, which covers religion, culture and all aspects
of history, is to run to 15,000 pages and be completed in
about ten years. The fifty-page article on Amida-Buddhism
is considered to be perhaps the most succinct and informative article on the subject to appear in English.

50 Encyclopedia of Religion and Ethics edited by J. Hastings,
        J. A. Selbie and others. New York: Scribner's,
        1908-1926. 12 volumes.

The aim of this work is to include articles on every religious belief or custom, every ethical movement, every philosophical idea, and every moral practice. Persons and places famous in the history of religion and morals are included. Particularly valuable is it for the comparative approach to Buddhism, Christianity, Hinduism, and Islam, etc.

51 Humphreys, Christmas. A Popular Dictionary of Buddhism. London: Arco Publications, 1962. 223 p.
       This work is based on a brief glossary of Buddhist terms by Arthur C. March, which was later expanded for inclusion in a Buddhist student manual in 1956. It is designed for the English-speaking student of Buddhism.

52 Japanese-English Buddhist Dictionary. Tokyo: Daito Shuppansha, 1965. 383 p.
       This is a reliable work based on a standard Japanese dictionary, with the terms translated into Roman letters and alphabetized.

53 Ling, T. O. A Dictionary of Buddhism: A Guide to Thought and Tradition. New York: Scribner's, 1972. 277 p.
       The author, who is a lecturer in comparative religion at the University of Leeds, presents clear and concise definitions of Buddhist terms, descriptions of Buddhist attitudes, historical surveys of the spread of Buddhism, and explanations of main Buddhist doctrine. Most entries are cross-referenced and it contains a bibliography, enabling the reader to pursue further study.

54 Nyanatiloka, B. Buddhist Dictionary, Manual of Buddhist Terms and Doctrines. Colombo, Ceylon: Frewin, 1950. 189 p.
       The author spent 38 years compiling this work. Although far from formidable in size, it seems to contain an exposition of most technical terms. Arranged by subject alphabetically, many articles are cited by the sources and are cross-referenced to other articles.

55 Sivananda, S. S. Yoga Vendanta Philosophy. Rishikesh, India: Yoga Vendanta Forest University, 1950. 144 p.
       This is a dictionary of Yoga terms, with definitions and terms in Sanskrit.

56 Soothill, W. E. A Dictionary of Chinese Buddhist Terms.

London: Kegan Paul, 1937. 510 p.
This dictionary contains Sanskrit and English equiva-
lents and a Sanskrit-Pali index. It has definitions in English
of Buddhist terminology.

57 Wood, E. Yoga Dictionary. New York: Philosophical
       Library, 1956. 177 p.
This work includes both definitions and longer notes.
All technical terminology is taken from Sanskrit works.

58 _____. Zen Dictionary. London: Owen, 1957.
       165 p.; New York: Philosophical Library, 1962.
       162 p.
This work covers all major aspects of Zen practice
and teaching, both Chinese and Japanese. The book interprets all Zen methods, history, and life in the Zen monasteries. It includes brief biographies and some quotations,
with a selected bibliography, by author and title only. The
diacritical markings are shown.

59 Zaehner, R. C. The Concise Encyclopedia of Living
       Faiths. London: Hutchinson, 1959. 431 p.
This work attempts to describe in a brief compass
those faiths which have withstood the test of time and seem
to correspond to some fundamental need in man. Buddhism
is discussed in three chapters. Judaism, Christianity,
Islam, Zoroastrianism, Hinduism, Jainism, Shinto, Confucianism and Taoism are also discussed. A final chapter
entitled "A New Buddha and a New Tao" deals with Jungian
psychology and Marxism.

INDEXES

60 American Theological Library. Index to Religious
       Periodical Literature: An Author and Subject Index
       to Periodical Literature, 1949/52- . Chicago:
       American Theological Library Association, 1953- .
This work indexes religious and archaeological peri-
odicals from the United States, Canada, England, France,
Germany, Japan, Scotland and other countries.

61 Annual Magazine Subject Index, 1907-1949. Boston:
       Faxon, 1908-1952. 43 v.
This is a subject index to a selected list of American
and English periodicals and society publications. It is an
index of subject only, not of authors or titles.

62 British Humanities Index, 1962- . London: London
        Library Association Quarterly.
    A continuation in part of the Subject Index to Periodi-
cals, this work indexes some 275 British periodicals including
many in local history.

63 Nineteenth Century Reader's Guide to Periodical Litera-
        ture, 1890-1899, with supplementary indexing, 1900-
        1922. New York: Wilson, 1944. 2 v.
    This is an author, subject, and illustrator index to the
material in 51 periodicals, mainly in the period from 1890
to 1899. The periodicals indexed are general, and the Guide
gives a total of about 25 articles on Buddhism.

64 Poole's Index to Periodical Literature, 1802-1881. Rev.
        ed. Boston: Houghton, 1891. 2 v. (Supplements
        continued through 1907)
    This is the pioneer index and, though now discontinued,
still an important index to American English periodicals, since
it covers the longest period (105 years) and indexes the large
total of about 590,000 articles in 12,241 volumes of 479
American and English periodicals.

65 Readers' Guide to Periodical Literature, 1900- . New
        York: Wilson, 1905, v. 1- .
    This work indexes United States periodicals of broad,
general and popular character and aims to provide a well-
balanced selection of most popular American magazines representing all the important subject fields.

66 Richardson, E. C. Periodical Articles on Religion: An
        Alphabetical Subject Index. New York: Scribner's,
        1907-1911. 2 vols.: subject volume, 1907, 1168 p.;
        author volume, 1911, 876 p.
    This is an index to 58,000 articles by 21,000 writers,
in more than 600 periodicals and transactions in English and
the principal foreign languages on the religions of the world.

67 Social Science and Humanities Index, formerly Interna-
        tional Index. New York: Wilson, 1916-74.
    An important index for the large or scholarly library,
it contains an author and subject index on the same plan as
the readers' guide, and it covers the more scholarly journals
in the humanities and social sciences.

68 Subject Index to Periodicals, 1915-1961. London: The
        Library Association, 1919-1962. Quarterly, 1954-
        1961, with annual cumulation.

An English index, begun in 1915 under the title
Athenaeum Subject Index, the work indexes more than 500
periodicals, principally British and American, and includes
many foreign titles.

GENERAL SURVEYS

69   Adams, C. J.   A Reader's Guide to the Great Religions.
     See entry No. 1.

70   Akiyama, A.   Buddhist Hand-Symbols.   Yokohama:
     Yoshikawa Bookstore, 1939.   86 p.
     The character of a man is betrayed by his looks.
Different Buddhas are all known by different hand-symbols,
which are regarded as mystic enigmas.   The aim of this
work is to solve the intricate puzzles of these symbols.

71   Alabaster, H.   The Wheel of the Law.   London: Trub-
     ner and Co., 1871.   323 p.
     This work gives three distinct essays or parts which
exemplify the sceptical phase, the traditionary phase, and
the ultra-superstitious phase.   The author tries to give a
picture of the modern Buddhist, a life of Buddha, and an
account of the Phrabat.

72   Asoka, King of Magadha.   Edicts of Asoka.   Edited and
     translated by N. A. Nikam and P. P. McKeon.
     Chicago: University of Chicago Press, 1959.   68 p.
     The Indian emperor Asoka's edicts were carved on
stone pillars and placed throughout India and Ceylon.   This
work helps to see the real points of contact and of divergence
between Eastern and Western cultures.

73   Barthelemy-Saint-Hilaire, J.   Life and Legend of Buddha.
     New York: Dutton, 1957.   384 p.
     A general view of the Buddhist doctrine is given.
Also included are a critical study on Buddhism, the legend
of the Buddha, the general character of Buddhist ethics
derived from the canonical writings of the councils, and
Buddhism in India in the seventh century of the Christian
era: its simplicity, the worship of statues and the important
part they play in Buddhism.

74 Beck, L. A. Life of the Buddha. London: Collins,
       1969. 287 p.
       The work contains the story and teaching of the
Buddha, intelligible and human, so that those who wish to
understand one of the greatest facets of history may not
find themselves entangled in a maze of scholarly terms,
and may perhaps be enabled to realize its strange coincidences with modern psychology and certain scientific verities.

75 Berry, T. Buddhism. See entry no. 369.

76 Bhikkhu, K. Buddhism Explained: An Introduction to
       the Teachings of Lord Buddha. Bangkok: Social
       Science Association of the Press of Thailand, 1968.
       184 p.
       This book has been written especially to answer
questions often raised by foreign visitors to Siam who have
no previous knowledge or conception of Buddhism. It is
recommended to all who want to read a good introductory
account of Buddhism. This work is a revised edition of the
previous work, What Is Buddhism?

77 _____ . What Is Buddhism? Bangkok: Social Science
       Association, 1965. 150 p.
       This is an instructive book for the enquirer and be-
ginner alike, clearly answering the questions and correcting
the many misconceptions. Most answers are concise and
very much to the point. The differences between the various
schools of Buddhism are well done. It is honored with a
Foreword by Princess Poon Diskul, President of the World
Fellowship of Buddhists.

78 Bisch, J. Why Buddha Smiles. Translated by Gwynne
       Vevers. London: Tapplinger, 1966. 158 p.
       The author writes as lightly as he travels. He was
looking for, and describes with humorous detachment, the
simple mechanics of Buddhism as a force directing men's
lives. He hardly touches at all its deeper philosophical and
religious aspects.

79 Brown, B. , ed. The Story of Buddha and Buddhism:
       His Life and Sayings. New York: McKay, 1927.
       209 p.
       The story has a threefold purpose--to tell the story
of Buddha's life, to explain the doctrine of Buddhism, and
to give selections from the teachings of Buddha and from the
legends about him.

80 Buddhism. Studia Missionalia XII. Rome: Universitatis
        Gregorianae, 1962. 181 p.
    This is a collection of nine articles, four in French,
four in English and one in German. The first three are
from the pens of fine Buddhist scholars who also happen to
be Roman Catholics. They describe the missionary activities of early Buddhism and the spread of the monasteries in
ancient Ceylon. The remaining six are the works of ec-
clesiastics who are not in the least interested in Buddhism
for what it is.

81 Buddhist Brotherhood in America. A General Outline of
        the Life and Teachings of the Lord Buddha. Los
        Angeles: The Buddhist House, 1943. 16 p.
    This is a textbook handed down from the Shakyamuni
Buddha, which strives to present the teachings in as simple
and clear a manner as possible in American terminology.

82 The Buddhist Lodge, London. What Is Buddhism?: An
        Answer from the Western Point of View. London:
        Buddhist Lodge, 1929. 240 p.
    Rather a popular manual than a scholarly treatise, the
whole book is in fact a compromise. Compiled by a group
of many minds of both sexes, both schools of Buddhism and
a dozen nationalities, it is based upon the Theravada point of
view, but borrows from the Mahayana sufficiently of its
principles to make of the whole a complete philosophy.

83 Byles, M. B. The Lotus and the Spinning Wheel. Lon-
        don: Allen and Unwin, 1963. 259 p.
    The author tells the stories of the two great teachers
whose follower she claims to be, Gotama the Buddha and
Mahatma Gandhi. She takes us on two Indian journeys, the
one to the Ganges Basin, to the places where the Buddha
lived and taught, and the other to Gandhi's ashram at
Sevegram. The larger half of the book is taken up with the
life of the Buddha. References are given at ends of chapters,
also sources. The book makes pleasant and interesting
reading and can be recommended as one approach to the Pali
scriptures.

84 Calcutta University. Journal of the Department of Letters.
        v. 1- . Calcutta: Calcutta University Press, 1920.
    This work contains contributions on various subjects,
notably India, Buddhism, ancient chronology, etc.

85 Cleather, A. L. Buddhism: The Science of Life.

Peking: China Booksellers, 1928. 183 p.
This work is composed of three articles republished
in book form: "Why I Believe in Buddhism, " "Some Thoughts
on Buddhism, " and "Tibetan Initiates on the Buddha. " It has
been rearranged and revised. Some of it comes directly
from the Tibetan initiates or their disciplines, especially
matters relating to the Buddha and his inner doctrine.

86 Conze, E. Buddhism: Its Essence and Manifestations.
New York: Harper, 1959. 212 p.
This is a statement of the fundamental principles of
Buddhism, with a study of its historical development and of
its various schools of thought.

87 Dahlke, P. Buddhism and Its Place in the Mental Life
of Mankind. New York: Macmillan, 1927. 254 p.
It is a logical, incisive, and clearly written exposition of the author's belief that Buddhism, as he understands
it, must be taken into serious consideration by those interested in solution of the deepest problems of life.

88 Davids, C. A. F. Rhys. Buddhism: A Study of the
Buddhist Norm. See entry no. 299.

89 _____ . Buddhism: Its Birth and Dispersal. London:
T. Butterworth, 1934. 255 p.
This is a general survey of Buddhism in its various
forms written as regards its original teaching. It may be
supplemented by her Manual of Buddhism (1932).

90 _____ . A Manual of Buddhism for Advanced Students.
New York: Macmillan, 1932. 341 p.
This work supplies earliest documentary references
to the Buddha with Pali and Sanskrit Buddhist scriptures.
It has wrought a service by diffusing knowledge about a
great and long-lived institution and by checking, in its historical sobriety, the growth of arising erratic impulses.

91 _____ . The Visuddhi-Maggot Buddhaghosa. London:
Oxford University Press, 1920. 768 p.
This, the first Roman-letter edition of a work bearing
the laurels of 14 centuries of renown, is based on a tran-
script made from the latest Burmese edition at the time.

92 _____ . Wayfarer's Words. London: Luzac and Co.,
1940. 3 v.
A collection of articles and reviews, lectures and

addresses published or delivered by Mrs. Rhys Davids, in a
variety of philosophical, religious and literary journals issued in three continents, it is an inestimable benefit, especially to students of original and early Buddhism.

93 Davids, T. W. Rhys. Buddhism. New York: Pott,
       Young Co., 1877. 252 p.
       This is a sketch of the life and teachings of Gautama,
the Buddha, published under the direction of the Committee
of General Literature and Education appointed by the Society
for Promoting Christian Knowledge.

94 _____ (translator). Buddhist Birth Stories; or,
       Jataka Tales. London: Trubner and Co., 1880.
       347 p.
       After Buddha's death 550 of his disciples put together
the Book of the 550 Jatakas or Births. The text and accom-
panying commentaries give for each Jataka an account of the
event in Buddha's life leading to his first telling that particular story. Both text and commentary were then handed down
intact in the Pali language. This is the oldest, most complete, probably the most important collection of folklore
extant.

95 de Bary, W. T. The Buddhist Tradition in India, China
       and Japan. New York: Modern Library Edition,
       1969. 417 p.
       The idea of this book is not so much to give an ac-
count of Buddhism in its historical development as to let
Buddhists give an account of themselves. Excerpts are
given here from basic scriptures and the major writings of
Buddhist thinkers, with necessary background essays and
commentary. For the most part these are texts reorganized
by Buddhists themselves as representing the mainstream of
Buddhist thought and practice.

96 Fausset, H. I. Flame and the Light: Meanings in
       Vedanta and Buddhism. New York: Abelard-Schuman,
       1958 (repr. New York: Greenwood Press, 1969).
       232 p.
       The author searches for knowledge and practice which
can resolve the self-centered tension in which most people
live. He has not addressed his book to scholars or experts
in Eastern philosophy so much as to people who are looking
for real meaning in their own experience and may find in
these ancient teachings an aid to wiser and happier living.

97 Gard, R. A. Buddhism. New York: Braziller, 1961.
       256 p. (Great Religions of Modern Man series.)
       This is an excellent handbook, written with consider-
able erudition and managing to cover an immensely wide
field. The author has done his best to cover most aspects,
from a sketch of the traditions concerning the life of the
Buddha to the present. He discusses the Buddha, the
Dharma, and the Sangha. There is a comparative study of
life in a Thai Theravada monastery and a monastery of the
Tibetan Vajrayana.

98 [Goddard, D., ed.] Buddha, Truth and Brotherhood; An
       Epitome of Many Buddhist Scriptures. Santa Barbara,
       Cal.: Dwight Goddard, 1935. 166 p.
       This work gives, in brief form, a good idea of the
major characteristics and aims of Buddhism, especially as
interpreted by the Japanese.

99 Gundry, D. W. Religions; A Preliminary Historical and
       Theological Study. London: Macmillan, 1958; New
       York: St. Martin's Press. 189 p.
       This gives a general survey of the living religions
with chapters on the origins of religions and the religious
quest of the ancient world.

100 Herbert, J. An Introduction to Asia. London: Allen
       and Unwin, 1964. 410 p.
       This is an encyclopedic work with wisdom and infor-
mation from the Mediterranean to Japan and from the Arctic
to Indonesia. The author covers religion from Shamanism
and other primitive forms, Zoroastrianism, Judaism and
Islam to Hinduism, Jainism, Confucianism, Taoism and
Buddhism. It also includes the mixing of concepts and rites
caused by the modern syncretic movement in the East.

101 Humphreys, C. Buddhism. Baltimore: Penguin,
       1968. 256 p.
       The author attempts to cover the whole field of Bud-
dhism, its history, development, schools, art and Buddhism
in the world today. The life of the Buddha and the development and present day teaching of the various schools of
Buddhism are described sympathetically for general readers,
with 16 illustrations, a glossary, a large bibliography, a
new translation of Pansil and an analysis of the scriptures.

102 _____. The Buddhist Way of Life. London: Allen
       and Unwin, 1968. 223 p.

The author, who is the most authoritative Buddhist
in Western countries, discusses various aspects of the Buddhist way of life. The essays are divided into four parts of
Buddhism: background, basic Buddhism, deeper truths, and
Zen Buddhism.

103 _____ . An Invitation to the Buddhist Way of Life
        for Western Readers. New York: Schocken Books,
        1970. 223 p.
        This work presents studies in the Middle Way as
leading towards that life of wisdom-love which is ever here
and now. This is an explicative text of the values, directions,
and spiritual growth the Buddhist practitioner seeks to attain.

104 _____ . Way of Action. See entry no. 331.

105 Khantipalo, B. Buddhism Explained. Bangkok: Thai
        Watana Panich Press, 1971. 310 p.
        There are many useful sections that can help the
Western Buddhist, for example, those on giving, virtue,
collectedness, mind-development as medicine, and practical
advice to meditators.

106 Lizanne, C. The Heritage of Buddha. New York:
        Philosophical Library, 1955. 120 p.
        The author has told the life of the Buddha more or
less in the form of a modern novel, bringing out the teachings of the Buddha in a way acceptable to people of the
present day.

107 Loehr, M. Buddhist Thought and Imagery. Cam-
        bridge, Mass.: Harvard University, 1961. 26 p.
        This is the Abby Aldrich Rockefeller Inaugural
Lecture at Harvard, February 24, 1961.

108 MacQuitty, W. Buddha. New York: Viking, 1970.
        128 p.
        This is a book of unusual pictorial and verbal beauty.
The author writes of the man Gautama Siddhartha, the peace
he offered his followers, and its diffusion and transfiguration
through time and geographical boundaries.

109 Monier-William, M. Buddhism in Its Connexion with
        Brahmanism and Hinduism, and Its Contrast with
        Christianity. London: J. Murray, 1889. 563 p.
        This is a description of the chief characteristics of
Buddhist images, based mostly on those of India and Tibet
but applicable also to those of China.

110 Morgan, K. W., ed. The Path of the Buddha. See
     entry no. 307.

111 Muzzey, D. S. Spiritual Heroes. New York: F.
     Ungar, 1959. 304 p.
     This is a study of some of the world's foremost
prophets.

112 Narada, T. A Manual of Buddhism: A Textbook of
     Buddhism for the S. S. C. Colombo: Associated
     Newspapers of Ceylon, 1953. 156 p.
     This is a textbook on Buddhism revised according
to the new syllabus for the S. S. C.

113 Radford, R. L. Many Paths to God. Wheaton: Theo-
     sophical Publishing House, 1972. 190 p.
     This is a good book for the beginner to obtain an
adequate working knowledge of most of the religions practiced
today. It seems significant, however, that at the end of
each chapter a list of books for further study is given. This
seems to indicate that the writer is only giving a rough outline of each religion based on her own interpretation of the
same; the serious student would need to go to the sources
for authentic material.

114 Rajagopal, D. Commentaries on Living. London:
     Victor Gollancz, 1960. 312 p.
     This book, the third series of Krishnamurti's talks
to enquirers, will be welcomed by all who are familiar with
his previous notebooks. By question and answer the enquirer is led to understand more clearly and deeply just
what his problem is and in that understanding he finds his
solution.

115 Ram, N. S. Seeking Wisdom. See entry no. 140.

116 Rieker, H. U. Beggar Among the Dead: Some Ex-
     periences of a Buddhist Monk in India. Translated
     from the German by Edward Fitzgerald. London:
     Rider, 1960. 224 p.
     The subtitle explains what the book is about. The
author, who is a native of Germany, started his penniless
journey in order to find the truth. He turned to the mountains, spurred on by the wise words of a Chinese and a
Punjabi. To seek in his own heart for truth he traveled
India and Tibet. It is all very dramatically told.

117 no entry

118 Ross, N. W. Three Ways of Asian Wisdom: Hinduism,
     Buddhism, Zen and Other Significance for the West.
     New York: Simon and Schuster, 1966. 222 p.
     This serves as an introduction to the major Oriental
religions. It shows not only history and practices, but how
they have been carried to the West and what their present
significance is to our culture. It also includes a bibliography.

119 Sa, U. P. A Brief Outline of Buddhism. Rangoon:
     n.p., 1956. 121 p.
     This booklet by the retired Deputy Commissioner of
Burma, who has also published The Venerable Anuruddha's
Abhidhammatthasangaha in Pali and Burmese, tells some of
the legends around the life of Buddha and intersperses this
with some very intricate enumerations from the Abhidhamma
or Further Teaching of Theravada Buddhism.

120 Saddhatissa, H. The Buddha's Way. See entry no.
     1249.

121 Sangharakshita, B. Crossing the Stream. Bombay:
     Chetana, 1960. 75 p.
     This little book contains a series of articles by the
author which appeared in Stepping-Stones, the Buddhist
Journal. The articles are of a simple nature and this would
be an excellent gift to someone who has just become interested in Buddhism, as it gives a picture of many facets of
the teaching.

122 _____. A Survey of Buddhism. Bangalore: Indian
     Institute of World Culture, 1957. 500 p.
     This work is based on enlarged versions of lectures
the author gave in 1954 under the auspices of the Indian
Institute of World Culture. It surveys in a wide sweep the
whole field of Buddhism in a manner reminiscent of Dr. E.
Conze's classic Buddhism. The attempt to place the personality of the historical Gautama Buddha against the background of tradition, and the basic principles of the Dharma
as displayed in the Pali Canon are explained and commented
on.

123 _____. The Three Jewels: An Introduction to
     Modern Buddhism. Garden City, N.Y.: Doubleday,
     1970. 269 p.
     The author gives various forms of Buddhism as
practiced today in the Buddhist countries. This work, while
not being very different from his earlier work, A Survey of

Buddhism, attempts to show the superiority of Mahayana
Buddhism. He also seems to favor the idealistic interpretation of the Buddha's teaching as presented by the Yogacara
school.

124 Soni, R. L. Life's Highest Blessings: The Highroad
      of Success and Happiness. Mandalay: World Insti-
      tute of Buddhist Culture, 1956. 146 p.
      The 38 blessings are elaborately classified and ex-
pounded, and the text of the Sutta is given in Pali, an
English word-for-word translation, and finally in a free
(English) rendering, with a full commentary which actually
takes in a great deal of basic Buddhism.

125 Stryk, L. World of the Buddha: A Reader from "The
      Three Baskets" to Modern Zen. Garden City, N.Y.:
      Doubleday, 1968. 423 p.
      This work is a collection of Buddhist writings
ranging from Jataka tales and legendary accounts of the
Buddha's life through a variety of excerpts from the Tripitaka and other Pali works dealing with different aspects of
early Buddhist philosophy, to passages exemplifying later
Mahayana development. In the latter part Tibetan, Chinese,
and Japanese writings are included. Special attention is
given to Zen poems, sermons, and anecdotes.

126 Thera, V. K. D. What Buddhists Believe. Kuala
      Lumpur: Buddhist Missionary Society, 1964. 86 p.
      This is a substantial and wide-ranging pamphlet de-
signed to give short, clear answers to the enquirer's questions. Topics dealt with include belief in God, birth control,
vegetarianism, as well as the basic tenets.

127 Thomas, E. J. The Life of the Buddha as Legend and
      History. New York: Knopf, 1927. 297 p.
      In this book all that is known of the life of the Bud-
dha from the texts is set forth in a Western form by an
authoritative writer. He does not confine himself to any one
body of Buddhist texts, but draws from Hinayana Pali sources
and Mahayana Sanskrit and Tibetan sources alike and uses not
only canonical books, but also the later commentaries.

128 _____ . The Road to Nirvana and the Quest of En-
      lightenment. London: Murray, 1950. 95 p.
      This is a new edition to the Wisdom of the East, a
series consisting of translations from the Pali Buddhist
scriptures in the case of the first and from the Sanskrit

Buddhist scriptures in the second. It gives informative and sympathetic introductory notes chosen as to give an account of the life of Gautama and an outline of his teaching, in each case from the standpoint of the Theravada and the Mahayana schools respectively. They make excellent introductions to Buddhism.

129 Walshe, M. O. Buddhism for Today. London: Allen and Unwin, 1962. 143 p.
       This book can answer for thoughtful people in the Western world what Buddhism holds and can do for them. The work tells how Buddhism can be used without ever losing sight of what it teaches and has a guide giving ideas for practicing it.

130 Walters, J. The Mind Unshaken. London: Rider and Co., 1960. 120 p.
       The author who is English visited the Far East as chief correspondent of a leading British national newspaper and came to know Buddhism and Buddhists in the Theravada countries of Ceylon, Burma and Thailand. A basic introduction to Buddhism, the blending of personal experience, lucid writing and the unambiguous statements of fact all are irresistible.

131 Ward, C. H. S. Buddhism: Hinayana (Vol. 1), Mahayana (Vol. 2). London: Epworth, 1947, 1952.
       These books are concise and comprehensive works on Buddhism meeting an urgent need for a modern scholarly text. Its clear style and simplicity of language should make it interesting to the general reader and give a real insight into the culture and fundamental outlook of the Buddhist peoples of Ceylon, Burma and Siam.

132 Zurcher, E. Buddhism: Its Origin and Spread. New York: St. Martin's Press, 1962. 97 p.
       One of the series of concise histories of world religions, this work gives a summary of Buddhist teaching. There are chapters on the life of the Buddha and the Dharma, followed by an examination of the modern world. It presents a comprehensive picture of the whole field of Buddhism.

ADDRESSES and ESSAYS

133 Arber, A. The Manifold and the One. London: John
      Murray, 1957. 146 p.
      The work is a synthesis, with many quotations,
about a central theme, which for want of a better term may
be called spiritual. It includes Plotinus' talking of one's
original face and the distinction between intellectual and
emotional mysticism.

134 Cameron, C. The Flowing Stream: Reflection on the
      Middle Way. London: Buddhist Society, 1939. 48 p.
      Reprinted from The Middle Way, a journal devoted to
Oriental philosophy and religion, the subject matter is of
general interest.

135 Dahlke, P. Buddhist Essays. Translated from the
      German by B. Silacara. London: Macmillan, 1909.
      361 p.
      This work deals with Buddha's life and teaching in
regard to life, sorrow, Nirvana, God, morality, asceticism,
etc. To these the author adds his own exegesis and conclusions. It is a full and reliable exposition of an exclusively
Oriental system of thought by an appreciative European con-
vert.

136 Dixon, B. Journeys in Belief. London: Allen and
      Unwin, 1968. 239 p.
      Anyone who has felt the pull of a new way of thought
and a different perception of the world will be in full sympa-
thy with the 18 authors of this book. They are describing,
with considerable honest searching of mind and heart, what
has occurred to them in their lifetime and how their beliefs
have grown and altered and led them onwards.

137 Howe, G. Cure or Heal? London: Allen and Unwin,
      1967. 234 p.
      The work shows us that time is the basic part of
our environment, the importance of which we hardly realize.
In a time environment we must make choices, and thus we
suffer. The author points out that the Buddhist way of acceptance and detachment and the realization of the existential
reality of the "Middle Way" between opposite extremes bring
a new illumination into being, but also involve suffering.

138 Humphreys, C. Studies in the Middle Way. London:
        Allen and Unwin, 1959. 168 p. [see also entry
        no. 570.]
        This volume is in great part a re-issue of essays
and addresses on the fundamental problems of life as seen
by a Buddhist and is dedicated to H. P. Blavatsky. There
is a chapter on theosophy and Buddhism (the author claims
he arrived at Buddhism by way of theosophy). This work
includes many poems.

139 Radhakrishnan. East and West: Some Reflections.
        London: Allen and Unwin, 1955. 140 p.
        This contribution by the Vice-President of India to
a better understanding between East and West consists of
three Beatty Memorial Lectures to McGill University. Each
lecture contains stimulating material for thought and an admirable addiction to epigram.

140 Ram, N. S. Seeking Wisdom. Wheaton: Theosophical
        Publishing House, 1971. 60 p.
        This is a collection of essays by a deeply perceptive
writer on essential truths with items such as: "Truth or
Semblance, " "Freedom from Opposites, " "Attention, "
"Interest, " and "Love. "

141 Sangharakshita, B. Crossing the Stream. See entry
        no. 121.

142 Wickramasinghe, M. The Buddhist Jataka Stories and
        the Russian Novel. Colombo: Associated News-
        papers of Ceylon, 1956. 173 p.
        This work contains 11 essays. The two major ones
deal with certain selected aspects of life and character as
found in a number of the Jataka stories. In the second essay
the author is at pains to show that the characters in Dos-
toievski's chief novels have spiritual and psychological affinities. The last essays are no more than very slight sketches
of Indian and Sinhalese art and culture and make easy reading.

ANTHOLOGIES

143 Burlingame, E. W. Buddhist Parables. See entry
        no. 794.

144   Burtt, E. A. (ed.).   The Teaching of the Compas-
         sionate Buddha.   See entry no. 1225.

145   Davids, C. A. F. Rhys.   Buddhism: A Study of the
         Buddhist Norm.   See entry no. 299.

146   Dickhoff, R. E.   Agharta.   Boston: Bruce Humphries,
         1951.   106 p.
         Agharta will be an organization operating on the
surface of the earth for all to see, nothing secret, nothing
hidden, and from the underground coming up will lead the
true Agharta with the creed that in this era of the Lord
Maitreya let Truth and Justice reign supreme.

147   Humphreys, C.   Wisdom of Buddhism.   New York:
         Random House, 1961.   280 p.
         One of the best anthologies available, it holds the
balance between the various schools of Buddhism.   It is a
comprehensive collection of Buddhist scripture extracts.
The passages quoted, covering the main teachings of Buddhism as found in the Theravada and Mahayana, and in
Chinese, Tibetan, and Japanese Buddhism, give an enquirer
a fair grasp of the whole field.

148   Reynolds, C.   An Anthology of Sinhalese Literature up
         to 1815.   See entry no. 427.

149   Ross, N. W.   The World of Zen: An East-West An-
         thology.   New York: Random House, 1960.   362 p.
         Miss Ross's anthology gives an impression of the
scope of Zen--its teaching and practice, its influence on
painting, poetry, architecture, gardening, drama, and ath-
letic arts, as well as its relevance to modern thought in
psychiatry and the philosophy of science.

150   Saunders, K. J.   The Heart of Buddhism.   London:
         Oxford University Press, 1915.   96 p.
         This work is a translated anthology of Buddhist
verse.

151   Suriyabongs, L.   A Buddhist Anthology.   Bangkok:
         Thai Watana Panich, 1957.   96 p.
         This is an excellent anthology from the Pali Canon
with four sections on the Buddha, the Dhamma, the Sangha
and the Lay-Disciple.

152   Walters, J.   The Mind Unshaken: A Modern Approach
         to Buddhism.   See entry no. 130.

153 Wright, D. A Manual of Buddhism. London: K. Paul,
        Trench, Trubner and Co., 1912. 87 p.
        This is a pocket book for earnest men, mainly in
the lucid and beautiful words of the Buddha himself.

154 Yohannan, J. D. The Treasury of Asian Literature.
        Atlanta: Phoenix, 1958. 488 p.
        This is a general collection of the sacred and secu-
lar literature of all Asia, chosen on no perceivable principle
from other men's translations of such works, and, as such,
can rank with any other anthology.

ART

GENERAL

155 Anesaki, M. Buddhist Art in Its Relation to Buddhist
        Ideas, with Special Reference to Buddhism in Japan.
        London: Houghton, 1916.
        Four lectures printed in this volume give a brief
account of the Buddha and of his two principal ideals of an
unbounded fellowship and dedication, and follows with an exposition of these as conceived by the Japanese and expressed
in their art--temples, sculpture of various sorts, and
painting--during different periods.

156 Bapat, P. V. (ed.). 2500 Years of Buddhism. See
        entry no. 365.

157 Bernstein, J. The Wildest Dreams of Kew--A Profile
        of Nepal. See entry no. 685.

158 Chetwode, P. Kulu: The End of the Habitable World.
        See entry no. 245.

159 Coe, S. The Art of Japanese Flower Arrangement.
        London: Herbert Jenkins, 1964. 158 p.
        The teachings of the Sogetsu School of Tokyo, the
largest and most popular of the many modern schools of
flower arranging in Japan, are propounded. The basic
principles of the art and instructions in the making of the
basic arrangements and their variations are clearly and
concisely given. The work includes the original classical

styles and another part on the latest modern free style, abstract and avant garde trends.

160 Coomaraswamy, A. K. Buddha and the Gospel of
      Buddhism. See entry no. 1227.

161 _____. Introduction to Indian Art. Edited by Mulk
      Raj Anand. London: Theosophical Publishing
      House, 1956. 123 p.
      This is a reprint with added chapters on Islamic
architecture and Sikh and modern painting, written by the
editor. It shows the development of art from Indo-Sumerian
forms to modern Indian paintings with a few photographs and
many pen and ink drawings.

162 Davidson, J. L. Lotus Sutra in Chinese Art; A Study
      in Buddhist Art to the Year 1000. New Haven:
      Yale University, 1954. 105 p.
      In this book the author has taken one of the pre-
rogatives of the art historian, which is to use the materials
of culture as a means of interpreting the fundamental thought
of a civilization. Because Lotus Sutra is the prime source
of Buddhist art, it is the author's central point of study.
Mahayana scriptures on Buddhist art have so far received
little attention. The Mahayana naturally also availed itself
of art to get its message across to the masses. The 40
illustrations at the end well show the striking beauty of
Chinese works of art. Useful bibliographical notes are
given at the end of the book.

163 Fink, R. A Short Introduction to Japanese Art. Lon-
      don: Seeley Service, 1954. 88 p.
      The author covers a thousand years of art develop-
ment in eighty pages, and the reader is therefore rushed
through the centuries at somewhat breakneck speed. But the
balance is remarkably maintained, and to all who are new
to the subject this is a reasonably accurate and helpful introduction.

164 Groslier, B. P. Indo-China; Art in the Melting-Pot
      of Races. London: Methuen, 1963. 245 p.
      This work covers Cambodia, Laos, Annam, Vietnam,
Burma, Siam, and much beside and is historically a fascinating complex of Hinduism, Mahayana Buddhism and then
the Theravada variety, all blended into a shifting kaleido-
scope of kingdoms, races and civilizations. As here set

out, the art forms and traditions make a fascinating study
for the Western reader.

165 Grousset, R. Chinese Art and Culture. Paris: Andre
         Deutsch, 1959. 331 p.
     This book deals with four thousand years of Chinese
art and civilization. The author does not simply discuss the
art of China, he delves into the mysteries of Chinese philosophy and religion, dealing with them as they affect the
art of the period. There are 16 color plates and 64 black
and white ones.

166 _____. In the Footsteps of the Buddha. See entry
         no. 355.

167 Hasumi, T. Zen in the Japanese Art; A Way of
         Spiritual Experience. New York: Philosophical
         Library, 1962. 113 p.
     Dr. Hasumi has studied Zen under German as well
as Japanese teachers and his treatment of the subject owes
much to German aesthetics, philosophy and terminology.
This work treats the subject scholarly, particularly in the
chapter on the artistic and spiritual history of Japan.

168 Herrigel, G. L. Zen in the Art of Flower-Arrange-
         ment. See entry no. 1081.

169 Hisamatsu, S. Zen and the Fine Arts. Tokyo: Ko-
         dansha International, 1971. 400 p.
     This is the first book to disclose the spiritual rela-
tionship between Zen and the fine arts and to show its in-
trinsic meaning. The author, former professor of religion
and Buddhism at Kyoto University, is one of the foremost
scholars in both Zen and art in Japan. 239 art plates and
explanatory notes are given.

170 Hurlimann, M. Asia: 289 Pictures in Photogravure,
         Four Colour Plates, Introductory Essay, Historical
         Notes. New York: Studio Publications, 1957.
         262 p.
     The author attempts to cover the whole of Asia in
photographs. The 24 pages of introduction can say nothing
in that space. This is virtually a scrapbook of photographs
from Turkey to Japan.

171 Kidder, J. E. Early Japanese Art. London: Thames
         and Hudson, 1964. 350 p.

For the study of Japanese art this is an admirable
introduction in terms of time, and certainly it is the first
work of its range yet to appear. The period covered ranges
from 600 B.C. to A.D. 600, just before the history of
Buddhism in Japan begins. The influence of Korea and
China is well brought out.

172 Kim, C. The Art of Korea. London: Thames and
        Hudson, 1966. 284 p.
     As a former Director of the National Museum of
Korea, the author can speak with much authority and it is
fair to describe the work as the first on Korean art by a
Korean. The work is fascinating, for Korean art is the
unique Oriental art from which Japanese art originates.
Most illustrations are excellent, and those in color are very
good.

173 Kramrisch, S. The Art of India; Traditions of Indian
        Sculpture, Painting, and Architecture. New York:
        Phaidon, 1954. 231 p.
     The introductory essay relates Indian art to the basic
religious concepts of the culture. A number of paintings are
reproduced in color. Photographs of temples and sculptural
details, while not always very clearly reproduced, are representative and many suggest the texture of the stone. Brief
notes are given for each plate, and a short bibliography is
included.

174 _____. The Art of Nepal. New York: H. N.
        Abrams, 1964. 159 p.
     An Asia House Gallery publication, this is a cata-
logue of an exhibition selected by Dr. Stella Kramrisch and
shown in the Asia House Gallery in the summer of 1964 as
an activity of the Asia Society. Most of the exhibits are
illustrated, some in full page and a few in color, and the
author's pioneer chronology is most interesting.

175 LeMay, R. The Culture of Southeast Asia. London:
        Allen and Unwin, 1953. 218 p.
     Dr. LeMay is a well-known writer on Buddhist art,
and in this volume he has made the first comprehensive
study of all art forms of Southeast Asia, dealing above all
with Buddhist sculpture and architecture. The History of
Indian and Indonesian Art, published in 1927 by Dr. Coomaraswamy, was the first in this area, but his emphasis is on
Indian art. Also at that time far less research had been
done, particularly in Siam and Indo-China. Dr. LeMay tries

to explain the difference between the Eastern and the Western
approach to art and culture in general, a matter which is of
paramount importance if we wish to derive a feeling of aesthetic satisfaction from a contemplation of Buddhist art.

176   Marshall, J.   Buddhist Art of Gandhara.   New York:
          Cambridge University Press, 1960.   112 p. and 111
          plates.
          There is so much confusion about the genesis and
nature of the Buddhist art of Gandhara.   However, Sir John
has great authority on this subject and he gives clearly the
considerable difference between the two schools of Gandhara
Buddhist art, that of the first and second centuries A.D. and
that of the fourth and fifth, which Sir John prefers to call
the Indo-Afghan school.

177   Munsterberg, H.   Chinese Buddhist Bronzes.   Tokyo:
          Tuttle, 1967.   192 p.
          This work gives information on the origins of Bud-
dhist sculpture in China, casting techniques, and modern
collections, as well as a list of major dated Chinese Buddhist
bronzes.

178   Olschak, B.   Bhutan, Land of Hidden Treasures.   See
          entry no. 496.

179   Rawson, P.   The Art of Tantra.   London: Thames and
          Hudson, 1973.   216 p.
          Tantric art, the art derived from the philosophy of
Tantra, has only recently made any impact on the West.
Coming from India, yet having links with recent trends in
Western art, Tantra combines eroticism, mathematics,
magic and metaphysics in a view of life which offers a
uniquely successful antidote to the anxieties of our time.
Many works exhibited, together with others not previously
reproduced, are illustrated in this book, which is the first
complete survey of Tantric art and the way it can be put to
practical use.

180   Ridley, M.   Far Eastern Antiquities.   London: John
          Gifford, 1972.   112 p.
          This work deals mainly from the prospective col-
lector's point of view with a vast and relatively unexplored
subject.   The author divides it into several sections: sculpture, bronzes, lacquer, miniature sculpture, jade and ivory.
The wide white margins and glowing jewel colors of the
beautifully set illustrations make the very opening of the book

a pleasure. Most of the illustrations are specifically Buddhist.

181   Rowland, B. The Art and Architecture of India: Bud-
         dhist, Hindu, Jain. Baltimore: Penguin, 1954.
         288 p.
         Brief factual surveys are given, not only of Indian
art and architecture, but also of the neighboring countries
that have been influenced by Indian styles. The text is well
illustrated with many drawings and photographs. It includes
a useful bibliography.

182   Rubissow, H. The Art of Asia. New York: Philo-
         sophical Library, 1955.   237 p. and 84 illustrations.
         Presented as a swift, far-flung survey of Oriental
art from the earliest times to the present, these pages contain a series of notes on the history of art in 16 centuries,
with illustrations from each, largely from specimens in
American museums.

183   Sawa, T. Art in Japanese Esoteric Buddhism. New
         York: Weatherhill, 1972. 151 p.
         The book contrasts the aims of exoteric and esoteric
Buddhist art. The former strives to give physical form to
the vast paradises in which the Buddha dwells, the latter devotes maximum attention to the rites and disciplines that
lead human beings to Buddhahood in this life.

184   Seiroku, N. The Arts of Japan: Ancient and Medieval.
         See entry no. 196.

185   Sickman, L. and Soper, A. The Art and Architecture
         of China. Baltimore: Penguin Books, 1955.   334 p.
         This is the third volume in the Pelican History of
Art series. It is in two parts, the first confined to painting
and sculpture, and the second treating architecture. The
author stresses the earlier dates for the greatest period of
Chinese art.

186   Suzuki, D. T. Zen Buddhism and Its Influence on
         Japanese Culture. See entry no. 1134.

187   Swaan, W. Lost Cities of Asia. London: Elek, 1967.
         175 p.
         The author is well known as an art historian and
travel-writer devoted to three cities: Ceylon, Pagan, and
Angkor. The volume is well done, in quality of text,

accurate observations and good photographs, mostly the
author's own. Altogether it contains 103 plates, 51 in
color, showing a great wealth of Buddhist art.

188 Swann, P. C. Japan: From the Jomon to the Toku-
        gawa Period. London: Methuen, 1966. 238 p.
        High-ranking works of art are here duly highlighted
and most beautifully illustrated. This work is part of the
Art of the World series. The quality of colored pictures
is exceptionally good, and the marginal references are most
helpful. Here the author gives the history of Japan, a
wealth of its art, much of its Buddhism, and is in every
sense most lovely reading.

189 Vincent, I. V. Sacred Oasis: Caves of the Thousand
        Buddhas. Chicago: University of Chicago Press,
        1953. 114 p.
        This is a well-illustrated account of a journey in
1948 by a young American woman to the Caves of a Thousand
Buddhas, near Tun Huang in China. One of the best descriptions of the site since Aurel Stein and Pelliot rediscovered
the Caves nearly fifty years ago, they and the present author
were equally affected on first entering the Caves. The site
of the Caves was for centuries one of the most important
cross-roads of Asia. North of Tibet, south of Mongolia,
west of China, and east of India, it was for every traveler
the gateway to a new civilization. From the photographs in
this work it is clear that this ready-made museum contains
much of the finest Buddhist art extant.

ARCHITECTURE

190 no entry

191 Hurlimann, M. Bangkok. London: Thames and Hud-
        son, 1963. 122 p.
        Founded in 1782, Bangkok is a city of temples.
The author gives a good introduction and includes many pictures with brief descriptions.

192 Kramrisch, S. The Art of India; Traditions of Indian
        Sculpture, Painting, and Architecture. See entry
        no. 173.

193 Le May, R. The Culture of Southeast Asia. See entry
        no. 175.

194 Ooka, M. Temples of Nara and Their Art. Translated
        by Dennis Lishka. New York: John Weatherhill,
        1973. 184 p.
        As an architectural study, the book is invaluable,
since it offers for the first time in English a wealth of information on the now vanishing structures from which Nara
derives its fame. The book discusses the art treasures
housed in these temples, giving primary attention to the
masterpieces of sculpture that have survived from the age
of Nara's greatness. At the same time, it carries the
history of each temple.

195 Rowland, B. The Art and Architecture of India: Bud-
        dhist, Hindu, and Jain. See entry no. 181.

196 Seiroku, N. The Arts of Japan: Ancient and Medieval.
        Translated and adapted by John Rosenfield. London:
        Ward, Lock and Company, 1966. 236 p.
        The author is a leading Japanese art historian, with
emphasis on aesthetics. The work is put forward as the
only book in which the arts of Japan are treated together in
terms of the spirit of the time and place where they were
produced. The contents are arranged geographically, for
90 per cent of the art described is architecture and its
attendant sculpture, ending with the Zen temples of Kyoto.

197 Sickman, L. The Art and Architecture of China. See
        entry no. 185.

198 Speiser, W. Oriental Architecture in Colour. New
        York: Viking, 1965. 504 p. Translated from the
        German by C. W. E. Kessler.
        This book contains 112 fine photographs of part of
the Architecture of the World series with explanatory text,
plans, and commentary.

199 Wheeler, M. Splendours of the East; Temples, Tombs,
        Palaces and Fortresses of Asia. London: Weiden-
        field and Nicolson, 1964. 288 p.
        The author emphasizes architecture in relation to
environment, but the result is an outstanding volume among
a welter of such. Here are beautiful, historic and representative buildings which are rightly famous, and rightly appear in a vast number of such pictorial anthologies. The
quality of the photographs in color and in black and white is
good, a blend of grand panorama and delicate vignette,
beautiful art.

200 Yoshida, T. The Japanese House and Garden. Trans-
         lated from the German by Marcus G. Sims. Lon-
         don: Architectural Press, 1955. 204 p. 249
         illustrations.
     The author gives account of how Zen Buddhism in-
fluenced Japanese architecture. Here is a chastity of taste,
a poverty of possession, and a simplicity of living which is
far nearer the Buddhist ideal than any other. In the present
book there is all one needs to know about its construction,
with a wealth of glorious detail of houses, new and old.
The author gives some of his own design too.

DANCE

201 Bowers, F. Theatre in the East: A Survey of Asian
         Dance and Drama. New York: Grove, 1956, 1960.
         374 p.
     This is a survey of Asian dance and drama as ob-
served by the author on a study-tour. Some of the material
has been previously published in the New Yorker, Saturday
Review, and Holiday. Illustrated by more than seventy
photographs with end papers showing exotic dancers in magnificent gilt, this book is an inspired creation, both in ap-
pearance and in subject matter.

202 Gordon, B. An Introduction to the Dance of India,
         China, Korea, and Japan. New York: Asia Society,
         1965. 8 p.
     This little book gives a handy introductory essay
and presents some fundamental facts about the dance in
South and East Asia. The last portion compares Asian and
Western dance.

DRAMA

203 Bowers, F. Theatre in the East: A Survey of Asian
         Dance and Drama. See entry no. 201.

204 Carus, P. The Buddha. Chicago: Open Court Pub.
         Co., 1911. 68 p.
     This is a drama in three acts and four interludes,
and it tells a tale of Buddha's life.

HYMNS

205 Hymns of the Faith. London: Trubner, 1902. 109 p.
    This is an ancient anthology preserved in the short
collection of the sacred scriptures of the Buddhists. The
work is translated from the Pali by Albert J. Edmunds.
Most of the poems are Buddhist devotional poetry, early
hymns by monks and popular poetic proverbs of India.

206 Robinson, R. Chinese Buddhist Verse. London:
        Murray, 1954. 85 p.
    This is a selection of 20 hymns that form part of
the Buddhist scriptures of China which, according to the
author, are read, believed and followed today. This work
contains a guide to pronouncing Sanskrit and Chinese terms,
and also a useful, brief introduction.

207 Wellesz, E. Ancient and Oriental Music. New York:
        Oxford University, 1957. 530 p.
    The second edition of the Oxford History of Music
presents the musicological studies, which has created a new
outlook. The first chapter gives an introduction to the essentials of all kinds of primitive music. The main part of
the volume, Chapters Two through Eight, gives a historical
survey of the music of the East. Under Chapter Two there
is a Buddhist music section which gives the early historical
development of Buddhist music.

PAINTING

208 Awakawa, Y. Zen Painting. Translated by John
        Bester. Tokyo: Kodansha, 1970. 184 p.
    This is a comprehensive survey of Zen painting,
which carefully approaches the meaning of Zen in poetry and
painting in its thirty-page preface but confuses, rather than
clarifies with the constant use of Sino-Japanese terms which
refer more to states of mind than conditions of artistic
reaction. Some 135 paintings are used as examples of Zen
painting in this study.

209 Bhikkhu, B. Teaching Dhamma by Pictures: Explana-
        tion of a Siamese Traditional Buddhist Manuscript.
        Bangkok: Social Science Association of Thailand,
        1968. 109 p.

This is a collection of 47 paintings taken from an
old manuscript found at Chaiya, in southern Thailand.   The
author has written for each of them an explanation of the
particular aspect of Dhamma illustrated.

210   Carus, P.   Portfolio of Buddhist Art, Historical and
        Modern.   Chicago: Open Court Pub. Co., 1906.
        31 plates.
        This collection of Buddhist pictures does not pretend
to be complete in any respect.   It consists of a few samples
only, which are chosen almost at random from a wealth of
innumerable art productions that have originated under the
influence of Buddhism.

211   Clark, W. E.   Two Lamaistic Pantheons.   New York:
        Paragon, 1937.   314 p.
        This invaluable book of Tibetan iconography has
been out of print for many years.   The hundreds of illustrations taken from statues and woodblock illustrations are
fully indexed in Sanskrit, Tibetan and Chinese.

212   Coomaraswamy, A. K.   Buddha and the Gospel of
        Buddhism.   See entry no. 1227.

213   Fontein, J.   Zen Painting and Calligraphy.   Boston:
        Museum of Fine Arts, 1970.   173 p.
        The ancient philosophy of Zen Buddhism, which had
its roots in India and traveled to China and Korea and
thence to Japan in the 12th and 13th centuries, has so
deeply penetrated the life of the Far East that it has affected many expressions of its culture.   This is the first
exhibition of Zen painting and calligraphy to be held in the
Western world; 27 masterpieces are included in this exhibition and are shown for the first time outside Japan.

214   Gray, B.   Buddhist Cave Paintings at Tun-huang.
        Chicago: University of Chicago, 1959.   86 p.   70
        plates.   Photos by J. B. Vincent, with a preface
        by Arthur Waley.
        In 1953 Mr. Vincent published The Sacred Oasis,
the record of a journey to the Tun-huang Caves which were
rediscovered in 1908.   Mr. Basil Gray of the British Museum, after examining the photography, paid a visit to the
caves and now gives a detailed account of the subjects,
dating, and importance of a large section of the pictures
found.

215 Hisamatsu, S. Zen and Fine Arts. Kyoto: Bokubisha,
        1958. 106 p. 290 plates.
        This work is devoted entirely to Zen and its impor-
tant relationship to the fine arts. It shows a magnificent
collection of plates dealing with Zen elements found in the
various forms of art, including paintings, calligraphy,
gardens, tearooms, tea utensils and temples.

216 Kramrisch, S. The Art of India; Traditions of Indian
        Sculpture, Painting and Architecture. See entry
        no. 173.

217 The New York Graphic Society. Japan: Ancient Bud-
        dhist Paintings. Paris: UNESCO, 1959.
        Published by the New York Graphic Society by ar-
rangement with UNESCO, the series is designed to bring
within the reach of artists, teachers, students and the wide
art-loving public, the finest quality color reproductions of
masterpieces of art which hitherto have been known to a
too limited few.

218 Sengai: The Zen Master. Edited by Daisetz Suzuki.
        London: Faber and Faber, 1971. 127 p.
        Gibbon Sengai (1750-1837) was one of the great
Japanese Zen masters of the old school. Calligraphy and
ink drawing constituted a part of his Zen training. He
devoted himself entirely to the art of brush. This book
contains his explanatory notes and texts to 127 scrolls
selected by Mr. Suzuki and the explanation of the historical
and spiritual background of the pictures.

219 Sickman, L. The Art and Architecture of China. See
        entry no. 185.

220 Silva, A. de. Chinese Landscape Painting in the Caves
        of Tun-Huang. London: Methuen, 1967. 240 p.
        Photographs by D. Darbois.
        The author brings in word and picture an almost
thousand-year history of Buddhist painting and sculpture.
Most of the exquisite color plates appear for the first time
in the West and a detailed commentary accompanies each.
The interwoven text provides explanation of the art techniques
deployed. The author works for UNESCO in Paris as editor,
author and journalist. This work is exceptionally good research of Tun-Huang.

221 Suzuki, D. T. Manual of Zen Buddhism. See entry
        no. 1128.

222 Wray, E. and Rosenfield, C. Ten Lives of the Buddha:
        Siamese Temple Paintings and Jataka Tales. New
        York: Weatherhill, 1972. 154 p.
        The wall paintings discussed in this book illustrate
the ten most important Jataka tales, stories of the Buddha's
previous lives in which he was still a bodhisatta striving to
accumulate a sufficient store of merits and wisdom to be
able to achieve Buddhahood by a supreme effort in his final
life. The authors review the plots of the ten Jatakas illustrated, and they give a brief history of the Jataka collection,
with the chief emphasis on Burma and Siam.

SCULPTURE

223 Bowie, T. The Sculpture of Thailand. New York:
        The Asia Society, Inc., 1972. 135 p.
        Here is a presentation of a thousand years of Thai
sculpture with a grand set of photographs, mostly of Buddha
images, many of recent discovery, and all expertly described by Mr. Subhadradis Diskul. Description of an image
in terms of its date, style and origin is for the expert only,
but anyone can see here the overall excellence of this Thai
art.

224 Coomaraswamy, A. K. Buddha and the Gospel of
        Buddhism. See entry no. 1227.

225 Cunningham, A. Stupa of Bharhut. Varanasi: Indo-
        logical Book House, 1962. 143 p.
        This concerns a Buddhist monument ornamented with
numerous sculptures illustrating Buddhist legend and history
in the third century B.C. with an introduction by Vasudeva
S. Agarwala.

226 Devendra, D. T. Classical Sinhalese Sculpture
        c. 300 B.C. to 1000 A.D. London: Alec Tiranti,
        1958. 179 p.
        To the people of Ceylon this work will be a most
helpful manual towards understanding their great heritage of
majestic sculpture. It gives a good survey of the materials
used and the approximate time of building these ancient monuments with their austere and beautiful sculpting, which were
all inspired by Buddhist devotion.

227 Kar, C. Classical Indian Sculpture, 300 B.C. to

<u>500 A.D.</u>   New York: Transatlantic Arts, 1950.
<u>36 p.</u> and 86 plates.

Most plates are excellently produced, and the text,
though not much more than notes of chronological sequence,
provide the would-be student with the basics of the subject.
So much of early Indian art is Buddhist art that the head-
notes to this series of reviews seem no exaggeration. It is
interesting to see how in different times and places the essential common element persists.

228   Kramrisch, S.   <u>The Art of India; Translations of</u>
        <u>Indian Sculpture, Painting, and Architecture.</u> See
        entry no. 173.

229   LeMay, R.   <u>The Culture of Southeast Asia.</u>   See entry
        no. 175.

230   Saunders, E. D.   <u>Mudra: A Study of Symbolic Gestures</u>
        <u>in Japanese Buddhist Sculpture.</u>   London: Routledge
        and Kegan Paul, 1959.   296 p.
        Many Buddhists who study chiefly the Theravada and
Zen schools of Buddhism do not appreciate what a large part
ritual and symbolic magic play in many schools.   This work,
which gives the historical background and explanation of
various types of symbolic gestures, may, by the great range
of Buddhist sculpture in Japan, send students to some of the
vast range of books set out in the good reference bibliography, concerning Japanese Buddhist Zen art.

231   Sickman, L.   <u>The Art and Architecture of China.</u>   See
        entry no. 185.

232   Spiegelberg, F.   <u>Zen, Rocks and Waters</u>.   Introduction
        by Sir Herbert Read.   New York: Pantheon Books,
        1961.   63 p.
        This is a collection of 16 woodcuts based on brush-
drawings whose genesis is seldom clearly specified.   The
artist and the period of his work, however, have little relevance to the theme, which is the great artist's power to express in brush-work his awareness of Zen.   It has a good
introduction by Sir Herbert Read; it is interesting to read a
Western mind on Eastern art.

233   Suzuki, D. T.   <u>Manual of Zen Buddhism; An Anthology</u>
        <u>from Original Sources; Reproductions of Buddhist</u>
        <u>Paintings, Drawings and Religious Statues.</u>   See
        entry no. 1128.

BIOGRAPHY

234 Agehananda Bharati, S. The Ochre Robe. Seattle:
         University of Washington, 1961. 294 p.
     This remarkable spiritual autobiography should be
read by everyone who is struggling to think through the
religious field. The main themes are communication between man and man, the potentialities of a humanistic-mysti-
cal religion, in which India could learn from the humanism
of the West, and a genuine bridge-building between East and
West by those who know the terrain at both ends. There is
a glossary of Sanskrit and Hindi terms.

235 Anesaki, M. Nichiren, the Buddhist Prophet. Cam-
         bridge, Mass.: Harvard University Press, 1916.
         160 p.
     This work gives a clear exposition of Nichiren's
personality and teaching which unified religion and ethics,
rescued pure Buddhism from the contamination of spurious
beliefs and restored it to the purity of its original high
ideals.

236 Aurobindo, S. Letters of Sri Aurobindo. London:
         Luzac, 1947. 416 p.
     This book constitutes a manual for the practical
pilgrim on the path of spiritual discovery. It consists of
letters written to disciples and postulants over a period of
about twenty years, and deals with their problems and questions. It is full of inspiration and help for the serious
student.

237 Barborka, G. A. H. P. Blavatsky, Tibet and Tulku.
         Madras: Theosophical Publishing House, 1966.
         476 p.
     The author produces new material on the life of
H. P. Blavatsky, an original analysis of her various methods
of writing, and a great deal of information on Tibetan Buddhism.

238 Blavatsky, H. P. Collected Writings 1888-1889.
         Volume X. Edited by B. de Zirkoff. London:
         Theosophical Publishing House, 1964. 461 p.
     This volume is largely taken up with a reprint of
Transactions of the Blavatsky Lodge, being the answers to
questions asked at meetings of the Lodge in London. The
editor gives Miss Blavatsky's views on the decadence of

Buddhism in the Eighties; of Colonel Olcott's successful efforts to revive it in Ceylon; her comments on an article,
"A Buddhist Prince's View of the Universe and the Nature
of Man" by a Thai prince; and an elaboration on Karma,
Tanha and the Skandhas as the triple cause of our rebirth.

239   Blofeld, J. E. C.   The Wheel of Life; Autobiography
         of a Western Buddhist.   London: Rider, 1959.
         263 p.
      This is a record of a spiritual pilgrimage to some
of the holiest and most inaccessible mountains in China.
His book ends with an account of his journey to a Vajrayana
monastery in the foothills of the Himalayas in a remote part
of Sikkim, and his final initiation there at the hands of the
Tangku Lama.

240   Brunton, P.   A Hermit in the Himalayas.   London:
         Rider, 1936.   322 p.
      The author wrote this work as an autobiography of
his experiences and journeys.   It tells of a lovely retreat
of several weeks in the Tehri-Garhwal State with the thoughts
and feelings which came during meditation about life in
general.   The author gives also the superficial view of the
Buddha's doctrine and comparison with that of Krishna.

241   Buddhaghosa, B.   The Minor Readings; The First Book
         of the Minor Collection, the Illustrator of Ultimate
         Meanings.   London: Luzac, 1960.   342 p.
      This is the last translation to be completed by the
late Bhikkhu Nanamoli.   It consists of the short text which
has been called the whole duty of a layman, together with
Buddhaghosa's famous commentary on it.

242   Bush, L.   The Road to Inamura.   London: Robert
         Hale, 1961.   238 p.
      This work is the author's own story of his life.
The author married a Japanese wife and lived in Northern
Japan and is now on his own, broadcasting, lecturing, and
writing.   If there is no Buddhism here, there is much of
the charm of a most lovable people presented by one who
has made their land his home.

243   Chang, C. C.   Practice of Zen.   See entry no. 1071.

244   Chaudhuri, H.   The Integral Philosophy of Sri Auro-
         bindo; Comparative Symposium.   London: Allen and
         Unwin, 1960.   352 p.

Essays by thirty scholars from universities of
England, Germany, America, and India have been collected
under five headings: philosophy, epistemology and psychology,
Yoga, ethics, and literature.

245 Chetwode, P. Kulu: The End of the Habitable World.
        London: John Murray, 1972. 230 p.
        This volume tells of the author's journey, the
people she met and much of the Hindu shrines to somewhat
obscure gods on which subject she has made herself an expert. Most of her book tells about Nicholas Roerich, who
spent the last eighteen years of his life in the Valley, dying
in 1947. A magnificent figure of a man, Roerich was ar-
chaeologist, botanist, explorer, writer, stage-designer, poet,
and above all the author of Himalaya (1926), which contains
a wide selection of his paintings in color, and Altai Himalaya
(1929), described as a travel-diary, which shows evidence of
his supreme quality.

246 Clark, J. M. Meister Eckhart. London: Thomas
        Nelson, 1957. 269 p.
        It has often been said that among Christian mystics,
the 14th-century German Master Eckhart comes closer to
the outlook of Mahayana Buddhism than any other. The first
part gives a sober and authoritative description of Eckhart's
life and teachings and the second part is a translation of
25 sermons.

247 Coates, H. H. and Ishizuka, R. Honen, the Buddhist
        Saint: His Life and Teaching. Kyoto: Chienin,
        1925.
        This is a translation of the life of the founder of the
Jodo sect, with historical instruction and notes, explanatory
and critical. A mine of information on Pure Land Buddhism
is contained here.

248 The Dalai Lama of Tibet (Dalai Lama XIV). My Land
        and My People. New York: McGraw-Hill, 1962.
        271 p.
        His Holiness the 14th Dalai Lama, spiritual and
temporal ruler of Tibet, was born a farmer's son two years
after the death of his previous incarnation, according to his
account. At that time his native region was already under
the control of the Chinese. His discovery by the priests
commissioned to seek out their new ruler, the ransom de-
manded by the Chinese governor for his release, his en-
thronement at Lhasa and the events of his young life make

interesting reading. In 1950 when he was only 16, his
people were threatened by Chinese Communist invasion. As
a Buddhist priest and a follower of Gandhi's doctrine of non-
violence, the Dalai Lama offered no resistance and sought a
treaty. His subsequent betrayal, the murder of many of his
people and their perilous escape into India form the bulk of
his moving and dignified account.

249 Dharmapala, A. Return to Righteousness. Ceylon:
       Ministry of Education and Cultural Affairs, 1965.
       875 p.
       This is a collection of speeches, essays and letters
of the Anagarika Dharmapala.

250 Ennin (Jikaku Daishi). Diary: The Record of a Pil-
       grimage to China in Search of the Law. Translated
       from the Chinese by Edwin O. Reischauer. New
       York: Donald, 1955. 454 p.
       Ennin was a Japanese Buddhist monk who went to
China for study in A.D. 838, and during a sojourn of nine
years recorded his experiences in a travel diary.

251 Evans-Wentz, W. Y. Tibet's Great Yogi Milarepa.
       London: Oxford University Press, 1951. 315 p.
       This is a biography from the Tibetan, being the
Jetsun-Kahbum, or biographical history of Jetsun-Milarepa,
according to the late Lama Kazi Dawasumdup's English
rendering, edited with introduction and annotation by W. Y.
Evans-Wentz.

252 Gage, A. The One Work; a Journey towards the Self.
       London: Vincent Stuart, 1962. 137 p.
       Miss Gage has written an account of her own search
for the reality of her self through rediscovering the meaning
of the traditional symbols pointing the way. Her journey
took her to India, where she walked through the Ajanta Caves
and round the holy mountain, Arunachala; to Angkor, where
she found in the structure of temples, with their stone faces,
a clear expression of the symbolic language; to Bali; to
Japan.

253 Grousset, R. In the Footsteps of the Buddha. See
       entry no. 355.

254 Guenther, H. V. The Life and Teaching of Naropa.
       See entry no. 736.

255 Hayakawa, S.   Zen Showed Me the Way; To Peace,
     Happiness, and Tranquility.   See entry no. 1080.

256 Hesse, H. Siddhartha. Translated from the German
     by Hilda Rosner. London: Vision Press, 1953.
     167 p.
     Brought up in an orthodox Brahmin family, Siddhartha
departed from his parents to become an ascetic. After many
years he found his problem still unsolved and he wandered on
until he came to Jetavana where he met Buddha and listened
to him in rapt attention. Nevertheless, he did not remain
with the Buddha as he had the deep realization that wisdom
must be obtained alone. This short, but very well-written
book will make a great appeal to all who, like Siddhartha,
set out on the quest for enlightenment.

257 Humphreys, C. Studies in the Middle Way. See entry
     no. 570.

258 Hwui-Li. The Life of Hiuen-Tsiang. Translated by
     Samuel Beal, with an introduction containing an
     account of the works of I-Tsing. London: K. Paul,
     Trench, Trubner, 1911.   218 p.
     This is a biography by a disciple which in many
places clarifies and supplements the records of the masters.

259 Jivaka, L. The Life of Milarepa. Wisdom of the East
     Series. London: Murray, 1962. 174 p.
     This version of the biography of Tibet's beloved
Yogi and reformer is condensed from the complete translation by W. Y. Evans-Wentz. Summarizing clearly his
teaching, it gives his early practice of sorcery, his family
feuds, tribulations as a disciple, physical and mental trials
in search of enlightenment and his human achievements.

260 Kanda, Y. The Ramayana of Valmiki. London: Shanti
     Sadan, 1959. 720 p. 3 volumes.
     The Ramayana is the record of the life and deeds of
Prince Rama, regarded by the Hindus as a divine incarnation.
The Ramayana is a work of inner meaning, and what on one
view is simply the enthralling story of a great man, on another is a description of the awakening of human consciousness
to divinity.

261 Merton, T. The Way of Chuang Tzu. See entry no
     989.

262 Nikam, N. A. and McKeon, R. The Edicts of Asoka.
       Chicago: University of Chicago, 1959. 69 p.
       The Buddhist Emperor Asoka is often referred to
as an example of how Buddhist ethical principles are applied
to the government of state. The text of the rock and pillar
Edicts and the cave inscriptions are supplied with explanatory footnotes where necessary, and the whole is somewhat
elaborately preceded by a Foreword, a Preface, and an Introduction.

263 Norbu, T. J. and Harrer, H. Tibet Is My Country.
       London: Rupert Hart-Davis, 1960. 264 p.
       This is an authentic autobiography of a Tibetan.
The eldest of the Dalai Lama's brothers narrated the story
to Heinrich Harrer. The story is simply told but richly
alive. The book contains a useful chronology of events and
also some fine colored illustrations.

264 Nott, C. S. The Teaching of Gurdjieff; the Journal of
       a Pupil; An Account of Some Years with G. I.
       Gurdjieff and A. R. Orage in New York. London:
       Routledge and Kegan Paul, 1961. 230 p.
       This book, liberally compiled from diaries and notes
on some of the talks given by Gurdjieff and A. R. Orage
during the years 1923 to 1928, together with descriptions of
the sacred dances staged by Gurdjieff, and also the author's
comments on his own personal experiences, combines to
form an interesting and varied picture of the teaching that
is claimed to integrate the wisdom of the East with the
science of the West.

265 Olcott, H. S. Hammer on the Mountain: The Life of
       Henry Steel Olcott. London: Theosophical Pub-
       lishing House, 1972.
       The author of the Buddhist Catechism and co-founder
with H. P. Blavatsky of the Theosophical Society writes a
well-illustrated biography that includes in its contents his
relationship with H. P. Blavatsky, and his work for theosophy and Buddhism.

266 Percheron, M. Marvelous Life of Buddha. Translated
       by Adrienne Foulke. New York: St. Martin's
       Press, 1960. 250 p.
       This biography combines the presumed facts of the
Buddha's existence with the tenets of his teaching and the
myths that have grown up around him. Included are selections
from Indian and Tibetan literature about Buddhism.

267   The Platform Sutra of the Sixth Patriarch: The Text
        of the Tun-huang Manuscript.   See entry no. 1260.

268   Plomer, W.   A Message in Code; The Diary of
        Richard Rumbold, 1932-1961.   London: Weidenfeld
        and Nicolson, 1963.   290 p.
        Mr. Rumbold as an R. A. F. pilot had moments of
spiritual happiness which he was not to know again until he
contacted Buddhism.   In search of its way of life he visited
first Ceylon and then Japan, and thus we have the diary of
an intelligent seeker, who without preconception of what he
would find, spent a substantial time in a Theravada and then
a Zen environment.

269   Radhakrishnan, S.   Ramana Maharshi and the Path to
        Self-Knowledge.   London: Rider and Company,
        1953.   207 p.
        This book purports to bring to the West the true
meaning of how the Eastern mind has found the answer to
life, and how in the pure life of Sri Bhagavan one can see
the path all the great sages have pointed to through the
ages.   The author has been a faithful devotee to carry to
the world the teachings of a pure sage.   By the study of
this book much can be learned with added enjoyment of an
interesting account of the lives of those who were in close
touch with the sage.   It also gives a good picture of the
life lived in the holy places of India.

270   Ramana, M.   The Collected Works of Maharshi Ramana.
        London: Rider, 1959.   200 p.
        The book includes works actually written by him,
mostly at the request of devotees, and verses which he borrows or adapts from the Gita and Shri Shankaracharya.   One
remarkable section is the hymn to Arunachala written from
the Dvaita level of the devotee.

271   The Recorded Sayings of Layman P'ang; A Ninth Cen-
        tury Zen Classic.   See entry no. 1110.

272   Sadhu, M.   In Days of Great Peace.   London: George
        Allen, 1958.   212 p.
        This work is an account of the impact made on the
author by Ramana Maharshi during a visit of many weeks,
as he says, "the real experience of an average man" in the

presence of a man who is more and more coming to be regarded as the great saint of modern times.

273 Sengai, G. Sengai; The Zen Master. See entry no.
      218.

274 Shattock, E. H. An Experiment in Mindfulness: An
      English Admiral's Experience in a Buddhist Monas-
      tery. New York: Dutton, 1960. 158 p.
      This is the account of a British Rear Admiral who
enters a Buddhist monastery for an experiment in intensive
meditation during a four-week leave. He tells of his daily
life at the monastery and how he reaches his religious ob-
jectives.

275 Smith, V. A. Asoka, the Buddhist Emperor of India.
      Oxford: Clarendon Press, 1909. 204 p.
      The fullest treatment in English is given here of
the history of Asoka, descriptions of the monuments, translations of the rock and pillar edicts, and the Ceylonese and
Indian legends.

276 Symonds, J. Madame Blavatsky. London: Odhams,
      1959. 250 p.
      The book is one long all-embracing sneer; it devotes
much prurient attention to such items as the malformation of
the subject's uterus and unsubstantiated gossip about her sex
life.

277 Thera, N. The Life of Sariputta. Ceylon: Wheel Pub-
      lications, 1966. 112 p.
      This work is based on Pali texts collected and trans-
lated by the author about the great sage Sariputta. The book
consists of five parts: first, from the birth to the attainment of sainthood; second, maturity of insight; third, the
further shore; fourth, discourses of Sariputta; fifth, Sariputta
in the Jatakas. There is also an Appendix providing a brief
historical account of the discovery of the relics of Sariputta.

278 Trungpa, C. Born in Tibet. London: George Allen
      and Unwin, 1967. 264 p.
      The author was only thirteen months old when he was
installed as Supreme Abbot of the Surmang district of monasteries in Tibet. Brought up in the strict but kindly seclusion

of the various monasteries and retreats to which he retired,
he proved a character of exceeding depth, both in kindness
and penetration, which endeared him to all his fellow Lamas
and the lay people.

279   Waley, A.   The Life and Times of Po Chu-i.   London:
          Allen and Unwin, 1949.   238 p.
          Po Chu-i was a Buddhist and had many friends
among the monks, more especially those of the Southern
Zen school.   This charming biography succeeds in presenting
a vivid picture of the poet, drawn partly from contemporary
records but mainly from his own works.

280   Watters, T.   On Yüan Chwang's Travels in India.
          London: Oriental Translation Fund, N. S. 1904-
          1905.   2 volumes.
          This is an extensive collection of very valuable notes
on the life and travels of Hsuang Chwang.   It is a most useful reference on specific questions.

281   Watts, A.   In My Own Way; An Autobiography.   New
          York: Pantheon Books, 1972.   400 p.
          Covering the years 1915 to 1965, the work describes
Alan Watts' childhood in England, his strict and traditional
schooling, his turn to Buddhism at age 15, his move to
America and finally the turn towards bringing together the
thought of East and West in his own life and philosophy.

282   Won Buddhist Half-Centennial Commemoration Commis-
          sion, Buddhist Federation of Korea.   The Canonical
          Textbook of Won Buddhism.   See entry no. 682.

283   Yale, J. R.   What Vedanta Means to Me; A Symposium.
          (Various contributors.)   London: Rider and Co.,
          1960.   224 p.
          Contributions are chiefly autobiographical, even if
mainly subjective.   They are very varied in background and
approach, but that of John Yale might be taken as fairly
representative.   It is a quite readable book, full of the tri-
umphant assertion of the divinity, for all these are, in the
spiritual sense, success stories.

284   The Zen Master Hakuin: Selected Writings.   Translated
          by Philip B. Yampolsky.   New York: Columbia Uni-
          versity Press, 1971.   253 p.
          The work contains a brief account of Rimzai Zen
Buddhism in Japan, three writings by Hakuin, and an appendix,

listing and describing Hakuin's works. Although composed
in an epistolary style, they are, in effect, sermons, dealing
with Zen, since Hakuin Ekaku (1686-1769) is one of the
major figures in the history of Japanese Zen Buddhism.

DOCTRINE

285 Anesaki, M. Katam Karaniyam, Lectures, Essays,
        and Studies. Boston: Marshall Jones Co., 1936.
        318 p.
        This is a part of the capital passage in the Pali
Canon describing the attainment of the Arahatta, the ideal
perfection of Buddhist training.

286 Appleton, G. On the Eightfold Path. London: Oxford
        University Press, 1961. 156 p.
        The author, who worked in Burma for twenty years,
essays to enter sympathetically into Buddhism, and to compare and contrast the main doctrines with that of Christianity,
basing his study of the former mainly on the Theravada
teaching.

287 Ashish, S. M. Man, Son of Man. London: Rider,
        1971. 352 p.
        The present work was begun by Sri Krishna Prem,
but handed over to Sri Madhava Ashish, who in due course
found it necessary to entirely rewrite it. Anthropogenesis
is noticeably different from the earlier cosmogenesis, but
shows deep scholarship, fortified assuredly with deep meditation. The author concentrates on this central theme, and
almost brushes aside those aspects of the stanzas concerned
with Rounds and Races, or the Continents of Atlantis and
Lemuria, and much beside, which does not seem to assist
this exposition.

288 Babbitt, I. The Dhammapada, Translated from the
        Pali with an Essay on Buddha and the Occident.
        London: Oxford University Press, 1936. 123 p.
        This work explains the meaning of Dhammapada as
a path of virtue and its relationship with law or norm.

289 Beal, S. Texts from the Buddhist Canon Known as
        Dhammapada. See entry no. 1156.

290 Bigelow, W. S. Buddhism and Immortality. Boston:
        Houghton, 1908.
        As an attempt to interpret Oriental ideas to Western
minds, the book deserves high praise. In particular the
exposition of "Karma" is admirable. The nobler side of
Japanese Buddhist doctrine is brought before the reader very
effectively.

291 Blavatsky, H. P. An Abridgement of the Secret Doc-
        trine. Edited by E. Preston and C. Humphreys.
        London: Theosophical Publishing House, 1965.
        288 p. [also see entry no. 1271].
        First published in two volumes in 1888 under the
title of The Secret Doctrine, this work is the basic document of the theosophical movement and contains the mystery
of its wisdom. Here all the teaching of the Buddhist scriptures are contained, and the way which the Buddha taught to
the perfection of the part made whole. A biography of H. P.
Blavatsky, the genesis of The Secret Doctrine, and a bibliography are given for further study.

292 Buddhaghosa. The Path of Purification. See entry
        no. 1158.

293 Burlingame, E. W. (translator). Buddhist Parables
        Translated from the Original Pali. See entry
        no. 794.

294 Carus, P. Amitabha. Chicago: Open Court Pub. Co.,
        1906. 121 p.
        This is a story of Buddhist theology explaining the
way of Buddhist salvation from evil by walking in the noble
eightfold path of moral conduct, consisting in right comprehension, right aspiration, right speech, right conduct, right
living, right endeavor, right discipline, and the attainment
of the right bliss.

295 _____. The Dharma or the Religion of Enlighten-
        ment. Chicago: Open Court Pub. Co., 1896.
        18 p.
        This is a brief summary of Buddhism, giving Bud-
dhist doctrines and Ten Commandments and Seven Jewels
of the Law.

296 Collins, R. The Theory of Eternal Life. London:
        Vincent, 1956. 126 p.
        No life is well lived unless it prepares for death,

and some knowledge of what we must expect to happen after death is certainly worth having. The author describes his beliefs on the experiences of the intermediary state between death and rebirth in the terminology of Mahayana Buddhism.

297   Conze, E.   Abhisamayalankara: Introduction and Trans-
        lation from Original Text, with Sanskrit-Tibetan
        Index.   See entry no. 1164.

298   _____.   Buddhism, Its Essence and Development.
        See entry no. 375.

299   Davids, C. A. F. Rhys.   Buddhism; A Study of the
        Buddhist Norm.   London: Williams and Norgate;
        New York: Holt, 1912.   255 p.
            This is a study of the Buddhist Dhamma, inter-
preted as a doctrine of the norm.   The London edition is
no. 44 of the Home University Library of Modern Knowledge
series.

300   Dayal, H.   The Bodhisattva Doctrine in Buddhist San-
        skrit Literature.   London: Paul, Trench, Trubner,
        1932.   392 p.
            This is the most important survey of Buddhist
doctrine relevant to the Bodhisattva, or savior.   The origin
of this concept, the thought of enlightenment, the perfections,
and the stages and last life before enlightenment of the
Bodhisattva are critically discussed with reference to original
sources.

301   Dutt, S.   The Buddha after Five Centuries.   London:
        Luzac, 1957.   259 p.
            This book should only be reviewed by an indologist
or an Arabat.   Its subject is the development of Buddhist
doctrine and practice during the first five centuries after
what the author calls the Buddha's enlightenment.   He treats
the legendary sources more critically than the practice
hitherto has been.

302   Facter, D.   Doctrine of the Buddha.   New York: Philo-
        sophical Library, 1965.   132 p.
            This is a brief and unpretentious summary of the
first principles of Theravada Buddhism, supported by quotations from contemporary writers.   The author is sincere,
wishes to proclaim the Dhamma, and for the beginner in
Buddhist studies helps to that purpose.

303   Grimm, G. Doctrine of the Buddha. Mystic, Conn.:
        Verry, 1965. 413 p.
      The four parts of this book deal with Buddhism's
Four Most Excellent Truths: the most excellent truths of
suffering, of the arising of suffering, of the annihilation of
suffering, and of the path leading to the annihilation of suffering.

304   Holmes, E. The Creed of Buddha. London: The
        Bodley Head, 1949. 260 p.
      The chief merits of the work, which is a brilliant
accomplishment, are boldness in specification, a wide outlook, and a wealth of original and suggestive ideas. Most
of it is interpretative. The book is eloquent, discerning,
worthy in purpose, and worthy for any thinking man.

305   Humphreys, C. A Western Approach to Zen. See
        entry no. 1087.

306   Khantipalo, P. Tolerance. A Study from Buddhist
        Sources. London: Rider, 1963. 191 p.
      The author presents not only the theories and
knowledge of the Dahamma of Buddha but a comparison with
the tolerance expounded by the other doctrines. This is a
wonderful book which will inspire the reader with the
Dhamma of tolerance.

307   Morgan, K. W. (ed.). The Path of the Buddha: Bud-
        dhism Interpreted by Buddhists. New York:
        Ronald Printing Co., 1956. 432 p.
      This is an earnest attempt on the part of 11 devout
Buddhist scholars to describe, 25 centuries after the Buddha,
the beliefs and practices of the Buddhist world, both Theravada countries, Burma, Ceylon, and Thailand, and Mahayana
countries, Tibet, China, Korea, and Japan. Ideally suited
to American college students.

308   Oldenberg, H. Buddha: His Life, His Doctrine, His
        Order. Translated from the German by William
        Hoey. London, Edinburgh: William and Norgate,
        1882. 454 p.
      This is an excellent, but somewhat outdated study of
Buddha and Buddhism in India during its earliest stages.
The Buddha's life and basic doctrines are accurately presented, based upon original source materials, by a highly
qualified scholar.

309 Powell, R. The Free Mind: The Inward Path to
       Liberation. New York: The Julian Press, 1972.
       190 p.
       The purpose of the work is to eliminate the en-
crusted "I" that we have created and to remove the prison
walls we have erected around ourselves. The author tries
to bring enlightenment to a disturbed world, which he feels
must change if it is to survive. He not only clarifies the
problems, but shows a possible way out for man.

310 Prajnaparamita, Selections. Selected sayings from the
       Perfection of Wisdom.... See entry no. 1204.

311 Saddhatissa, H. The Buddha's Way. See entry no.
       1249.

312 Santideva, S. A Compendium of Buddhist Doctrine.
       London: John Murray, 1922. Translated from the
       Sanskrit by C. Bendall and W. H. D. Rouse.
       This work is compiled chiefly from earlier Mahayana
Sutras.

313 Shcherbatskoi, F. I. The Central Conception of Bud-
       dhism and the Meaning of the Word "Dharma." 2nd
       ed. Calcutta: Gupta, 1956. 96 p.
       This is a critical study of the concept of dharma
(doctrine or element of reality) which is basic to Buddhist
thought. This concept together with that of the aggregated
skandhas, which constitute man, are fundamental elements
of ancient Buddhism and are pivotal points for the entire
doctrine. An appendix dealing with the eminent Mahayana
Buddhist philosopher, Vasubandhu, is also provided.

314 Spiro, M. E. Burmese Supernaturalism. See entry
       no. 512.

315 Story, F. The Four Noble Truths. Kandy, Ceylon:
       Buddhist Publication Society, 1961. 64 p.
       This is one of the best sets of instructions on Bud-
dhism. Starting from the standpoint of the Westerner dis-
satisfied with Western explanations of the nature of things,
it tries to lead him firmly to see that where they fail Buddhism points the way forward.

316 Suzuki, D. T. The Essentials of Zen Buddhism. See
       entry no. 1124.

317 Thomas, E. J. The History of Buddhist Thought. 2nd
      ed. See entry no. 405.

318 Tripitaka (English selections). The Vedantic Buddhism
      of the Buddha. See entry no. 1214.

319 Van Gorkom, N. Buddhist Outlook on Daily Life.
      Bangkok: Abhidhamma Foundation of Mahadhata
      Vidyalaya, 1971. 67 p.
      This book is a compilation of four radio talks given
by the author. Published in both English and Thai, it forms
a useful introduction and outline to Abhidhamma teaching as
applied to daily life that wisdom can only be developed through
self-purification and the practice of good deeds and helpfulness
towards others.

320 Walshe, M. O. Buddhism and Death. London: The
      English Sangha Trust, 1972. 20 p.
      The author describes the three main views on the
subjects of death, the Christian, the secular, and the Buddhist as a wise middle way between the first two. He deals
with the folly of refusing to face the fact of death and turns
to the Buddhist teaching on the subject. He discusses spiri-
tualism and then turns to the Buddhist doctrine of rebirth.

321 Wei, W. W. Ask the Awakened; The Negative Way.
      London: Routledge and Kegan Paul, 1963. 282 p.
      The thought of Wei Wu Wei is concerned with the
original doctrine taken by Bodhidharma to China, a teaching
which contained strong elements of Taoism. The book is
divided into four parts under the respective headings of the
Crossroad, the Negative Way, Absolute Absence and an Epi-
logue. Considering the intangibility of the subject matter,
it is remarkably readable. The author's main attack made
from many angles is upon the I-concept which causes all
the evil in the world and all the unhappiness.

                              EDUCATION

322 Amore, R. C. The Concept and Practice of Doing
      Merit in Early Theravada Buddhism. New York:
      Columbia University Press, 1970. 178 p.
      This study discusses the formative era of Theravada

Buddhist ethics.   The author emphasizes the heart of lay
Buddhist ethics, the concept and practice of doing merit.

323   Bapat, P. V. (ed.).   2500 Years of Buddhism.   See
          entry no. 365.

324   Dutt, S.   Buddhist Monks and Monasteries of India.
          See entry no. 767.

325   Hoftiezer, R. J.   Zen as Educational Praxis: A Study
          of the Educational Characteristics of the Practice of
          Zen Buddhism.   Buffalo: State University of New
          York at Buffalo, 1972.   202 p.
          This study was carried out to identify the practical
characteristics of Zen Buddhism in such a way that the educational qualities are clearly outlined.   From this study two
facets of Zen application stand out as significant for Western
education, Zen as value-ambience and Zen as praxis.

326   Hung, T. T.   Buddhism and Politics in Southeast Asia.
          Claremont, Cal.:   Claremont Graduate School, 1970.
          482 p.
          This author examines the social and political teachings
of the Buddha, and then he traces the evolving relations of
Buddhism and politics throughout the political history of Southeast Asia.   Throughout his study the author finds that Buddhism is a flexible current of belief and practice capable of
adapting to a variety of circumstances without departing from
its essential principles.

327   Kobayashi, M. S.   The Educational Implications of
          Existentialism and Buddhism.   Columbus: Ohio State
          University Press, 1971.   394 p.
          This study identifies certain of the basic relation-
ships between these philosophical perspectives and explicates
the implications they have for educational theory and practice.
The investigation, itself, is best described as a philosophical-
logical inquiry involving both analysis and synthesis.

ETHICS

328   Conze, E.   Buddhist Scripture.   See entry no. 1165.

329   Dhammapada.   The Dhammapada Translated by Narada
         Thera; Sayings of Buddha.   See entry no. 1174

330   Hopkins, E. W.   Ethics of India.   See entry no. 594.

331   Humphreys, C.   The Way of Action: A Working
         Philosophy for Western Life.   London: Allen and
         Unwin; New York: Macmillan, 1959.   195 p.
         The purpose of this book is to find out and to
demonstrate what is right acting and to guide the reader in
the attempt to make every one of his actions right.   The
book is divided into two parts; the first is an analysis of
action and the second gives practical advice.

332   King, W. L.   In the Hope of Nibbana: An Essay on
         Theravada Buddhist Ethics.   La Salle, Ill.:   Open
         Court, 1964.   298 p.
         The author is a Christian theologian who has already
written an interesting study of Buddhism and Christianity.
The first part of his book discusses the framework of self-
perfection, the more theoretical aspects of the Theravada
Buddhist ethic, including the ethical implications of the doctrines of Karma, Rebirth and Anatta.   The second part attempts to show that ethic in practice and to consider its
social implications both in ideal and in practice.

333   Krishnamurti, J.   The Urgency of Change.   Edited by
         Mary Lutyens.   New York: Harper and Row, 1971.
         154 p.
         In each of the chapters of this his tenth book,
Krishnamurti brings his questioners, whether they are asking
about fear or morality, suicide or self-expression, the religious life or how to live in this world, surely and patiently
to an understanding of the roots of their problem.   He skill-
fully probes the questioner's understanding to reveal the
source and eventual solution of their problems.

334   Saddhatissa, H.   Buddhist Ethics: Essence of Buddhism.
         London: Allen and Unwin, 1970.   232 p.
         Emphasizing ethical behavior, the author examines
the background to Buddhism, its unique doctrines, the nature
of the Buddhist "trinity"--Buddha, Dhamma (Teaching), Sangha
(Community of Monks)--and a brief analysis of the written
scriptures in their present form.   The author is head of the
London Buddhist Vihara and an eminent leader.   Buddhism is
presented as an ethicophilosophy to be practiced by each
adherent in the expectation that only by an arduous spiritual

struggle can happiness and perhaps ultimately Nibbana be attained.

335   no entry

336   Saunders, K. J.   The Ideals of East and West.   New
            York: Macmillan, 1934.   246 p.
            An account of the ethical systems of East and West,
with illustrative reading, is given here.

337   Tachibana, S.   The Ethics of Buddhism.   New ed.
            Colombo: The Buddha Sahitya, 1962.   215 p.
            This is a new edition of Ethics of Buddhism, which
first appeared in 1926.   This book has long been a classic
on Buddhist morality and includes a useful index.

338   Thera, P.   The Buddha's Ancient Path.   London:
            Rider, 1963.   239 p.
            The author clearly explains how, where, and why
one or more of the standards of moral teaching are handed
down in the Pali Canon and connected with others.   The
book is well written with a firm and clear understanding.
The numerous quotations are all apt and most of them carefully translated.

FICTION

339   Coatsworth, E.   The Cat Who Went to Heaven.
            Drawings by Kiddell-Monroe.   New York: Mac-
            millan, 1930.   57 p.
            Those who want a story for children that is Buddhist
in spirit have here a delightful Chinese example.   All but
the very youngest will be charmed and moved by the story of
the artist who loved his cat so much that in defiance of tradition he risked ruin by including a cat among the animals
depicted as being blessed by the Buddha on his death.

340   Gazdanoy, G.   Buddha's Return.   Translated from the
            Russian by N. Wreden.   New York: Dutton, 1951.
            224 p.
            A 23-year-old student in Paris gives a beggar a ten-
franc note; he is captured and released by Kafkaesque secret
police; he has erotic visions with all the force of reality; he

is accused of murdering the beggar, now rich (a clue is a
statuette of Buddha); he seems to live more lives than one;
he finally inherits and enjoys a fortune.

341 Payne, P. S. R. Yellow Robe: A Novel of the Life
        of Buddha. New York: Dodd, 1948. 308 p.
        A fictional life of Gautama Buddha, the book is
divided into two parts, the first relating his worldly life as
a young prince, the second devoted to his life as a pilgrim
and mendicant preacher.

342 Reynolds, C. An Anthology of Sinhalese Literature up
        to 1815. See entry no. 427.

343 Stern, S. M. Three Unknown Buddhist Stories in an
        Arabic Version. London: Cassirer, 1972. 38 p.
        These are three short previously unpublished stories
in the Jataka tradition but coming from Sanskrit via middle
Persian and Arabic. It is fascinating how stories have been
tailored to different religious thinking in Arabic culture.
The work is primarily for scholars, the Arabic text being
printed in full alongside the translation.

                        GAUTAMA BUDDHA

344 Bapat, P. B. (ed.). 2500 Years of Buddhism. See
        entry no. 365.

345 Barlaam and Josaphat. The Balavariani; A Tale from
        the Christian East. Translated by D. M. Lang;
        introduction by I. V. Abuladze. Berkeley: Univer-
        sity of California Press, 1966. 187 p.
        This "is a Christianized version of a legendary
biography of the Buddha. It is an outstanding piece of evidence of cultural diffusion from East to West during the first
millennium A.D. The present edition is a translation from
the Georgian text, which represents the oldest and most complete account of the legend hitherto known. The Georgian
text is the source of the Greek text, attributed to St. John
of Damascus, which is available with an English translation
in the Loeb Classical Library (translated by G. R. Woodward and Harold Mattingly, Harvard University Press, 1914).
Besides an English translation with critical notes, the present

edition includes an introduction giving the history of the text
and a useful bibliography.   Thus it provides a fundamental
resource for the study of the relationship of Buddhist and
Christian asceticism and folklore"--Choice.   The manuscript
was discovered by Mr. Abuladze, director of the Institute of
Manuscripts of the Georgian Academy of Sciences, who provides the introduction.   This is one of the UNESCO Collection of Representative Works.

346   Beck, L. A.   The Splendour of Asia; The Story and
            Teaching of the Buddha.   New York: Dodd, Mead,
            1926.   269 p.
      The life of Gautama Buddha is told in the rich ca-
dence of an Oriental prose poem including his painless birth,
the princely pleasures of his youth, his felicitous marriage
crowned by the birth of a son.

347   Brewster, E. H.   The Life of Gotama the Buddha.
            New York: Dutton, 1926.   243 p.   Introductory
            note by C. A. F. R. Davids.
      The author has compiled the life of Buddha from the
Pali Canon which is composed of the rules and sayings of
their leader as collected and preserved by the early Buddhist
monks.   This is an excellent presentation of all the biographical materials in the Pali texts.

348   Buddha's Words of Wisdom.   See entry no. 1152.

349   Byles, M. B.   Footprints of Gautama the Buddha,
            Being a Story of Portions of His Ministerial Life.
            London: Rider, 1957.   227 p.
      This simply told life of the Buddha fulfills a dif-
ferent purpose from that of the scriptures of the Pali Canon
and of the Mahayana, the two chief sources for the material
used.   All the stories told paint a moral so that there is a
good picture of the philosophical and ethical tenets of the
Theravada teaching and to a lesser extent that of the Mahayana.   The photographs of scenes of modern India and Nepal
help to bring his life story nearer to us.

350   Coomaraswamy, A. K.   Gotama the Buddha.   London:
            Cassell, 1948.   224 p.
      This work contains two introductory essays, one on
the life of Gotama and the other on Buddhist doctrine.   The
anthology is composed almost entirely of extracts from the
Pali Canon, the earliest recorded sayings, compiled about
80 B.C. in Ceylon.   A very clear idea of the canonical

doctrine can be gained from these words of the Buddha. The
author's emphasis is on the training and theological background of Buddhist doctrine.

351 DaCunha, J. G. Memoir on the History of the Tooth-
        Relic of Ceylon. London: W. Thacker Co., 1875.
        70 p.
        This is a preliminary essay on the life and systems
of Gautama Buddha, his systems dealt with more from a
synthetic than from an analytical point of view.

352 Davids, T. W. R. Buddhist Birth Stories. See entry
        no. 94.

353 Edwards, M. A Life of the Buddha. London: Folio
        Society, 1959. 188 p.
        It would have been more appropriate if the pub-
lishers of this book had called it "A Legendary Life of the
Buddha, " for in this translation of an early 19th-century
Burmese manuscript, legend, myth and fairy tale take
precedence over doctrine.

354 Griswold, A. B. Dated Buddha Images of Northern
        Siam. Paris: Artibus Asiae, 1957. 134 p.
        The author made a discovery of considerable im-
portance in being able to run to earth 90 images in northern
Siam bearing dates ranging from A.D. 1470 to 1596, with a
further 18 in the 17th, 18th and 19th centuries.

355 Grousset, R. In the Footsteps of the Buddha. Trans-
        lated from the French by Mariette Leon. London:
        George Routledge and Sons, 1932. 352 p.
        The book has history, travel, adventure, topography,
art, archaeology, and as its core, devout Buddhism. In
A.D. 629 Hsuan-tsang, the master of the law, determines
to go West to walk in the footsteps of the saints and sages,
a journey that was to take 16 years. The book ends with a
sympathetic exposition of Mahayana mysticism and the
Bodhisattva ideal.

356 Hoontrakool, Y. The Path of Light. Bangkok: 1956.
        245 p.
        It is a treatise of the life and teaching of the Bud-
dha. The author devotes his life to the study of the Dhamma.
The results of many years of study under two teachers are
embodied in this book.

357 Ludowyk, E. F. C. The Footprint of the Buddha.
London: Allen and Unwin, 1958. 182 p.
This is an informative book on Ceylon where the
Buddha, according to legend, has left a giant footprint on
the highest mountain. This book is concerned with the
Buddha only in so far as his teaching has influenced the
history and art of Ceylon. It also gives a wealth of information which would be immensely helpful as a travel
guide.

358 Oldenberg, H. Buddha; His Life, His Doctrine, His
Order. See entry no. 308.

359 Prajnaparamita, Selections. Selected Sayings from
the Perfection of Wisdom. See entry no. 1021.

360 Radhakrishnan, S. Gautama the Buddha. London:
British Academy, 1938. 47 p.
This is an annual lecture on a master mind
given in London, giving a brief discussion of Buddhist
philosophy.

361 Saunders, K. J. Gotama Buddha: A Biography. New
York: The Association Press, 1920. 113 p.
This is a biography based on the canonical books of
the Theravadin. An attempt is made to bring order into the
confusion which still exists as to the person of Gotama and
as to his essential teachings.

362 Tripitaka. The Quest of Enlightenment; A Selection
of the Buddhist Scriptures. See entry no. 1212.

363 Warren, H. C. Buddhism in Translations; Passages
Selected from the Buddhist Sacred Books. See
entry no. 1220.

364 Wong, J. Buddha; His Life and Teaching. Mount
Vernon: Peter Pauper. 269 p.
This book is actually in the form of a series of
stories: first the story of the birth, life, and enlightenment of Prince Siddhattha who renounced the world and became the Buddha; then the stories of the first disciples,
the establishment of the order, the first schism, the great
questions and Buddha's answers, his parables, and his
last days.

HISTORY

365 Bapat, P. V. (ed.). 2500 Years of Buddhism. New
        Delhi: Government of India, 1956. 503 p.
        This is a collection by Indian scholars on many
sides of Buddhism, including its origin, the Buddha's life
and teachings, the councils, Asoka and the expansion of
Buddhism, the principal schools and sects, Buddhist literature, education, art, and the history of Buddhistic studies,
etc. A glossary, a bibliography, charts, maps, and illustrations are also included.

366 _____ . Vimuktimarga Dhutaguna-nirdesa. London:
        Asia Publishing House, 1964. 123 p.
        Professor Bapat re-edits a Tibetan text clearly
showing its dimensions and noting the variants found in five
different block-prints. This English edition seems much
superior to the one which Rev. Ehara made from the Chinese. The introduction is well worth reading and contains
conclusive evidence that Upatissa's work belongs to the
Abhayagiri school. There is also a glossary of Tibetan
words.

367 Beal, S. Romantic Legend of Sakya Buddha. London:
        Trubner and Co., 1875. 395 p.
        This work is a translation of the Chinese version
of the "Abhinishkramana Sutra," done into that language from
Sanskrit by Djnanakuta, a Buddhist priest from North India.
This gives a complete historical sketch of Buddhism.

368 _____ . Texts from the Buddhist Canon Known as
        Dhammapada. See entry no. 1156.

369 Berry, T. Buddhism. New York: Hawthorn Books,
        1967. 192 p.
        This work is an account of the history and philosophy
of Buddhism. The author divides it into three parts: first,
an exposition of the life and important teachings of the Buddha; second, the development of Buddhism and specifically
Mahayana Buddhism; and last, the Buddhist expansion from
India to all Asian countries and recently into Western culture.

370 Bird, J. Historical Researches on the Origin and
        Principles of the Buddha and Jaina Religions. Bom-
        bay: American Mission Press, 1847. 72 p.
        This work embraces the leading tenets of their

system as found prevailing in various countries. It illus-
trates, by descriptive accounts of the sculptures in the caves
of Western India.

371   The Blue Annals.   Translated by George N. Roerich.
        Bengal: The Royal Asiatic Society of Bengal, 1949.
        15 vols.
        The Blue Annals, a history of Buddhism, were com-
posed between A.D. 1476 and 1478.   This work contains 15
books, the first containing an account of the original of the
Sakyan race, and the beginning of the Buddhist doctrine.
The second book deals with the later period of the propagation of the doctrine; the third gives an account of the early
translations of the Tantra into Tibetan. . . .   The Blue Annals,
besides their great attention to dates and their historical
character, contain many episodes in the lives of monks.
The text is tremendously important as a historical document.

372   Ch'en, K. K. S.   Buddhism in China: A Historical
        Survey.   See entry no. 36.

373   Chou, H. K.   A History of Chinese Buddhism.   Alla-
        habad, India: Indo-Chinese Literature Publications,
        1955.   264 p.
        This book is the first history of Chinese Buddhism,
dating from about A.D. 65 up to recent times.   The original
purpose of the book is to show how much India contributed
to the intellectual heritage of Asia, and to produce mutual
respect and helpful comradeship between the inheritors of
the two most ancient and yet most continuously vital civilizations of the world.

374   Chula, Prince H. R. H.   Lords of Life.   London:
        Alvin Redman, 1960.   352 p.
        Lords of Life could only have been written by Prince
Chula, who is well known as an exponent of the history and
present condition of the Buddhist monarchy.   This is a great
book to all historians and particularly so to students of Buddhist history in modern times.   The work covers the history
of the Chakri Dynasty that lasted 150 years.

375   Conze, E.   Buddhism, Its Essence and Development.
        New York: Philosophical Library, 1951.   212 p.
        This is a penetrating study of the essential nature
and teaching of Buddhism in the several phases of its development.   It is an excellent modern survey of Buddhism, its
monastic and popular forms, and its philosophical, devotional,

and magical schools. A discussion of non-Indian development is given also.

376 _____ . A Short History of Buddhism. Bombay:
       Chetana, 1960. 117 p.
       The author masterly surveys the whole history of
Buddhism with all its major schools and several minor ones,
and contrives to say something succinct, memorable and
precise about all of them. The book is divided into four
chapters covering the traditional four periods of Buddhist
history which are: old Buddhism or Hinayana, Mahayana,
Tantra, and Zen since A.D. 1000.

377 Cunningham, Sir Alexander. The Stupa of Bharhut.
       2nd ed. Varanasi: Indological Book House, 1962.
       143 p.
       This work concerns a Buddhist monument ornamented
with numerous sculptures illustrating Buddhist legend and
history in the third century.

378 Davids, C. A. F. R. Outlines of Buddhism; A His-
       torical Sketch. London: Methuen and Company,
       1934. 117 p.
       This is a historical sketch of the development of
Buddhism in India and its effect on Indian social science
and humanities.

379 Davids, T. W. R. History and Literature of Bud-
       dhism. Mystic, Conn.: Verry, 1962. 230 p.
       This work presents the origin and growth of religion
as illustrated by some points in the history of Indian Buddhism.

380 Dutt, S. Buddhism in East Asia: An Outline of Bud-
       dhism in the History and Cultures. Bombay:
       Indian Council for Cultural Relations; New York:
       Humanities, 1966. 225 p.
       This work was sponsored by the Indian Society for
Cultural Relations to produce an outline of the history and
culture of Buddhism in East Asia. The work was not to
consist of fundamental research but was to be presented in
broad outline and to hold the readers' interest. Although
history is the main theme, the work covers a wide range
of subjects including teachings, legends, the building of
stupas, architecture, pagodas, and temples. The author
fails to give any information about Buddhism in Korea which
had vital influence in developing Japanese Buddhism.

381   Eliot, C. N. E.   Hinduism and Buddhism: An His-
          torical Sketch.   London: Routledge and Kegan Paul,
          1921 (repr. New York: Barnes and Noble, 1954).
          3 vols.
          Pali Buddhism is covered in vol. 1, book 3; the
Mahayana is covered in vol. 2, book 4; and Buddhism outside India is covered in vol. 3, book 6.   This work is a
general readable account of major religious concepts of
Hinduism and Buddhism both in the Indian subcontinent as
well as in greater Asia.   The work also includes short discussions of Western religious influences.   The material is
based on traditional works and historical data and is given
with an intimate personal knowledge of both faiths and a
critical investigation of the texts.

382   Frazier, A. M.   Buddhism.   Philadelphia: Westminster
          Press, 1969.   304 p.
          This work contains general essays on Buddhist tra-
dition and selections from Buddhist literature.   The essays
start with Campbell's "The Dialogue in Myth of East and
West."   The second essay is a selection from Buddhism:
Its Essence and Development by Edward Conze.   The third
essay is a selection from D. T. Suzuki's Outlines of Mahayana Buddhism.   The fourth essay is a reprint from Zimmer's Philosophy of India.   Then the editor ends up with a
historical sketch of Buddhism.

383   Gard, R. A.   Buddhism.   See entry no. 97.

384   Goodrich, L. C.   A Short History of the Chinese
          People.   See entry no. 542.

385   Grousset, R.   In the Footsteps of the Buddha.   See
          entry no. 355.

386   Guenther, H. V.   The Royal Song of Saraha; A Study
          in the History of Buddhist Thought.   Seattle: Uni-
          versity of Washington Press, 1969.   214 p.
          Saraha is one of the earliest historical figures in
Tantric Buddhism.   Tradition has it that he was the teacher
of Nagarjuna, meaning, of course, the Tantric Nagarjuna.

387   Hsuan-tsang.   Si-yu-ki; Buddhist Records of the
          Western World.   New York: Paragon Book Repr.
          Corp., 1968.   2 vols.
          This work is translated from the Chinese of Hiuen
Tsiang by Samuel Beal.   A historical sketch of Buddhism's
development from Asia to the Western world is given.

388   Humphreys, C. <u>Buddhism</u>. Rev. ed. See entry no.
        101.

389   I-ching. <u>Record of the Buddhist Religion as Practiced</u>
        <u>in India and the Malay Archipelago, A.D. 671-695.</u>
        Translated by J. Takakusu. New Delhi: Munshiram
        Manoharlal, 1966. 240 p.
        This work contains a clear description of the sects
of the day and an especially full account of the regulations
and practices of the monks.

390   McCullough, H. C. <u>The Teiheiki, a Chronicle of</u>
        <u>Medieval Japan.</u> See entry no. 646.

391   Miauno, K. <u>Primitive Buddhism.</u> Translated and an-
        notated and compiled by Kosho Yamamoto. Tokyo:
        Karinbunko Press, 1971. 295 p.
        This work for the first time makes clear the rela-
tion between the Buddhism of Sakyamuni Buddha and Mahayana. This is a unique work helpful for Westerners to understand primitive Buddhism.

392   Morgan, K. W. <u>The Path of the Buddha; Buddhism</u>
        <u>Interpreted by Buddhists.</u> See entry no. 307.

393   Nyanaponika, V. <u>Pathways of Buddhist Thought.</u> See
        entry no. 25.

394   Pachow, W. <u>A Comparative Study of the Pratimoksa.</u>
        See entry no. 1015.

395   Pardue, P. A. <u>Buddhism: A Historical Introduction</u>
        <u>to Buddhist Values and the Social and Political</u>
        <u>Forms They Have Assumed in Asia.</u> New York:
        Macmillan, 1972. 203 p.
        This work may be called a historical narrative plus
a survey of the development of doctrine, devotion and philosophy, plus a sketch of the political, social and cultural
backgrounds with Buddhism's repercussions on them, plus a
Buddhist dictionary.

396   <u>Report of the Fifth General Conference of the World</u>
        <u>Fellowship of Buddhists.</u> Bangkok: Buddhist Asso-
        <u>ciation of Thailand, 1960.</u> 170 p.
        All the reports here are the messages from in-
numerable Buddhist Societies and all the work of the various
committees. All the presentations are listed in detail and
the resolutions too.

397 The Revolt in the Temple. London: Sina Publications,
        1953. 700 p.
        The purpose of this book is to commemorate the
history of the Buddhist faith, the Sinhalese race and the
land of Ceylon. It is both unique and versatile in as much
that it deals with the history, religion and ethics of the
Sinhalese race. It also contains throughout its pages a message to mankind of all races and religions.

398 Reynolds, C. An Anthology of Sinhalese Literature up
        to 1815. See entry no. 427.

399 Ronaldshay, L. D. Lands of the Thunderbolt. Boston:
        Houghton, 1923. 267 p.
        A considerable portion of this book is filled with a
history of Buddhism in India and a consideration of the effect
of Buddhism on the nature-worship that it partially super-
seded in the countries to which the book relates.

400 Saunders, E. D. Buddhism in Japan: With an Outline
        of its Origins in India. Philadelphia: University
        of Pennsylvania Press, 1964. 328 p.
        "The history and doctrines of Buddhism are clearly
sketched from the time of Gautama himself until the arrival
of the religion in the Japanese Islands 1000 years later....
(Professor) Saunders also carries the evolution of Buddhism
in Japan forward to the new sects of the mid-20th century....
Recommended"--Library Journal.

401 Saunders, K. J. Epochs in Buddhist History. Chicago:
        University of Chicago Press, 1924. 243 p.
        The Haskell Lectures for 1921 from a history of
Buddhism in India, Ceylon, Burma, Siam, China, Korea,
Japan, Nepal, and Tibet are contained here. The book is
an attempt to describe the process by which the stream of
Buddhism, which had its sources in the complex system of
Brahmanism, spread out over the Eastern world.

402 Schuon, F. In the Tracks of Buddhism. Translated
        from the French by Marco Pallis. New York:
        Hillary, 1968. 168 p.
        The author, as a convinced universalist, sees Bud-
dhism as a valid, important and original way of salvation
but not as the one and only way. One part of the book reviews the range of Buddhism manifested in its various
schools, noting that the esoteric aspect is discernible in the
Theravada texts as well as others. The last section deals

with various aspects of the Mahayana, in particular with the
mystery of the Bodhisattva and its relation to the Pure Land
School whose fascination lies in its seeming remoteness from
earlier ideals.

403   Smith, F. H.   Buddhist Way of Life, Its Philosophy
           and History.   New York: Hutchinson's University
           Library, 1951.   189 p.
      Beginning with the teaching of the Pali scriptures,
the Buddhist tradition is examined and interpreted.   The
differences in the various schools and councils are considered, and the development of the movement as a world
religion is reviewed.   There is a brief and somewhat superficial comparison between Christianity and Buddhism.

404   Thapar, R.   Asoka and the Decline of the Mauryas.
           London: Oxford University Press, 1961.   283 p.
      "The Beloved of the Gods" as he calls himself,
King Asoka of the Maurya Dynasty, is one of the greatest
figures in Buddhist history.   This work is written for the
academic market as historical material.

405   Thomas, E. J.   The History of Buddhist Thought.   2nd
           ed.   New York: Barnes and Noble, 1951.   316 p.
      This is an excellent survey of the development of
Buddhist thought from the early schools, the ascetic ideal,
Yoga, etc., through the basic doctrines of the Buddha to
the Mahayana conception of the Bodhisattva and metaphysical
schools.

406   Warder, A. K.   Indian Buddhism.   New Delhi: Motilal
           Banarsidass, 1971.   622 p.
      The author is already well known for his original
work Introduction to Pali and Pali Metre and for his translation work for the Pali Text Society in London.   Indian
civilization before and during Buddha's lifetime is first
covered.   Then the life of Buddha is traced from the extant
literature and a commendable effort is made to sort the
likely facts from the forest of legends which have subse-
quently grown up.   The teaching of Buddha takes up two
lengthy chapters.   Attempt has been made to see which
factors are common to both the Theravada and Mahayana
scriptures of the various schools.   The Chinese, Tibetan
and Pali writings have been fully consulted.   Other important
aspects covered include the collecting of the Tripitaka, the
popularization of Buddhism, the schisms and the evaluation
of the Mahayana and Madhyamaka.

JATAKAS

407   Davids, T. W. R.   Buddhist Birth Stories.   See entry
         no. 94.

408   Horner, I. B.   Ten Jataka Stories.   London: Luzac,
         1957.   93 p.
         From a wealth of Buddhist tales dealing with the
previous lives of the Buddha, ten stories have been chosen
here by the author who is the greatest living authority on
the Pali language and its literature.   Each story deals with
one of the ten perfections and the introduction provides the
necessary background to them.

409   Jatakas, N. K.   Jataka Tales.   London: Murray, 1956.
         105 p.
         These are birth stories of the Buddha retold by
Ethel Beswick with a foreward by Edward Conze.

JUVENILE LITERATURE

410   Carus, P.   Karma, a Story of Buddhist Ethics.   Chi-
         cago: Open Court Pub. Co., 1903.   46 p.
         This Buddhistic tale seems to shed light on a new
side of the two fundamental truths revealed by Christianity.
This is rather children's literature.

411   Dahlke, P.   Buddhist Stories.   London: Kegan Paul,
         1913.   330 p.
         This is one of the famous storybooks about Buddha
from his childhood to his adult work.   It is highly recom-
mendable as children's literature.

412   Herold, A. F.   Life of Buddha.   Rutland, Vt.:   Tuttle,
         1954.   286 p.
         This is a translation from the French of a story of
the life of Buddha based on Sanskrit sources of the first and
second centuries B.C.   It is excellent as a children's book,
although a mature person will perceive the motive underlying
the tales.

413   James, G.   The Bodhi Tree.   London: Geoffrey Chap-
         man, 1972.   94 p.

This storybook for children tells the story of the life of Buddha; it is beautifully produced and has lovely illustrations by Joanna Troughton.

414 Jivaka, S. Growing Up into Buddhism. Calcutta:
         Maha Bodhi Society, 1960. 128 p.
     This work tells the basic teachings of the Buddha, the Eightfold Path, the Four Noble Truths and a clearer understanding of the "I" concept, so gently and simply that even a beginner could understand them. The author wrote it for teen-agers and parents.

415 Kelen, B. Gautama Buddha, in Life and Legend. New
         York: Lothrop, 1968. 194 p.
     This work presents a portrait of a rather spoiled young aristocrat who becomes a great religious teacher through suffering and the desire to find answers to the most basic questions of human existence. The teachings of Buddhism, its place within the Hindu tradition, and its so-called atheism are all clearly explained.

416 Serage, N. The Prince Who Gave up a Throne; A
         Story of Buddha. New York: Crowell, 1966. 62 p.
     This is the life story of Siddhartha Gautama Buddha "based on the Buddha Karita of Asvaghosa, the Buddhist Sutras and other studies."

                              LAMAISM

417 Anuruddha, R. P. An Introduction into Lamaism.
         Hoshiarpur: Vishveshvaranand Vedic Research In-
         stitute, 1959. 212 p.
     This work gives the history of Tibetan Buddhism, then two useful chapters on Tibetan Iconography which needs illustrations and then a chapter on Lamaistic ritual which loses heavily in translation. The remaining chapters are useful essays on the subject.

418 Gould, B. J. The Jewel in the Lotus. London: Chatto
         and Windus, 1957. 252 p.
     The author, who spent nearly all his life as a political officer under the British Indian Government in the smaller countries to the north of India, has much to say of

Sikkim, Bhutan and Tibet. The installation ceremonies of
the four-year-old Dalai Lama are set out in greater detail
than anywhere else described.

419 Peissel, M. Lords and Lamas. See entry no. 497.

420 Shen, T. L. Tibet and the Tibetans. See entry no.
       749.

421 Yutang, L. The Wisdom of Laotse. London: Michael
       Joseph, 1958. 303 p.
       The two main exponents of what may be called
classical or philosophical Taoism are Laotse and Chuangtse.
All translations are by the editor; literal meanings of difficult terms are given in footnotes. The editor's comments
in italics and his excellent, long introduction blend har-
moniously with the texts.

LITERATURE

422 Bapat, P. V. (ed.). 2500 Years of Buddhism. See
       entry no. 365.

423 Collins, R. Theory of Conscious Harmony. London:
       Vincent Stuart, 1958. 211 p.
       This is taken from the letters of the author Rodney
Collins. The main theme running through the letters is that
of each person representing a certain pattern and of the
necessity to find out what is one's pattern and to live according to it. Each man's duties are different from those
of the others. The Buddhist would say, "Work out your own
salvation with diligence."

424 Coomaraswamy, A. K. Buddha and the Gospel of Bud-
       dhism. See entry no. 1227.

425 Hsieh, L. The Literary Mind and the Carving of
       Dragons. New York: Columbia University, 1959.
       298 p.
       This book is a study of thought and pattern in
Chinese literature which is mainly Buddhist. The carving
of dragons is a figurative term for literary and artistic em-
bellishment and is itself a good example of the kind of

allusiveness to be met with in the treatise. This is translated with an introduction and notes by Vincent Yu-chung
Shih.

426 Nariman, G. K. Literary History of Sanskrit Bud-
         dhism. Bombay: Taraporevala, 1920.
     This is a variable discussion of the literature of
late Buddhism.

427 Reynolds, C. An Anthology of Sinhalese Literature up
         to 1815. London: Allen and Unwin, 1971.   377 p.
     This volume of Sinhalese verse and prose centers
on the Buddha's teachings as recorded by Buddhist monks
and has been selected by the UNESCO National Commission
of Ceylon. It is an anthology of great literary merit, which
has been produced with loving care by an international group
of translators. Many of the stories will be familiar to Buddhists and all are of considerable literary interest to non-
specialist readers. A useful outline precedes each group of
subjects and describes the chronology, themes, and origins
of many historical and mythological incidents associated with
the Buddha's life.

428 Rider, A. The Learners. London: The Bodley Head,
         1963. 240 p.
     This novel will provide Buddhist readers with
interest as well as entertainment. A learned refugee Lama
is brought to an English university under the patronage of a
young scholar who has a foot in both worlds himself.

429 Stacton, O. Segaki. London: Faber and Faber, 1958.
         198 p.
     This is a novel of Zen. The story is set in medieval
Japan, at a time when the country was overrun with predatory
warriors engaged in civil war.

430 Waley, A. Ballads and Stories from Tun-huang. Lon-
         don: Allen and Unwin, 1960.   276 p.
     Tun-huang Caves were discovered in 1900 and dis-
closed many scriptures and manuscripts covering the period
from A.D. 400 to 1000. But there were also some eighty
specimens of popular literature, including ballads and stories,
some being Buddhist scriptures in story form. The author
has chosen four short stories and one long one here.

431 Yasuda, K. The Japanese Haiku. See entry no. 855.

MEDITATION

432 Baba, M. God to Man and Man to God. Edited by
      C. B. Purdom. London: Gollancz, 1955. 272 p.
      Although the author is not a Buddhist, his teachings
as a master are those of the Buddha. He reveals all stages
of becoming, as far as it is possible to do so in systematic
form. Emphasis is placed on meditation of the heart, which
the author deems the most important of all.

433 Bendit, L. J. The Transforming Mind. London:
      Theosophical Publishing House, 1971. 90 p.
      This work considers a major change beginning to
take place in the collective mind, the emergence of a new
mind, unitary, universal in quality, influenced from the
numinous level.

434 The Buddhist Lodge, London. Concentration and Medi-
      tation. London: The Lodge, 1943. 343 p.
      This is a textbook on Buddhism which would suit the
needs of Western students. The materials for this production are drawn partly from the actual experiences of members
of the Lodge. The book is compiled as a progressive course
of mind-development.

435 Byles, M. B. Journey into Burmese Silence. London:
      Allen and Unwin, 1962. 215 p.
      The course of the meditation and its results are
vividly described, and one is left with no doubt of the great
benefits which can be gained. The center the author first
visited, and where she mainly stayed, was in her opinion
also the best she saw, but she gives interesting pictures of
some others, as well as fascinating sidelights on Burmese
life. This book is not intended to be a technical guide to
Burmese meditation methods, but it gives vivid insight into
life at the center.

436 _____. Paths to Inner Calm. New York: Hillary,
      1965. 208 p.
      The author has traveled through Burma and Japan
and gives some of her experiences among monks, nuns and
lay meditators. She attempts to bring together Burmese
meditation, Zen, and the new Japanese religion Ittoen, as
paths to inner calm. This is her actual participation and
experience in these methods at the various meditation centers.

437 Conze, E. Buddhist Meditation. London: Allen and
        Unwin, 1956. 183 p.
        Some most outstanding original documents are here
translated from Pali, Sanskrit and Tibetan. This work deals
with the meaning of Buddhist meditation, its range and
principal divisions, chief literary documents and the relation
of its methods and presuppositions to modern psychology.

438 _____. Buddhist Scriptures. See entry no. 1165.

439 Coulson, R. G. The Way into God; A Method of Con-
        templative Meditation. With a foreword by the Dean
        of St. Paul's. London: John Murray, 1948. 200 p.
        In this book the author describes the gap between
religious and secular thought in the West today, and facing
the fact of the degeneration of Christian thought and power,
suggests a remedy. It is meditation, whereby the individual
draws on the deeps of his own experience and by its power
leads others to that sole, eternal spring.

440 Daing, U. T. Cittanupassana (Meditation on Mind) and
        Vedananupassana (Meditation on Feeling). See
        entry no. 500.

441 Dhammasudhi, C. K. S. Insight Meditation. Rangoon:
        Committee for the Advancement of Buddhism, 1967.
        144 p.
        The author explains clearly and precisely the prac-
tice of Mindfulness, or Satiputthana, as taught by Maha-Si
Sayadaw. The text of 16 lectures given by Chao Khun during
1967, added as a supplement to this edition, makes a more
complete volume.

442 Dhiravamsa, V. R. A New Approach to Buddhism, An
        Introduction to the Meditative Way of Life. Hind-
        head: India, Vipassana Centre, 1972. 67 p.
        This is a collection of a series of lectures by the
author. Seven chapters are entitled: Life and Death, Integration of the Intellectual and Spiritual Life, Freedom and
Love, Anatta: no Self, the Meditative Way of Life, What
Buddhism Has to Offer the West, and the Problems of Con-
flict.

443 Dogen. A Primer of Soto Zen: A Translation of
        Dogen's Shobogenzo Zumimonki. Translated by
        Reiho Masunaga. Honolulu: East-West Center,
        1972. 119 p.

This book consists largely of brief talks, hortatory
remarks, and instructional and cautionary comments by the
Japanese Zen master Dogen Kigen (1200-1253), as recorded
by his disciple, Ejo. Dogen is considered one of the greatest
thinkers in the history of Japanese Buddhism.

444 Eaglesfield, F. Silent Union; A Record of Unwilled
     Communication. London: Stuart and Watkins,
     1967. 95 p.
     The author describes incidents he has encountered
during his own search for enlightenment, showing how a
process of wordless communication is carried from one
person to another by individuals acting as transmitters. He
makes no attempt to explain this, saying, "It is better to
know that we can enter the universal consciousness than to
know how we do it."

445 Ehara, the Rev. N. R. M. The Path of Freedom
     (Vimuttimagga). Colombo, Ceylon: D. Roland
     D. W., 1962. 363 p.
     The original text in Pali of the work is no longer
in existence, but it has survived in sixth-century translation
by Tipitaka Sanghapala of Funan from which the Rev. N. R.
M. Ehara, Somathera and Kheminda Thera have compiled
this work. The Vimuttimagga, being a practical book of
instruction, will be of much value to those seeking an understanding of the teachings of the Buddha Dhamma.

446 Fausset, H. I. Fruits of Silence; Studies in the Art
     of Being. London: Abelard Schuman, 1963.
     244 p.
     The purpose of this work is to indicate how much
we experience the fullness of the dynamic Middle Way, how
wisdom and love, the fount of all creation and all service,
are only to be drawn upon at the center of the being which
is related to being itself.

447 Gregg, R. B. Self-Transcendence. London: Victor
     Gollancz. 1956. 224 p.
     This book demonstrates how we all start off from
certain basic assumptions before we start reasoning about
anything and that it is worthwhile to try to find out just what
these basic assumptions are. It shows the importance of
having one's basic assumptions mutually consistent.

448 Hayakawa, S. Zen Showed Me the Way: To Peace,
     Happiness and Tranquility. See entry no. 1080.

449 Huber, J. Psychotherapy and Meditation. See entry
      no. 870.

450 King, W. L. A Thousand Lives Away. See entry no.
      1010.

451 Krishna, G. Kundalini; The Evolutionary Energy in
      Man. London: Stuart and Watkins, 1971. 252 p.
      Some Yogis claim that it is possible to draw up the
spine towards the brain a torrent of radiant energy known as
Kundalini. This is an account of the author's life and development which has been dominated by the unexpected and
unintended arousing of this elemental force. This book will
be of absorbing interest to the serious students of Yoga,
meditation and of the works of Ouspensky.

452 Lang-Sims, L. A Time to Be Born. London: Andre
      Deutsch, 1971. 252 p.
      Perceptive self-analysis makes this book compulsive
reading for anyone interested in the tortuous convolutions of
character-development.

453 Lindenberg, V. Meditation and Mankind. London:
      Rider and Co., 1959. 206 p.
      This work aims to describe practices in prayer and
meditation throughout the world, and though each summary
cannot be quite correct in detail, there is much to tell any
of us about the rest of us.

454 Lounsbery, G. C. Buddhist Meditation in the Southern
      School. New York: Knopf, 1936. 177 p.
      This work contains practical instruction in the
methods of Buddhist meditation devised for Westerners.
The author makes the meditations of Asia more intelligible
and logical than they appear in many attempted expositions.

455 Luk, C. The Secret of Chinese Meditation. London:
      Rider, 1970. 240 p.
      The author describes all the methods used by the
different schools of Buddhism in China to obtain self-realization. Mr. Luk himself seems to be most sympathetic to the
Chan (Zen) school. This book is a fascinating and well
thought out series of descriptions of aims and practices.

456 Mindfulness of Breathing. Buddhist texts from the Pali
      Canon and extracts from the Pali commentaries,

translated from Pali by B. Nanamoli. 2nd ed.
Kandy: Buddhist Publication Society, 1964. 125 p.
   Mindfulness when breathing in and breathing out is
one of the methods of penetrating the Four Noble Truths on
which all aspects of the teaching converge. This subject is
therefore not at all neglected in the Pali Pitakas or suc-
ceeding literature. It finds its most comprehensive treatment in the 118th discourse of the Majjhima-nikaya which is
devoted entirely to this subject of meditation.

457 Radhakrishnan, S. Ramana Maharshi and the Path to
      Self-Knowledge. See entry no. 269.

458 The Recorded Sayings of Layman P'ang; a Ninth
      Century Zen Classic. See entry no. 1110.

459 Reichelt, K. L. Meditation and Piety in the Far East;
      Religious Psychological Study. London: Lutter-
      worth Press, 1954. 171 p.
   Dr. Reichelt had forty years of missionary work in
the Far East, mainly in China, but he traveled widely and
visited all the main Buddhist countries. During this time he
had intimate contact with a number of men who had achieved
some degree of religious experience. In this book he has
chosen the experience of meditation as the nucleus around
which religious systems could be discussed. On Chinese
Buddhism, Taoism and Confucianism Dr. Reichelt writes as
an authority. He discusses many subjects but emphasizes
Dhyana Meditation, ethics, mind training of the Noble Eightfold Path and Nirvana. His chapter on Taoism is a fascinating and scholarly one, including long quotations with a commentary and some account of famous Taoists. His account
of the Confucian worthies is a noble one. At last the author
discusses the relation between Christianity and Buddhism.

460 Saddhatissa, H. The Buddha's Way. See entry no.
      1249.

461 Sadhu, M. Concentration. London: Allen and Unwin,
      1958. 175 p.
   The author previously wrote In Days of Great Peace,
which was a great contribution to this subject. For a layman to devote these specialized ten-minute periods regularly
each day, and note the development of his practice, is most
excellent and these experiences should be worth following.

462 _____. Samadhi. London: Allen and Unwin, 1962.
      182 p.

Having learnt from the author's previous work <u>Con-</u>
<u>centration</u> the rudiments of concentration and mind con<u>trol</u>
and being brought to the threshold of meditation itself, one
now is taken step by step to the spiritual heights of Samadhi.
Every direction is clear and to the point, nothing necessary
being omitted and nothing unnecessary put in.

463 _____ . <u>Ways to Self-Realization.</u>   London: Allen
            and Unwin, 1963.   242 p.
This work is a clearly written and well balanced
account of the steps in the path of Maha Yoga, particularly
the steps for beginners.   The author is a follower of Ramana
Maharshi and a deeply devoted disciple.   Because this way
of life is the center of his existence, his book becomes
really alive and full of a deep understanding when he describes the Maharshi and the essence of the Maharshi's
teaching.

464 Sarukkali.   World Revolution through Buddhist Medita-
            tion.   Calle, Ceylon: F. Abeysuriya, 1961.   72 p.
This work contains short essays on the doctrine
with comments from sages and psychologists.

465 Sayadaw, L.   <u>Manual of Insight</u>.   London: Wheel Pub-
            lications, 1961.   87 p.
This is a technical treatise on Abhidhamma lines,
written in 1915 for Westerners by a famous Burmese master,
and for this new translation we must be grateful.   Abhidhamma is both the result of and the basis for meditation.
This book will be of value to those who know how to unlock
its secrets.

466 _____ .   <u>The Progress of Insight</u>.   Translated by
            N. Thera with the Pali original.   Ceylon: Forest
            Hermitage, 1966.   58 p.
This work is a descriptive key to the insight knowledge resulting from the form of Satipatthana meditation
taught by Mahasi Sayadaw of Rangoon.   The author is a very
experienced meditator and his work is based on the classical
Seven Stages of Purification of the Visuddhimagga, and is
written in what might be called Buddhaghosa phraseology.

467 Senzaki, N.   <u>Buddhism and Zen</u>.   See entry no. 1115.

468 Shastri, H. P.   <u>Scientist and Mahatma</u>.   London:
            Shanti Sadan, 1955.   141 p.
The author is a founder of the Shanti Sadan, a London

group devoted to the teaching of Yogi meditation as a basic
way of life. The book can be recommended to anyone who
wishes to know how the Buddhist's spiritual life is actually
lived in the present age.

469   Shibayama, A. Z. A Flower Does Not Talk. Trans-
         lated by S. Kudo. New York: C. E. Tuttle Co.,
         1971. 264 p.
         The author demonstrates that training in self-
awakening demands a will strong enough to eliminate ignorance and discrimination, and although special facilities
are normally required, the ordinary person can make considerable progress if his faith is sufficiently strong. There
is a detailed analysis and interpretation of the Song of Zazen
by Hakuin and explanatory essays on the Six Oxherding pictures. The practical and philosophical nature of Zen is
epitomized in the verse by the author which introduces the
last section of the book. The six illustrations of the Ox-
herding pictures, the eight photographs of flower arrangements, and the 12 paintings by Hakuin are of high quality
in this work.

470   Suzuki, D. T. Zen Buddhism; Selected Writings. See
         entry no. 1136.

471   Suzuki, S. Zen Mind, Beginner's Mind. New York:
         John Weatherhill, 1971. 134 p.
         This work contains informal talks on Zen meditation
and practice by Shunryu Suzuki edited by Trudy Dixon. The
book is about how to practice Zen as a discipline and religion, about posture and breathing, about basic attitudes and
understanding of Zen. The author's comments are clear and
practical. He states that we should begin with enlightenment and proceed to practice, and then to thinking. This
work is one of the Soto Zen school.

472   Swearer, D. K. Secrets of the Lotus: Studies in Bud-
         dhist Meditation. New York: Macmillan, 1971.
         This work discusses Buddhist meditation texts and
commentaries, contemporary interpretations of them and it
also gives a description of a recent Buddhist meditation experiment.

473   no entry

474   Thera, N. The Heart of Buddhist Meditation. 2nd ed.
         London: Rider, 1962. 223 p.

This is a second and expanded edition of the already famous work published in Colombo, Ceylon, in 1953, with a foreward by E. G. Howe. The present edition consists of three parts. The first part explains the aims and methods of mindfulness (Satipatthana). The second part contains the text of the greater discourse on the foundations of mindfulness (the "Satipatthana Sutra") from the Digha Nikaya, with notes. And the last section, which is entirely new, contains an anthology of texts from both Theravada and Mahayana sources on the subject of mindfulness.

475 Thera, P. V. M. Buddhist Meditation in Theory and
        Practice. Colombo, Ceylon: Gunasena, 1963.
        498 p.
      This book is for those who are sincere and ardent in their desire to achieve enlightenment. The author stresses meditation as a central position in Buddhist teaching. And he explains that meditation in practice has been developed into two complex systems known as Samadhi and Vipassana, both of which he analyzes in their fundamental principles.

476 Trungpa, C. Meditation in Action. London: Stuart
        and Watkins, 1968.   74 p.
      The author Lama Trungpa is the leading figure in Tibetan Buddhism in England. The work expresses the Tibetan doctrine and Tibetan point of view. An important part of the work is meditation. Lama says, "Meditation is dealing with purpose itself. It is not for something, it is dealing with the aim."

477 Warren, H. C. Buddhism in Translations; Passages
        Selected from the Buddhist Sacred Books. See
        entry no. 1220.

478 Wei, W. W. Open Secret. Hong Kong: Hong Kong
        University Press, 1965.   194 p.
      The purpose of all the Sutras is to teach people to empty themselves. The author explains so patiently and carefully the fact of our essential absence.

479 Willis, J. D. The Diamond Light of the Eastern
        Dawn: Collection of Tibetan Buddhist Meditations.
        New York: Simon and Schuster, 1972.   124 p.
      This work is an introduction to the practice of Tibetan Buddhist meditation that lies at the heart of a religious philosophy increasingly studied and followed around the world today. This collection of meditations presents the

Mantra, Yantra, Mudra, and Mandala and explores the importance of the Guru, the actual practice.

480 Wood, E. E. Mind and Memory Training. See entry
      no. 883.

MISSIONS

GENERAL

481 Bose, P. The Indian Teachers in China. Madras:
      Ganesan, 1923.
          This is an excellent compilation and organization of
available facts concerning the Indian Buddhist missionaries
to China.

482 Buddhism. Studia Missionalia XII. See entry no. 80.

483 no entry

484 Giles, H. A. The Travels of Fa-hsien; or The Record
      of the Buddhist Kingdoms. London: Routledge,
      1956. 96 p.
          This is a famous story of the Chinese pilgrim's
journeys in Buddhist India, about A.D. 400. The translation was first published in 1923. It is full of fascinating
information.

485 Pratt, J. B. The Pilgrimage of Buddhism and a Buddhist Pilgrimage. New York: Macmillan, 1928.
      758 p.
          This is one of the best synthetic estimates of Buddhism, describing the organic unity of its life and growth,
based on two visits to Buddhist lands as well as on an intimate knowledge of the literature.

486 Raven-Hart, R. Where the Buddha Trod: A Buddhist
      Pilgrimage. Colombo: Cave, 1965. 133 p.
          This book should prove most useful for its detailed
accounts of how to get to the various monuments and shrines
which are described most fully, both in the text and by
pictures. This work has the qualities of a study of the
Dhamma in the place of its birth and nurture.

ASIA

487   Chen, K. K. S. Buddhism, the Light of Asia. New
         York: Woodbury, 1968. 297 p.
      This is a concise, comprehensive history of Bud-
dhism in India, Southeast Asia, China, Tibet, and Japan.
It gives an analysis of Buddhist philosophy, literature, art,
and ceremonies and a description of the monastic community.

488   Dutt, S. Buddhism in East Asia. See entry no. 380.

489   Humphreys, C. Via Tokyo. London: Hutchinson,
         1949. 200 p.
      This is not only a travel book, but also a special
inquiry in search of Buddhism in the countries of Japan,
China, Siam, Burma, India and Ceylon, which the author
visited. He describes a great number of people with vivid
descriptions of customs and places. There is a helpful
index of names and places and also a glossary of Buddhist
terms.

490   Parrinder, E. G. An Introduction to Asian Religions.
         London: S. P. C. K., 1957. 138 p.
      This work presents the main facts about the living
religions of Asia as a sample guide to further study.

491   Saunders, K. J. Buddhism and Buddhists in Southern
         Asia. New York: Macmillan, 1923.
      The author describes Buddhist influence in modern
Ceylon and considers it in relation to Christian influence.

492   _____. The Gospel for Asia. New York: Mac-
         millan and Company, 1928. 245 p.
      This is a study of three religious masterpieces:
Gita, Lotus, and the Fourth Gospel. In this work the author
has made a comparative study of the three great sacred
texts. He describes sympathetically the striking similarity
among them.

493   Schecter, J. The New Face of Buddha; Buddhism and
         Political Power in Southeast Asia. See entry no.
         858.

494   Spencer, R. F. Religion and Change in Contemporary
         Asia. Minneapolis: University of Minnesota Press,
         1971. 172 p.
      This volume presents case studies of the contemporary

role of religion in seven Asian nations; China, Japan, Vietnam, India, Burma, Pakistan, and Indonesia. Each essay is by a specialist with long-term, firsthand experience in the area; the contributors represent various academic disciplines, including anthropology, history, political science, and history of religions.

BHUTAN

495 Gould, B. J. The Jewel in the Lotus. See item no. 418.

496 Olschak, B. Bhutan, Land of Hidden Treasures.
       London: Allen and Unwin, 1971. 58 p. and 80
       illustrations.
          The photography is by Ursula and Auguste Gansser.
Until recently Bhutan, a small Buddhist kingdom in the
northeast corner of the Himalayas, was closed to all foreigners. The text tells us more of the life of the people
and, in particular, of their love of dancing, mostly religious
in form.

497 Peissel, M. Lords and Lamas. London: Heinemann,
       1971. 192 p.
          Although he is not a Buddhist, the author is sincerely sympathetic with Buddhists' philosophy. In Bhutan he
finds a living faith which permeates their lives, where the
moral and spiritual values are more important than the material, and where architects and craftsmen still create anonymously to the glory of Buddha. This is a remarkable book
of travel in Bhutan monasteries.

498 Rahul, R. Modern Bhutan. New York: Barnes and
       Noble, 1971. 173 p.
          The author describes the land and the people of
Bhutan and the dynamics of its social system. Then he discusses Bhutan's system of government, including its structure
and functioning. He goes into the various aspects of the Buddhism of Bhutan, especially the impact of the religion on the
life and culture of the people.

BURMA

499 Byles, M. B. Paths to Inner Calm. See entry no.
       436.

500   Daing, U. T. <u>Cittanupassana (Meditation on Mind) and
        Vedananupassana (Meditation on Feeling)</u>. Rangoon:
        n.p., 1971. 120 p.
        This work, based on the Pali Canon, lays great
stress on the importance of the doctrine of Dependent Origination and the Four Noble Truths, especially in respect to
Vipassana meditation. Some Western readers may find the
presentation somewhat repetitive, but this can be very useful
in driving home salient points. The author uses quite a
number of Pali terms which will help to achieve a basic
understanding of them.

501   Edwards, M. <u>A Life of the Buddha</u>. See entry no.
        353.

502   Fielding-Hall, H. <u>The Inward Light</u>. New York:
        Macmillan, 1908.
        An account of Burmese Buddhist life in the late 19th
century is given here.

503   King, W. L. <u>A Thousand Lives Away</u>. See entry
        no. 1010.

504   Mannin, E. <u>The Living Lotus</u>. London: Jarrolds,
        1956. 320 p.
        This gives a very delightful picture of the life in
Burma, and it tells of the Nat worship practiced by the
gentle Burmese people. The story itself is of the life of
an Anglo-Burmese child brought up in Burma at the time of
the Japanese invasion, and who married at an early age to
a native of Burma.

505   Pulley, S. <u>A Yankee in the Yellow Robe</u>. New York:
        Exposition Press, 1968. 130 p.
        The author went to a meditation center in Rangoon
as a magazine writer. Later he became a monk and received full ordination. The book is a factual account of the
way of life in a community of monks in Rangoon.

506   Sa, U. P. <u>A Brief Outline of Buddhism</u>. See entry
        no. 119.

507   Schecter, J. <u>The New Face of Buddha; Buddhism and
        Political Power in Southeast Asia</u>. See entry no.
        858.

508   Slater, R. H. L. <u>Paradox and Nirvana</u>. New York:

Columbia University Press, 1950.   145 p.
This is an analysis of Burmese Buddhism, comparing it to Mahayana Buddhism and Christianity.   The
author's thesis is that the Nat cult in Burma is related to
Burmese Buddhism in such a way as to make the two a
consistent and inseparable part of Burmese culture.   This
comparative study has possible applications wherever primitive and higher religions co-exist in a society.

509   Smith, D. E.   Religion and Politics in Burma.   Prince-
          ton: Princeton University Press, 1965.   350 p.
Professor Smith examines in detail the interaction
between Buddhism and the state in Burma, from the period
of King Anawrahta to the dramatic events of the 1962 coup
d'etat.   The author tries to discover Buddhism's role in
Burma and he states that Burmese people cannot think of
nationality apart from the religion that they hold, for it is
Buddhism which has welded the Burmese together and the
idea of nationhood owes its inception to Buddhism.

510   Soni, R.   A Cultural Study of the Burmese Era.
          Mandalay: World Institute of Buddhist Culture,
          1956.   200 p.
This gives the historical background of Burmese
culture which was profoundly influenced by the teaching of
the Buddha.   The author expresses the wish that this work
will propagate inter-religious understanding and also international goodwill.

511   Spiro, M. E.   Buddhism and Society: A Great Tra-
          dition and its Burmese Vicissitudes.   See entry
          no. 995.

512   _____ .   Burmese Supernaturalism; A Study in the
          Explanation and Reduction of Suffering.   Englewood
          Cliffs, N.J.:   Prentice-Hall, 1967.   300 p.
This gives an account of the Burmese folk religion
and its relation to the traditional Buddhism of the country.
The subject is examined in relationship both to its historical,
social, and political background and to its effect on society,
culture and personality in modern Burma.

513   Thera, N.   The Heart of Buddhist Meditation.   See
          entry no. 473.

CAMBODIA

514 Audric, J. Angkor and the Khmer Empire. London:
         Robert Hale, 1972. 207 p.
         In 1861 Henri Mouhot, a French naturalist, dis-
covered Angkor, the lost city and former capital of the
Khmer Empire for which historians over the centuries had
searched. This empire had cradled the most brilliant,
cultured and advanced civilization of Southeast Asia, including all modern Cambodia and parts of Laos, Vietnam,
and Thailand. The author gives every detail of the rise
of the Khmers and their ruins. He also endeavors to solve
the intriguing mystery of the lost capital.

515 Schecter, J. The New Face of Buddha; Buddhism and
         Political Power in Southeast Asia. See entry no.
         858.

CEYLON

516 Baptist, E. C. Nibbana or the Kingdom. See entry
         no. 914.

517 Buddhaghosa. The Path of Purification. See entry
         no. 1158.

518 Cave, H. W. The Book of Ceylon. New York: Cas-
         sell and Co., 1908. 664 p.
         This is an attractive traveler's guide with maps
and 756 photographs. The work weaves history and archaeological description together instructively.

519 Copleston, R. S. Buddhism, Primitive and Present in
         Magadha and in Ceylon. New York: Longmans,
         Green, 1908. 301 p.
         This work gives the history and description of that
particular stock or branch of Buddhism. It is of interest to
the general reader and accurate enough to be of value to the
scholar.

520 Gombrich, R. F. Precept and Practice, Traditional
         Buddhism in the Rural Highlands of Ceylon. London:
         Oxford University Press, 1972. 366 p.
         This work is a thesis on the Pali Canon from which
the author gained the Ph.D. at Oxford. He gives very extensive interviews, comparing and analyzing the ideas and

statements of beliefs held by both monks and laity in and around the Sinhalese village of Migala.

521 Keith, A. B. Buddhist Philosophy in India and Ceylon.
       See entry no. 816.

522 Ludowyk, E. F. C. The Footprint of the Buddha.
       See entry no. 357.

523 Pieris, P. E., Translator. Religious Intercourse between Ceylon and Siam in the 18th Century.
       Ceylon: American Ceylon Mission Press, 1908, 1914.
       I. (1908) An account of King Kirti Sri's Embassy to Siam in Saka, 1672, is given here. II. (1914) This tells of Syamupadasampada, the Adoption of the Siamese Order of Priesthood in Ceylon, in the Saka Era, 1673.

524 Rahula, W. History of Buddhism in Ceylon: The Anuradhapura Period, Third Century B.C.-Tenth Century A.D. Colombo: M. D. Gunasena, 1956. 351 p.
       The scholarly work is mainly based on references from its seven main sources: the Pali Scriptures, Asokan Edicts, Ceylon Inscriptions, Pali Chronicles, Pali Commentaries, folktales, and miscellaneous works in Pali and Sinhalese. The work balances changes in the monastic world with the ever-changing social and economic conditions of the life of the laity in the Anuradhapura period.

525 The Revolt in the Temple. See entry no. 397.

526 Schecter, J. The New Face of Buddha; Buddhism and Political Power in Southeast Asia. See entry no. 858.

527 Williams, H. Ceylon, Pearl of the East. London: Hale, 1950. 460 p.
       The book opens with a short history of Lanka, giving appreciation to the Buddhist Sangha for preserving culture and teaching a religion of toleration, peace and simplicity. There are excellent descriptions and photographs of the countryside and detailed accounts of many famous places, mostly temples.

528 Wirz, P. Exorcism and the Art of Healing in Ceylon.
       Leiden: Brill, 1954. 253 p.
       This gives a study and survey of various ceremonies

and practices in Ceylon relevant to exorcism, devil dancing,
and the art of healing. Much of the material derives from
original sources with occasional references to Buddhist
culture. Spells, magic diagrams, etc. are included in their
Sinhalese original and in English translation.

529 Wriggins, W. H. Ceylon: Dilemmas of a New Nation.
        Princeton, N. J.: Princeton University Press, 1960.
        505 p.
        This study is the result of two years' investigation
by the author into Ceylon's economic, constitutional, religious and social problems. The religious chapter gives
some interesting facts relating to the Sangha, and it also
endeavors to state briefly the basic tenets of Theravada
Buddhism.

CHINA

530 Beal, S. Abstract of Four Lectures on Buddhist Lit-
        erature in China Delivered at University College.
        London: Trubner, 1882. 185 p.
        This work contains early translations of Buddhist
books in China on the method of Buddha's teaching as exhibited in the Vinaya Pitaka, and it relates coincidences between Buddhism and other religious systems.

531 _____. Buddhism in China. New York: E. and
        J. B. Young and Co., 1884. 263 p.
        Although old, this is one of the most systematic
treatments of the subject. It deals with various important
topics of Buddhism such as Nirvana, Kwang-yin, and
Amitabha, as well as some of the Buddhist texts that exist
in China.

532 _____. A Catena of Buddhist Scripture from the
        Chinese. See entry no. 34.

533 Blofeld, J. Jewel in the Lotus, an Outline of Present-
        day Buddhism in China. London: Sidgwick and
        Jackson, 1948. 193 p.
        The historical background, the philosophy, and the
different sects of Buddhism in contemporary China are
clearly described by a specialist in Chinese Buddhism who
bases his work on much original research in China. The
influence of various Buddhist sects on the life of the Chinese
people is also competently discussed.

534   Chang, C. C.   The Buddhist Teaching of Totality.
        University Park: Pennsylvania State University,
        1972.   270 p.
        The doctrines of Hwa Yen Buddhism provide a
unique philosophical system which explains man, the world,
and life as they are intuitively experienced in the practice of
Zen.   The school, widely regarded as the very crown of
Buddhist thought, arose in seventh-century China and is here
fully revealed for the first time to Western readers.

535   Ch'en, K. K. S.   Buddhism in China: A Historical
        Survey.   See entry no. 36.

536   Davidson, J. L.   Lotus Sutra in Chinese Art: A
        Study in Buddhist Art to the Year 1000.   See entry
        no. 162.

537   De Groot, J. J. M.   The Religion of the Chinese.
        New York: Macmillan, 1910.   230 p.
        This work gives an analysis of Chinese religion as
a native product, the primeval forms of which were never
swept away by any other religion, with a long chapter devoted
to the importation, Buddhism.

538   _____ .   Sectarianism and Religious Persecution in
        China.   Amsterdam: J. Müller, 1903-1904.   2 vols.
        This work is based largely on imperial decrees, the
texts and translations of which are given.

539   Dumoulin, H.   The Development of Chinese Zen after
        the Sixth Patriarch in the Light of Mumonkan.
        Translated from German by R. F. Sasaki.   New
        York: First Zen Institute, 1953.   146 p.
        This is a concise study of Zen Buddhism in its
golden age in China during the Tang and Sung dynasties, by
a Jesuit priest.   It contains two highly useful glossaries of
Sanskrit terms: one in romanized Japanese, the Chinese
characters, and romanized Chinese; and the other in romanized Chinese, the Chinese characters, and romanized
Japanese.

540   Feng, Y. L.   The Spirit of Chinese Philosophy.   Trans-
        lated by E. R. Hughes.   London: Paul, Trench,
        Trubner, 1947.   224 p.
        The book provides the historical background for Dr.
Feng's system of thought.   Major schools of philosophy, including Buddhism and neo-Confucianism are systematically
discussed.

541   Forke, A. The World-Conception of the Chinese; Their
        Astronomical, Cosmological and Physico-philosophi-
        cal Speculations. London: Probsthain, 1925. 300 p.
        The Chinese conception of the universe, the heavens,
Yin and Yang, and the five elements in both ancient and
modern times are explained on the basis of the writings of
major religions and schools of philosophy.

542   Goodrich, L. C. A Short History of the Chinese
        People. London: Allen, 1957. 250 p.
        Buddhist missionaries of both Hinayana and Mahayana
schools came to China, and by the sixth century A.D. Buddhism was at the height of its influence in China. This work
discusses its purely historical aspects and then the cultural
and religious developments within that.

543   Grousset, R. Chinese Art and Culture. See entry
        no. 165.

544   Hai, H. The Path to Sudden Attainment; A Treatise
        of the Chan (Zen) School of Chinese Buddhism. See
        entry no. 1078.

545   Hodous, L. Buddhism and Buddhists in China. New
        York: Macmillan, 1924. 84 p.
        Professor Hodous, who has seen sixteen years of
missionary service in Foochow, reproduces in this volume
the actual thinking of a trained Buddhist mind in regard to
the fundamentals of religion.

546   Hughes, E. R. Religion in China. New York: Hutchin-
        son's University Library, 1950. 151 p.
        This work gives a general survey of the religious
situation in China from the beginnings of Confucianism and
its background and the influence of Taoist mysticism to the
coming of Buddhism.

547   Hui-Neng. The Sutra of Wei Lang. Translated from
        Chinese by Wong Mou-lam. New edition by C.
        Humphreys. London: Buddhist Society, 1944.
        128 p.
        The only sutra spoken by a native of China, this
records the sermons and sayings of Wei Lang (A.D. 638-713),
the famous Zen master of the Tang dynasty.

548   Johnston, R. F. Buddhist China. New York: Dutton,
        1914.

This work covers fully and scientifically all phases
of what seems to be the surviving religion of China. The
author, who spent fifteen years in China, discusses three
China religions, and he believes that only Buddhism can be
considered as a serious rival to Christianity.

549 Jong, J. W. de. Buddha's World in China. Canberra:
     Australian National University, 1968. 29 p.
     This is the George Ernest Morrison Lecture in
ethnology on Chinese Buddhist literature, history, and criticism.

550 Li, S. C. Popular Buddhism in China. Shanghai:
     Commercial Press, 1940. 75 p.
     This work gives translations of 10 Buddhist poems,
32 Buddhist proverbs, Hsuan Tsang's "Essence of the Wisdom Sutra," and Kumarajiva's "Diamond Sutra," by Shao
Chang Li.

551 Moore, C. A. The Chinese Mind, Essentials of
     Chinese Philosophy and Culture. Honolulu: Uni-
     versity of Hawaii, 1968. 402 p.
     The Chinese Mind includes proceedings from four
East-West Philosophers' Conferences which took place on
United States territory. This work gives four of the papers
by Wing-Tsit Chan who emphasizes Buddhism, although he
contends there has been no significant development in the
last 800 years.

552 Pratt, J. B. The Pilgrimage of Buddhism and a Bud-
     dhist Pilgrimage. See entry no. 485.

553 Reichelt, K. L. Meditation and Piety in the Far East;
     Religious Psychological Study. See entry no. 459.

554 _____ . The Transformed Abbot. London: Lutter-
     worth Press, 1954. 157 p.
     This is the story, told by a Norwegian Lutheran
missionary, of the life of a Formosan Buddhist who was un-
able to find any lasting satisfaction in his own Buddhist tradition. The book ends with a short biographical note about
Tai-Hsu, the great reviver of Chinese Buddhism, who died
in 1947.

555 _____ . Truth and Tradition in Chinese Buddhism.
     2nd ed. Translated from the Norwegian by V. W.
     Bugge. New York: Paragon Book Reprint Corp.,
     1968. 330 p.

The author describes general characteristics of
Chinese Prahayana Buddhist literature, with special attention to certain classics in current use.

556 Robinson, R. Chinese Buddhist Verse. See entry no.
         206.

557 Schecter, J. The New Face of Buddha; Buddhism and
         Political Power in Southeast Asia. See entry no.
         858.

558 Soothill, W. E. The Three Religions of China. 3rd
         ed. London, New York: Oxford, 1951. 271 p.
         The fundamentals of the three major religions, Bud-
dhism, Confucianism, and Taoism, are presented. The
author explains the ideas of God, soul, sin, and ancestor
worship. This is based on lectures delivered at Oxford
before a group of students designated for mission work in
China.

559 Stein, Sir M. A. Sand-Buried Ruins of Khotan.
         London: T. F. Unwin, 1903. 2 vols.
         This is a personal narrative of explorations in
Chinese Turkestan. A large, two-volume set with numerous
illustrations, color plates, panoramas, and maps, it gives
a description of the central Asian territory through which
the pilgrims passed on their way to India.

560 Suzuki, D. T. The Zen Doctrine of No-mind; Signifi-
         cance of the Sutra of Hui-neng. See entry no. 1137.

561 Vajrachchedika. The Diamond Sutra; or, the Jewel of
         Transcendental Wisdom. Translated from Chinese
         by A. F. Price. 2nd ed. London: Buddhist So-
         ciety, 1955. 74 p.
         This gives an annotated translation of the Chinese
version of the Vajrachchedika Prajnaparamita, one of fifty
extant undertakings of the fifth century Buddhist missionary
to China, Kumarajiva, who worked with Chinese monks to
put into Chinese some 300 Buddhist works. The "Diamond
Sutra" is an especially valued Buddhist work in China.

562 Vincent, I. V. Sacred Oasis: Caves of the Thousand
         Buddhas. See entry no. 189.

563 Wei, S. Treatise on Buddhism and Taoism. Trans-
         lated from Chinese by L. Hurvitz. Kyoto: Kyoto

University, 1956. 103 p.
This work is a richly annotated translation, with
numerous passages reproduced in the original Chinese for
specialists, of the text of the Shih-lao-chih of the fifth
century Yung Kang Caves.

564 Welch, H. H. Buddhist Revival in China. With a
        section of photographs by Henri Cartier-Bresson.
        Cambridge: Harvard University Press, 1968.
        385 p.
The second of a projected three-volume series on
Buddhism in China, with emphasis on the revolutionary
changes, this work cites the history of the various move-
ments in Chinese Buddhism during the period from 1850 to
1950.

565 _____. The Practice of Chinese Buddhism, 1900-
        1959. See entry no. 775.

566 no entry

567 Wright, A. F. Buddhism in Chinese History. Stanford,
        Cal.: Stanford University Press, 1965. 144 p.
Chinese Buddhism is strikingly different from its
Indian ancestral form. Professor Wright's book brings out
the reciprocal influences of Chinese tradition on the message from India, as well as the profound impact of the Buddhist faith on the civilization of China.

568 Zurcher, E. Buddhist Conquest of China. New York:
        Humanities, 1959. 468 p. 2 vols.
In an introductory chapter the author gives a survey
of the little that is known about the history of Chinese Buddhism during its period of incubation to about A.D. 300. The
main subject of the book is the Buddhism of the upper classes
in Southern China roughly between the years 300 and 400.

ENGLAND

569 Humphreys, C. The Development of Buddhism in Eng-
        land. London: Buddhist Lodge, 1937. 103 p.
        This is a history of the Buddhist movement in London.

570 _____. Studies in the Middle Way. New York:
        Verry, 1959. 136 p. [see also entry no. 138.]

These essays are the result of forty years' experience in fields of thought including religion, philosophy, psychology, mysticism, morality and much more, which concerns what the Buddha called the Middle Way, between all opposites and extremes.

571 _____ . A Western Approach to Zen. See entry no. 1087.

572 _____ . Zen: A Way of Life. See entry no. 1088.

INDIA

573 Archer, J. C. The Sikhs in Relation to Hindu, Moslems, Christians, and Ahamadiyyas. See entry no. 984.

574 Barth, A. The Religions of India. London: Kegan Paul, 1932.
This book remains one of the clearest and most concise accounts of the religions of India as a whole.

575 Bennett, J. C. Long Pilgrimage. London: Hodder and Stoughton, 1964. 190 p.
This work is the teaching of an Indian sage, Shivapuri Baba. He stresses three disciplines to be acquired as a foundation before enlightenment can come: (1) care of the body to ensure physical welfare; (2) care of the mind so that time is not wasted looking for happiness; and (3) discipline of the will obtained through meditation.

576 Buffet, E. P. The Layman Revato. New York: Douglas C. McMurtrie, 1914. 106 p.
This is a story of a restless mind in Buddhist India at the time of Greek influence. Archaeological research, however, reveals that the Greco-Buddhist buildings and sculputres of Gandhara and other districts were Oriental ideas carried out with a classic technique.

577 Chennakesavan, S. The Concept of Mind in Indian Philosophy. See entry no. 805.

578 Chetwode, P. Kulu: The End of the Habitable World. See entry no. 245.

579 Conze, E. Buddhist Thought in India. See entry no. 807.

580   Coomaraswamy, A. K.   Introduction to Indian Art.
           Edited by Mulk Raj Anand. See entry no. 161.

581   Cranmer-Byng, L.   Legends of Indian Buddhism.
           London: John Murray, 1911. 128 p. (The Wisdom
           of the East series.)
           Three legends in this volume forcefully illustrate
the doctrine of Karma: the story of King Asoka's son,
Kunala; the story of Kunala's contemporary, Sundara; and
the story of Asoka's brother, Vitasoka. This work illus-
trates fundamental Buddhist doctrines, reveals the civilizing
influence of Buddhism and tells the history of Asoka.

582   Cunningham, Sir A.   The Bhilsa Topes or Buddhist
           Monuments of Central India.   Varanasi: Indological
           Book House, 1966. 236 p.
           This work comprises a brief historical sketch of
the rise, progress, and decline of Buddhism, with an account of the opening and examination of the various groups
of topes around Bhilsa. It gives bibliographical footnotes.

583   Dasgupta, S. N.   A History of Indian Philosophy.
           London: Cambridge University, 1922-1955. 5 vols.
           This work gives extensive descriptive accounts of
Indian philosophical systems, Vedic and Brahmanical specu-
lations, Hindu classical systems, Buddhist and Jain philosophy, materialistic ideas, religious works, etc.   The work is
highly technical and reflects a slightly personalized interpretation, but it is a valuable exposition by an Indian author
and helpful for the discrimination of terms.

584   Davids, T. W. R.   Buddhist India. Essex, England:
           Gupta, 1957. 332 p.
           This work describes ancient India during the period
of Buddhist ascendancy, more from the point of view of the
Rajput than of the Brahmin.

585   De Bary, W. T.   The Buddhist Tradition in India,
           China, and Japan. See entry no. 95.

586   _____.   Sources of Indian Tradition. New York:
           Columbia University, 1964. 2 vols. 962 p.
           This is an excellent selection of texts intended "to
provide the general reader with an understanding of the
intellectual and spiritual traditions of India and Pakistan."
It includes not only religious and philosophical, but also
political, social, and economic selections.

587   De Riencourt, A. <u>The Soul of India</u>. London: Jona-
         than Cape, 1961. 431 p.
         This is a philosophical interpretation of the history
of India which covers some 5000 years. Buddhism at its
inception is represented as a joyless, pessimistic and world-
negating doctrine, which coincided with the twilight of Indian
cultural development.

588   Eliot, C. N. E. <u>Hinduism and Buddhism</u>. See entry
         no. 948.

589   Farquhar, J. N. <u>An Outline of the Religious Literature
         of India</u>. London, New York: Oxford, 1920. 451 p.
         This gives a useful survey of Indian religious litera-
ture from the time of Vedic religion through the theistic
developments, philosophies, and devotional sects. Muslim
influence is also extensively treated, as are the Indian religions of Buddhism and Jainism.

590   Ganhar, J. N. <u>Buddhism in Kashmir and Ladakh</u>.
         New Delhi: P. N. Ganhar, 1956. 245 p.
         This is a good attempt to examine the history of
Kashmir in the light of Buddhism, and the best extant description of the people and religion of Ladakh is found here.
How large a part this northwest corner of India has played
in the long history of Buddhism, and how it helped to lay
the foundations of Buddhism in China are discussed.

591   Graham, D. A. <u>The End of Religion</u>. See entry no.
         704.

592   Hiriyanna, M. <u>The Essentials of Indian Philosophy</u>.
         London: Allen and Unwin, 1949. 216 p.
         This short textbook, highlighting the distinguishing
characteristics of Vedic religion and philosophy, Buddhist
and Jain philosophies, and the six classical schools of Hindu
philosophy, is a useful but very general treatment. A short
glossary of technical Sanskrit philosophical terms is included.

593   _____. <u>Outlines of Indian Philosophy</u>. London:
         Allen and Unwin, 1932. 419 p.
         This is a comprehensive account of Indian philosophy
based on the author's lecture series at Mysore University.
Vedic and Upanishadic philosophies, the Bhagavadgita, Buddhism, Jainism, materialism, and the six classical schools
of Hindu philosophy are treated. This work is more detailed
than the author's <u>Essentials of Indian Philosophy</u>.

594 Hopkins, E. W. Ethics of India. New Haven: Yale
          University Press, 1924. 265 p.
     This work is an excellent and competent study of
ethics in India from the Rig Veda, Upanishads, legal literature, and Buddhist ethics. The important concept of religious devotion and its relation to morality is also discussed,
and a final general evaluation is given. The value of the
work is even more enhanced by its virtual exclusiveness in
dealing with this aspect of Indian religion and philosophy.

595 Joshi, L. Studies in the Buddhistic Culture of India.
          Delhi: Motilal Banarsidass, 1967. 538 p.
     The purpose of this volume is "to present authentic
materials for the historical reconstruction and critical appreciation of some aspects of Buddhistic culture in India
during the seventh and eighth centuries A.D."

596 Keith, A. B. Buddhist Philosophy in India and Ceylon.
          See entry no. 816.

597 _____. The Samkhya System; A History of the
          Samkhya Philosophy. See entry no. 817.

598 Kosambi, D. D. The Culture and Civilization of Ancient
          India: An Historical Outline. London: Routledge
          and Kegan Paul, 1964. 210 p.
     This is a basic outline of Indian history from 2500
B.C. to the 13th and 14th centuries A.D. It was during the
period of the rise of the many religions of India that the
country formed its finest cultural highlights. The author
mentions Buddhism as the finest product ever turned out of
India.

599 Law, B. D. Indological Studies. Parts I and II, Cal-
          cutta: Indian Research Institute, 1950. Part III,
          Allahabad: Ganganath Research Institute, 1952.
     This is a study of India and its people as seen
through its languages, literature, history, philosophies,
customs, and antiquities.

600 Markham, P. Road to Katmandu. See entry no. 689.

601 Mehta, P. D. Early Indian Religious Thoughts: An
          Introduction and Essay. London: Luzac, 1956.
          532 p.
     This description of early Indian religious thought is
a work of true understanding and mature scholarship, which

expresses in a striking way the author's personal philosophy
and convictions on the human situation and the significance
of spiritual endeavor. The chapters on the Buddha and his
teachings, God-conception, and religion are especially recommended.

602 Moore, C. A. The Indian Mind: Essentials of Indian
         Philosophy and Culture. Honolulu: University of
         Hawaii, 1968. 458 p.
     The 18 papers in this symposium deal with Indian
metaphysics and epistemology, with problems of ethical,
social, religious, and political philosophy. Each has been
written by an expert born in the tradition on which he writes
and all are accompanied by an invaluable introduction by the
author.

603 Nikhilananda, S. The Upanishads: Translated from
         Sanskrit.... See entry no. 1201.

604 Oldenberg, H. Buddha, His Life, His Doctrine, His
         Order. See entry no. 308.

605 Radhakrishnan, S. Indian Philosophy. New ed. London:
         Allen, 1948. 2 vols. [also see entry no. 824.]
     This work gives a clear and rational account of the
highest conception of Buddhism and Hinduism.

606 _____. A Source Book in Indian Philosophy.
         Princeton: Princeton University, 1957. 683 p.
     This is an extremely useful anthology of Hindu
philosophical works of the Vedic, Epic, and Classical
Periods. Selections indicate the philosophies of materialism,
Jainism and Buddhism, and those of contemporary thinkers.
Short introductory notes precede each major section of se-
lected, translated texts.

607 Rajn, P. T. The Philosophical Traditions of India.
         London: George Allen, 1972. 256 p.
     The author covers the pre-Aryan Mohenjo-daro
civilization of about 3000 B.C. Then he takes the reader
through the Aryan religion of sacrifices, and the rise of
Jainism and Buddhism to the advent of Christianity in the
17th century. In the final chapter the author explains contemporary Indian religions and philosophical trends.

608 Renou, L. Religions of Ancient India. London: Uni-
         versity of London, 1953. 139 p.

These are reliable, authoritative, and critical essays, based on a lecture series at the School of Oriental
and African Studies at the University of London in 1951.
Buddhism, Hinduism, and Jainism are briefly, but competently, treated from the standpoint of the main problems
these religions faced and the present status of such problems.

609 Schweitzer, A. Indian Thought and Its Development.
        Translated by Mrs. Charles E. B. Russell. Glou-
        cester, Mass.: Peter Smith, 1962. 272 p.
        The work begins with the general principles of
Indian thought, which are opposed to those of Western philosophy. It shows what practical effects they have upon
human life, how the extreme fanatics lived and still do live,
and how the principles were compromised to include practical
morality.

610 Sen, A. C. Buddhist Remains in India. New Delhi:
        Indian Council for Cultural Relations, 1956. 140 p.
        As a brief description of the extant remains of Bud-
dhist culture in India it should prove an excellent introduction. It is designed for a further contribution by India to
Buddha Jayanti. Many illustrations and an excellent map
are included.

611 Snellgrove, D. L. Buddhist Himalaya. See entry no.
        1046.

612 Thera, H. S. Handbook of Buddhists. See entry no.
        29.

613 Vasto, L. del. Return to the Source. London: Rider
        Books, 1971. 320 p.
        This is the account and the long awaited translation
of the author's search for spiritual reality, a search that led
him to India and encounters with both Ramana Maharshi and
Gandhi.

614 Warder, A. K. Indian Buddhism. See entry no. 406.

615 Weber, M. Religion of India: The Sociology of Hin-
        duism and Buddhism. New York: Macmillan, 1958.
        392 p.
        This work is part of a vast comparative study which
Weber had originally entitled, Die Wirtschaftsethik der Welt-
religionen. Weber made his general intentions clear in the
introduction to his first volume. These studies do not claim

to be complete, but they deliberately emphasize the elements
in which the various cultures differ from Western civilization.

616   Wood, E. E.   Practical Yoga, Ancient and Modern.
        See entry no. 1290.

617   Woodcock, G.   The Greeks in India.   London: Faber,
        1968.   199 p.
        This is a historical sketch of how the Greeks visited,
invaded, governed, settled and flourished in the regions now
forming Afghanistan, India, and Pakistan.   The appeal of
Buddhism to their logical minds and their own stimulating
influence on local art, both religious and secular, as well
as on manners and customs, has supplied material for a
fascinating survey.

618   Younger, P.   Introduction to Indian Religious Thought.
        London: Darton, 1972.   142 p.
        The book deals with the overall Indian pattern and
the author does not neglect Buddhism in both its aspects, as
a part of the tradition and as a departure from it.

619   Zimmer, H. R.   Philosophies of India.   New York:
        Meridian, 1956.   687 p.
        This is a readable, interesting, but often unreliable
and overly generalized discussion of major concepts of
Indian civilization.   Included are political, aesthetic, social,
and religious philosophies.   Jainism, Buddhism, Brahmanism,
and Tantra, as well as classical Hindu philosophies, are
treated.

JAPAN

620   Anesaki, M.   A History of Japanese Religion.   London:
        Kegan Paul, Trench, Trubner, 1930.   423 p.
        This is an account of the general features of Shinto,
its mythology, cults and communal life, together with the
introduction and establishment of Buddhism, and the subsequent
course of events.   It amounts to a historical survey of the
development of Shinto, Buddhism, Confucianism, and Christianity up to 1930.

621   Bellah, R. N.   Tokugawa Religion.   New York: Free
        Press, 1957.   249 p.
        The author, a sociologist trained in Japanese history
and language, analyzes the traditional value system and

concludes that ethical and religious ideas have deeply influenced patterns of social and economic behavior, rather
than vice versa.

622   Brameld, T.   Japan: Culture, Education and Change
         in Two Communities.   New York: Holt, Rinehart,
         1969.   316 p.
      This is a book with an anthropological orientation.
The author emphasizes the principle that all learning and
teaching must be understood in the cultural and social context, so these functional interdependencies are not neglected.
It presents the Japanese people's basic cultural background
as Buddhism.

623   Brannen, N. S.   Soka Gakkai: Japan's Militant Bud-
         dhists.   Richmond: John Knox Press, 1968.   181 p.
      The Soka Gakkai movement is the third largest po-
litical force in Japan today and worthy of American attention.
The book is "a study in depth of (its) beliefs and practices"
by an assistant professor of linguistics at International
Christian University, Tokyo, who is an American Baptist
missionary.

624   The Buddhist Church of America.   Buddhism and Jodo
         Shinshu.   See entry no. 761.

625   Bush, L.   The Land of the Dragonfly.   London: Robert
         Hale, 1959.   216 p.
      This is a comprehensive survey of the development
of the Japanese nation and way of life from the earliest times
to the present day by an English author.   The effects of the
two major impacts, first of Buddhism and secondly of
Western ideas, are well covered.

626   Byles, M. B.   Paths to Inner Calm.   See entry no. 436.

627   Coe, S.   The Art of Japanese Flower Arrangement.
         See entry no. 159.

628   Dogen.   A Primer of Soto Zen.   See entry no. 443.

629   Dunn, C. H.   Everyday Life in Traditional Japan.   New
         York: Putnam, 1972.   191 p.
      In seven chapters, packed with detail and illustrations,
the author, a reader in Japanese at the London School of
Oriental and African Studies, covers almost the whole of society from "The Samurai" to "Actors and Outcast."   The

eighth chapter deals with everyday life in Edo.   In chapter
six, Buddhism and the growth of the Pure Land School are
discussed, and the Nicheren set is also briefly discussed.

630   Earhart, H. B.   Japanese Religion: Unity and Diversity.
        Belmont: Dickenson, 1969.   115 p.
        This work presents the general reader and teacher
with an introduction to the religions of Japan in the context
of their historical unity.   It is conceived and written as an
introduction to the history of religion in Japan, and can be
read as a first book in this area.

631   Eliot, Sir C. N. E.   Japanese Buddhism.   London:
        Edward Arnold, 1959.   449 p.
        This work recounts the rise of Buddhism in India,
and it deals briefly with Buddhism in China.   The author
summarizes the history of Japanese Buddhism in chronological fashion.   He follows the fortunes and expounds the doctrines of the chief Buddhist sects, relating them to Shinto
and the cultural life of Japan.

632   Fink, R.   A Short Introduction to Japanese Art.   See
        entry no. 163.

633   Graham, A.   Conversations, Christian and Buddhist:
        Encounters in Japan.   See entry no. 920.

634   Hall, R. K.   Shushin: The Ethics of a Defeated Nation.
        New York: Bureau of Publications, Columbia Uni-
        versity, 1949.   244 p.
        This is an annotated translation of official ethics
textbooks in use in Japanese schools immediately prior to
World War II.

635   Hanayama, S.   Buddhism in Japan, in the Path of
        Buddha.   Edited by K. W. Morgan.   New York:
        Ronald Press, 1956.
        This is a short treatise by a leading Japanese
scholar, emphasizing the uniquely Japanese character of
Japanese Buddhism.

636   Holzman, D.   Japanese Religion and Philosophy: A
        Guide to Japanese Reference and Research Ma-
        terials.   See entry no. 39.

637   Japanese National Commission for UNESCO.   Philosophi-
        cal Studies of Japan.   See entry no. 813.

638   Johnston, W.   Christian Zen.   See entry no. 926.

639   Keene, D.   Living Japan.   London: Heinemann, 1959.
      224 p.
      The author, a well-known scholar of Japanese
literature, both old and new, has given us a book which is
much more than a picture-travelogue.   Buddhism, for all
its present decline, is a presence we are aware of, and it
may be much deeper rooted than present conditions lead us
to consider.   That is the message received and firmly believed by this compiler.

640   Kidder, J. E.   Early Japanese Art.   See entry no. 171.

641   _____ .   Japan Before Buddhism.   London: Thames
      and Hudson, 1959.
      This is the best single book on prehistoric Japan,
with discussions of the religious implications of the diverse
archaeological evidence.

642   Kitagawa, J. M.   Religion in Japanese History.   New
      York: Columbia University Press, 1966.
      The most complete, up-to-date account of Japanese
religion in a single volume, this work combines Japanese
and Western materials with the recent insights of the study
of religion.

643   _____ .   Studies of Esoteric Buddhism and Tantrism.
      Koyasan: Koyasan University, 1965.   p. 1-26.
      This work was compiled in commemoration of the
1150th anniversary of the founding of Koyasan.   The article
"Master and Savior" in it is a valuable biography of Kobo
Daishi, emphasizing his significance for popular religion.

644   Knox, G. W.   The Development of Religion in Japan.
      New York: Putnam, 1907.   204 p.
      The purpose of this work is to exhibit the continuity
and development of the religious life of the Japanese people.
The author shows how the religious feelings have been excited
and how in the course of the ages they have changed and pro-
gressed.

645   Lloyd, A.   Creed of Half Japan: Historical Sketches
      of Japanese Buddhism.   New York: Dutton, 1912.
      This is an argument to show the parallelism between
Buddhism and Christianity.   It tells the story of the triumphs,
reverses, kinships and achievements of Buddhism.

646   McCullough, H. C.   The Teiheiki; A Chronicle of
        Medieval Japan.   New York: Columbia University
        Press, 1959.   400 p.
        The interest to the Zen student is that it is in this
period, when the seat of power was Kamakura, and every
man of note was a warrior or a priest--or both--that Zen
Buddhism took root in Japan.   The three main factors of
the day, the court, the monks, and the warriors, are alike
most helpfully analyzed and explained in a long and admirable
introduction.

647   Moore, C. A.   The Japanese Mind: Essentials of
        Japanese Philosophy and Culture.   Honolulu: East-
        West Center, 1967.   357 p.
        The book sets out to distinguish the mental and
spiritual traits peculiar to the Japanese people; it was produced by the East-West Philosophers' Conference at the University of Hawaii.   At the last part the author, who is the
initiator and organizer of the conference, writes that the
Japanese mind is distinguished by two fundamental traits:
direct experience and direct thinking.

648   Otani, K. K. N.   Tannisho; A Tract Deploring Heresies
        of Faith.   Tokyo: Higashi Honganji, 1961.
        This work is a commemoration of the 700th anni-
versary of the death of Shinran, the Japanese Buddhist saint,
and it is a very welcome gesture by the author as president
of the Translating Committee, of which Dr. Suzuki is the
chairman.

649   Pratt, J. B.   The Pilgrimage of Buddhism.   See entry
        no. 485.

650   Price, W.   Journey by Junk.   London: Heinemann,
        1953.   223 p.
        This is primarily an account of a six-week trip
by junk on the beautiful Inland Sea.   In the intervals of
adventures the author writes on many aspects of Japan today--
social and political problems and the position of women.

651   Reischauer, A. K.   Studies in Japanese Buddhism.   New
        York: Macmillan, 1917.   361 p.
        This is a pioneer work on Japanese Buddhism by an
early student of the subject who served as a Christian missionary to Japan.

652   _____ .   The Task in Japan.   Chicago: Fleming H.

Revell, 1926.   231 p.
This is a popular presentation of Japanese Buddhism
from a missionary point of view which throws into relief
certain aspects of present-day Buddhism.

653 Satomi, K.   Japanese Civilization.   New York: Dutton,
      1924.   238 p.
The book is an exposition of the doctrine of Nichi-
renism, a Japanese sect of Buddhism, and its relation to
the national principles of Japan and its spiritual civilization.
A sketch of Nichiren's life is given and many of his writings
are summarized.

654 Saunders, E. D.   Buddhism in Japan.   See entry no.
      400.

655 _____ .   Mudra; A Study of Symbolic Gestures in
      Japanese Buddhist Sculpture.   See entry no. 230.

656 Sawa, T.   Art in Japanese Esoteric Buddhism.   See
      entry no. 183.

657 Schecter, J.   The New Face of Buddha; Buddhism and
      Political Power in Southeast Asia.   See entry no.
      858.

658 Shinoda, M.   The Founding of the Kamakura Shogunate,
      1180-1185.   New York: Columbia University Press,
      1960.   385 p.
The author, professor of Japanese history at the
University of Hawaii, has taken most of his material from
The Mirror of Eastern Japan which he calls a semi-official
history in diary form from the first shogunate, from 1180
to 1266.   The five years he has chosen and illustrated by
extracts from this diary are vital in Japanese history, not
least in the history of Japanese Buddhism.

659 Shunjo Honen, the Buddhist Saint: His Life and
      Teaching.   Translated by H. H. Coates and R.
      Ishizuka.   Kyoto: Society for Publication of Sacred
      Books of the World, 1949.   955 p.
This translation of the official biography of the
founder of Jodo Buddhism in the 12th century is especially
valuable for its copious footnotes.   It is virtually an encyclopedia of medieval Japanese Buddhism.

660 Sources of the Japanese Tradition.   Compiled by

R. Tsunoda, W. T. De Bary and D. Keene. New
York: Columbia University, 1958. 928 p.

This work is intended to provide the general reader
with an understanding of the background of contemporary
Japanese civilization, especially as this is reflected in intellectual traditions which remain alive today.

661   Steinilber-Oberlin, E. Buddhist Sects of Japan, Their
History, Philosophical Doctrines and Sanctuaries.
New York: Macmillan, 1938. 303 p.

The history, doctrines and sanctuaries of the diverse
Buddhist sects in Japan are described in this translation of
the French edition, written in collaboration with the Japanese
companion who accompanied the author during his visit to
Japan, and in the consultations with the monks, bonzes and
professors from whom the information was obtained.

662   no entry

663   Suzuki, D. T.   Essays in Zen Buddhism.   See entry
no. 1123.

664   _____. Shin Buddhism. New York: Harper and
Row, 1970. 93 p.

This work consists of five lectures presented by
Dr. Suzuki at the New York Buddhist Church in the spring
of 1958. The lectures concentrated on the ideas of Shinran's
teachings as interpreted by Suzuki and are titled: "Love
and Compassion as Infinite Light," "The Enlightenment of
the Inner Self," "The Reality of Faith," "The Futility of
Pride," and "The Excellence of Man."

665   _____.   Training of the Zen Buddhist Monk. New
York: University Books, 1959. 161 p.

Originally published in 1934, now with the addition
of the author's early memories which appeared exclusively
in The Middle Way in November 1954, the text is interwoven
with Zen stories and illustrations, and there are appendices
of monastery verses, rules, and regulations and a glossary
of Japanese terms.

666   _____.   Zen and Japanese Buddhism. Rev. ed.
Rutland: Tuttle, 1962. 150 p.

A concise introductory handbook sponsored by the
Japan Travel Bureau, it attempts to define Zen, its position
in Buddhist thought, some central ideas and schools, together with accounts of some Zen masters.

667 _____ . Zen and Japanese Culture. New York:
        Pantheon Books, 1958. 478 p.
        In 11 essays the author explains how Zen has af-
fected every phase of Japanese culture, noting its dominant
impulse toward simplicity and including art, the caste of the
Samurai, swordsmanship, the study of Confucianism, the
art of tea, and the love of nature.

668 _____ . Zen Buddhism and Its Influence on Japanese
        Culture. See entry no. 1134.

669 _____ . Zen Buddhism, Selected Writings. See
        entry no. 1136.

670 Swann, P. C. Japan: From the Jomon to the Tokugawa
        Period. See entry no. 188.

671 Von Durckheim, K. G. The Japanese Cult of Tranquil-
        lity. London: Rider and Co., 1959. 106 p.
        This brief work is little more than a long essay
and three brief translations from German. It concerns the
author's thesis that the Japanese may be noted for a profound
tranquillity, but it adds little to our knowledge of Japan or
Zen.

672 Watanabe, S. Japanese Buddhism: A Critical Ap-
        praisal. Translated by Alfred Bloom. Tokyo:
        Kokusai Bunka Shinkokai, 1968.
        This is an important postwar criticism of Buddhism
by a Buddhist priest who has made a frank analysis of "The
Strong and Weak Points of Japanese Buddhism."

673 Yamaguchi, S. Dynamic Buddha and Static Buddha.
        Tokyo: Risosha, 1958. 93 p.
        The essays of this volume consist of the translations
of Dobutsu to Seibutsu, which were originally delivered as
special summer lectures at Jojunjin in Kobe, Japan, in 1947.
Their first step is to describe the nature of the Buddha; the
second is the description of the three concrete aspects of
the Buddha.

674 Yasuda, K. The Japanese Haiku. See entry no. 855.

KOREA

675 Blyth, R. H. Zen and Zen Classics. See entry no.
        1069.

676 Clark, C. A. Religions of Old Korea. New York:
        Revell, 1932. 295 p.
     This is a broad-visioned, comprehensive view of all
religions, past and present, of Korea. It shows patient research and sympathetic treatment. The author surveys Buddhism, Confucianism, Shamanism, the Chuntokyo Cult and
other miscellaneous cults.

677 Hulbert, H. B. The History of Korea. London:
        Routledge and Kegan Paul, 1905. 2 vols.
     The author gives a chronicle of Korea from pre-
historic times to the 20th century in Western language. No
attempt is made to indicate the nature and scope of Eastern
philosophies generally, and of Buddhism in particular, but
it shows how much Buddhism has influenced Korean culture
and social life.

678 Hyun, P. Voices of the Dawn; A Selection of Korean
        Poetry. See entry no. 846.

679 Kim, C. The Art of Korea. See entry no. 172.

680 Lee, J. H. A Handbook of Korea. Seoul: Office of
        Public Information, 1955. 360 p.
     This rather comprehensive handbook of Korea des-
cribes the land and people, government, agriculture, industry,
transportation and communication, finance and trade, social
welfare, religions and culture of Korea.

681 Starr, F. Korean Buddhism: History--Condition--Art.
        Boston: Jones, Marshall Co., 1918. 294 p.
     This work is comprised of three lectures concerned
respectively with the history, condition, and art of Korean
Buddhism. They are accompanied by 37 full-page illustrations from photographs and a bibliography.

682 Won Buddhist Half-Centennial Commemoration Commis-
        sion, Buddhist Federation of Korea. The Canonical
        Textbook of Won Buddhism. Seoul: Won Buddhist
        Federation of Korea, 1971. 384 p.
     This book concerns the teaching of the Won (Dhar-
makaya) school of Korean Buddhism and the sayings of one
of its masters, Tai-san Soh, who died in 1943. The teachings include the advocacy of keeping a regular diary, not
only as a record of one's meditational development, but to
act, by rereading, as a check that one is using his life
wisely. This is a useful book for students of Buddhism.

LAOS

683 Halpern, J. M. Aspects of Village Life and Culture
        Change in Laos. New York: Council on Economic
        and Cultural Affairs, 1958. 143 p.
        A report based on personal observation and an-
thropological field study with emphasis on family life and
cultural changes, the work makes suggestions to the United
States on using aid funds to improve immigration facilities.
The importance of Buddhism in Lao-Siamese life is also
stressed.

MONGOLIA

684 Bisch, J. Mongolia: Unknown Land. London: Allen
        and Unwin, 1963. 160 p.
        The Danish author is a professional traveler and
writer with a flair for good photography, and he writes a
balanced, objective and sympathetic account of the country
today, with enough of its history to show the immense and
swift advance into the materialistic comforts. The traditional Buddhism is beginning to disappear and leaves behind
a fine cultural legacy.

NEPAL

685 Bernstein, J. The Wildest Dreams of Kew--A Profile
        of Nepal. London: Allen and Unwin, 1972. 186 p.
        Illustrated in color and black and white photographs,
this is an impressionistic account of the history, land and
people of Nepal. The work is a graphically rich rendering
of the case of ten million Nepalese who moved from the age
of the wheel to the age of the airplane with no steps in between. It gives an interesting account of three Westerners
who trek across Everest and discover the social patterns
and philosophical insights of another world.

686 Forbes, D. The Heart of Nepal. London: Robert
        Hale, 1962. 185 p.
        This serves as a good traveler's handbook on Nepal.
The author surveys the fascinating mixture of old and new
in thought and practice, Buddhist and Hindu temples and observances, ancient tradition and modern planning.

687 Hagen, T. Nepal: The Kingdom in the Himalayas.

Berne: Kummerli and Fry, 1962. 117 p.
The author spent seven years on a geological survey
of Nepal, and the text contains an account of almost every
facet of the country, its geological structure, most interest-
ingly described for the layman, its people and their distribution, its history, including the present political situation.
All this is illustrated with numerous sketches and photographs
including 29 color plates, 42 monochrome plates, and 18
sketch maps.

688 Kramrisch, S. The Art of Nepal. See entry no. 174.

689 Markham, P. Road to Katmandu. New York: Mac-
     millan, 1972. 160 p.
This accounts the journey to Katmandu by some
young people of every race and nationality which is perhaps
the modern equivalent of the 18th century grand tour. They
travel on foot, bus or lorry. Their plans for the journey
appear to be minimal, and the impression they create on the
local peoples they meet must be one of wonder.

690 Murphy, D. The Waiting Land; A Spell in Nepal.
     London: John Murray, 1968. 213 p.
The author describes her seven-month travel in
Nepal on a bicycle. She does not explain too much about
cities, but rather about the mountains, the people, and the
intimate details of daily life among the scenery, which at
times she describes very beautifully.

691 Sekelj, T. Window on Nepal. Translated by M.
     Boulton. London: Robert Hale, 1959. 190 p.
This book comes as a thrilling reminder of the
loveliness of Nepal. The author tries to cover every aspect
of this remote valley, from its geography, history, agriculture, politics, and to what must have been even more
difficult, its religions. As the author says, the religion of
the people is so interwoven with their daily life, it would be
impossible to see them apart from their religious beliefs and
festivals.

692 Simpson, C. Katmandu. London: Angus and Robert-
     son, 1968. 104 p. 32 illustrations, 16 in color.
This is a lively, reasonably accurate account of the
cities which comprise most of the culture and art of Nepal.
These cities were till the 18th century independent kingdoms
and the place of each in Nepal is of the greatest interest.

693   Snellgrove, D. L.   Buddhist Himalaya.   See entry
      no. 1064.

694   _____ . Himalayan Pilgrimage.   London: Bruno
      Cassirer, 1960.   300 p.
      This is the fruit of the author's seven-month jour-
ney through western Nepal.   It is a diary of the trip, with
his faithful Sherpa, Pasang, to study the many peoples of
the area, and their religious beliefs and practices.   This is
supplementary to his previous work, Buddhist Himalaya, but
there is much more new material on Buddhism and on the
iconography of the various sects.

695   Tucci, G.   Nepal; The Discovery of the Malla.   Trans-
      lated from Italian by Loveth Edwards.   London:
      Allen and Unwin, 1962.   96 p.
      Professor Tucci is the most famous Italian Buddhist.
He managed to tramp some 12,000 miles through the Himalayas in thirty years, and this popular description of a four-
month tour in western Nepal in 1954 proves that he was still
on the march in search of Buddhist history.   He found it in
the extinct kingdom of the Mallas who, from the 11th to the
14th century, dominated not only western Nepal, but also
western Tibet.

696   Von Furer-Haimendorf, C.   The Sherpas of Nepal,
      Buddhist Highlanders.   London: John Murray, 1964.
      298 p.
      The author is an Asian anthropology professor at
the University of London.   He spent over two years in Nepal
while he and his wife lived with the Sherpas, visiting all
their main villages.   He gives very detailed accounts of
customs and morals ranging from a survey of environment
and economy to accounts of religious rites and of the local
version of Buddhism based on the scriptures of the Nyingmapa Sect.   All the illustrations and photographs of the
people, the monasteries and the mountains are very good.

SIAM (i.e., THAILAND)

697   Audric, J.   Siam, Land of Temples.   London: Robert
      Hale, 1962.   190 p.
      This is probably the best book on Thailand for the
general reader.   It is not a mere travelogue, for the writer
was commissioned to advise on a new scheme of secondary
education for the whole country.   Here is a quite factual

and relevant description of the life of the people today, at
all levels.

698   Bhikkhu, B.   Teaching Dhamma by Pictures: Explana-
        tion of a Siamese Traditional Buddhist Manuscript.
        See entry no. 209.

699   Blofeld, J.   People of the Sun.   London: Hutchinson,
        1960.   192 p.
        The author has lived and worked nine years in
Thailand and he feels the urge to tell Westerners something
of the people he has grown to love.   He tells not only
charmingly, but accurately, as is vouched for by Prince
Chula in a typical foreword.   This is a friendly, happy book
with lovely illustrations.

700   Busch, N. F.   Thailand; An Introduction to Modern
        Siam.   London: D. Van Nostrand, 1960.   166 p.
        It is not surprising that the Thai people are some
of the happiest on earth, and the author makes it clear that
their religion is a prime factor in that happiness.   Siam's
history, politics, government, religion, and art are the main
themes of the author.

701   Chula, Prince H. R. H.   Lords of Life.   See entry
        no. 374.

702   _____.   The Twain Have Met.   London: Foulis,
        1956.   299 p.
        This is the autobiography of Prince Chula Chakra-
bongse.   It contains six sections: (1) The history of the
Thai race and the Chakri dynasty; (2) Prince Chula's childhood; (3) Education at Harrow and Cambridge; (4) The
rituals of royalty; (5) Motor racing with Prince Bira; and
(6) His marriage.

703   Exell, F. K.   Siamese Tapestry.   London: Robert
        Hale, 1963.   192 p.
        The author, who is a mathematician at Chulalongkorn
University, gives some account of life as it was yesterday in
Siam.   Buddhism is not stressed, but he gives an interesting
picture of Siamese life and customs with many illustrations
as well as maps.

704   Graham, D. A.   The End of Religion.   New York:
        Harcourt Brace, 1972.   268 p.
        This book is a journal of the author's travels in

India, Thailand and other points both East and West. Written
with warmth, wisdom, humility and humor, we get an insight
into the author himself, what he calls the "personal equation."
In his dealings with scholars and monks from Hindu and Buddhist traditions, the author opens out to such an extent that
one at times forgets he is a Catholic monk. His knowledge
of Buddhist principles is sound as is his ability to see the
best of both worlds. Anyone undergoing a crisis of religious
belief or disbelief should read this book.

705 Griswold, A. B. Dated Buddha Images of Northern
        Siam. See entry no. 354.

706 _____ . King Mongkut of Siam. New York: The
        Asia Society, 1960. 59 p.
        This is a readable and fascinating paperback which
effectively dispels what are claimed to be a series of gro-
tesque caricatures of King Mongkut arising from misrepre-
sentations of an English governess employed for a time at
his court.

707 Kaufman, H. Bangkhuad: A Community Study in Thai-
        land. Locust Valley, New York: 1960. 235 p.
        This is a broad study of community life in a village
in Thailand. The author spent a year in Thailand obtaining
information from field work, and the function and structure
of the Buddhist church is given a thorough study.

708 Landon, K. P. Siam in Transition. Chicago: Uni-
        versity of Chicago Press, 1939.
        This is a brief survey of cultural trends in the five
years after the revolution of 1932.

709 Nagel's Guide to Thailand and Angkor. English version
        by Maurice O. Walshe. Geneva: Nagel, 1971.
        344 p.
        As is usual with the Nagel series, this guide is full
of facts about the countryside, the arts, the history and the
culture of the people of Thailand.

710 Schecter, J. The New Face of Buddha; Buddhism and
        Political Power in Southeast Asia. See entry no. 858.

711 Tambiah, S. J. Buddhism and the Spirit Cults in
        Northeast Thailand. See entry no. 1238.

712 Van Gorkom, N. Buddhist Outlook on Daily Life. See
        entry no. 319.

713 Wauell, S. The Naga King's Daughter. London: Allen
        and Unwin, 1964. 247 p.
        This is a travel guide by one of four young men who,
sponsored by the Cambridge Explorers' and Travellers' Club,
found a corner of the world where romantic legend and ad-
venture still obtained and had not been written up. The purpose of the trip, up the east coast of Malaya and south Thailand, was to settle a host of archaeological and cultural
riddles about the early kingdoms which once ruled the country.
It gives many lovely shots of Thai temples and interviews
with monks.

714 Wray, E. and Rosenfield, C. Ten Lives of the Buddha:
        Siamese Temple Paintings and Jataka Tales. See
        entry no. 222.

SIKKIM

715 Gould, B. J. The Jewel in the Lotus. See entry
        no. 418.

TIBET

716 Anuruddha, R. P. An Introduction into Lamaism, the
        Mystical Buddhism of Tibet. See entry no. 417.

717 Barber, N. The Flight of the Dalai Lama. London:
        Hodder and Stoughton, 1959. 160 p.
        This vivid account of the events leading up to the
flight of the Dalai Lama and the story of the flight itself
told by a British journalist will be received with considerable
interest. The book deals with a growth of religion in Tibet
from A.D. 630 to the Dalai Lama of the present day. The
volume ends with a comment by the Dalai Lama and his re-
plies to questions put to him by the press.

718 Bardo, T. The Tibetan Book of the Dead. London:
        Oxford University Press, 1927. 248 p.
        The sub-title of this well-known classic is The
Afterdeath Experience on the Bardo Plane, According to
Lama Kazi Dawa-Samdup's English Rendering, and it is
unique in all literature. The author says that if we have
courage, we may sooner be released from the Wheel of Birth
and Death.

719   Bell, Sir C. A. The Religion of Tibet. London: Ox-
        ford University Press, 1931.
        This is an account of Lamaism, the Tantric form
of Mahayana Buddhism associated with the Lamas or priest-
kings of Lhasa in Tibet.

720   Chang, G. C. C. Teachings of Tibetan Yoga. See
        entry no. 1275.

721   Chögyam, T. Born in Tibet. New York: Harcourt,
        1968. 246 p.
        This is the story of the early life and escape from
the Chinese of a young Tulku of Tibet. Trungpa Tulka was
installed at the age of 13 months as the tenth successive
religious head and supreme abbot of the Surmang group of
monasteries.

722   Csoma, S. Tibetan Studies. Calcutta: Baptist Mission
        Press, 1912. 172 p.
        This is a reprint of the articles contributed to the
Journal of the Asiatic Society of Bengal by Alexander Csoma
de Körös. It contains notices on the different systems of
Buddhism and remarks on trans-Himalayan Buddhist amulets.

723   Dainelli, G. Buddhists and Glaciers of Western Tibet.
        New York: Dutton, 1934. 304 p.
        This book contains the author's day-by-day account
of a trip he made in 1930 during which he explored the
Siachen Glacier.

724   The Dalai Lama of Tibet. My Land and My People.
        See entry no. 248.

725   Das, S. C. Indian Pandits in the Land of Snow. Cal-
        cutta: K. L. Mukhopadhyay, 1965. 134 p.
        This book is a reprint of four lectures delivered in
1893 before the Asiatic Society of Bengal. This work gains
much from an excellent introduction by Dr. N. C. Sinha,
Director of the Namgyal Institute of Tibetology at Gangtok,
Sikkim. A large part of the lectures is concerned with the
propagation of the Buddhist teachings, not only in Tibet, but
also in China and other countries by Indian saints.

726   David-Neel, A. Initiations and Initiates in Tibet. 2nd
        ed. Translated by Fred Rothwell. New York: Uni-
        versity Books, 1959. 222 p.
        This is an account of Tibetan mysticism by a

Frenchwoman, herself a practicing Buddhist and lama who
has spent many years in Tibet. It serves as a sequel to
her earlier Magic and Mystery in Tibet.

727 _____ . Secret Oral Teachings in Tibetan Buddhist
        Sects. San Francisco: City Lights, 1967. 128 p.
        The author gives the basic teachings of the Tibetan
Buddhist sects, especially of Theravada. The topics she
treats are: the nature of the individual and of the phenome-
nal world, prajna; dependent origination, pratityasamutpada;
storehouse consciousness, alayavijnana; enlightenment, sum-
yata or doctrine of the world.

728 de Nebesky-Wojkowitz, R   Oracles and Demons of
        Tibet. London: Oxford University Press, 1956.
        666 p.
        The first half of his book is devoted to the classi-
fication, description and enumeration of a staggering number
and variety of "protective deities," while the second half is
concerned with their cult, worship and propitiation.

729 Ekvall, R. B. Religious Observances in Tibet: Pat-
        terns and Functions. Chicago: University of
        Chicago Press, 1964. 313 p.
        This serves as an attempt to bring to life the re-
ligion of the Tibetans as a subjective response expressed in
a pattern of behavior which makes sense in the context of
the world view, as an answer to personal and societal needs.

730 Evans-Wentz, W. Y. The Tibetan Book of the Great
        Liberation; The Method of Realizing Nirvana Through
        Knowing the Mind. London: Oxford University
        Press, 1954. 261 p.
        There is a general introduction by Dr. Evans-Wentz
that testifies to the author's close acquaintance with the
wisdom tradition of mankind. The ideas of the Nyingmapa
are very much at variance with our own habits of thought,
but Evans-Wentz succeeds in gently leading us on to at least
a tentative appreciation of their apparent absurdities. There
is some more discussion about Tibetan lamas, the biography
of Padmasambhava, the knowing of the mind in its realities
which expounds the innermost secrets of Yoga, and the poem
of Phadampa Sangay. Included is a psychological commentary
by C. G. Jung.

731 _____ . Tibet's Great Yogi Milarepa. See entry
        no. 251.

732   Gordon, A. K.   Iconography of Tibetan Lamaism.   2nd
         rev. ed.   New York: Paragon Book Reprint, 1967
         (c1959).   131 p.
      This work gives the student interested in Tibetan
iconography a general idea of the development of Buddhism
into Lamaism, and it makes easier the identification of the
various deities of the Tibetan Pantheon.

733   Gould, B. J.   The Jewel in the Lotus.   See entry
         no. 418.

734   Govinda, A. B.   Foundations of Tibetan Mysticism.
         See entry no. 779.

735   Govinda, L. A.   The Way of the White Clouds: A
         Buddhist Pilgrim in Tibet.   New York: Hutchinson,
         1966.   305 p.
      The author was in Tibet as a Buddhist pilgrim, and
it is in the appropriate spirit of reverent understanding and
observation that he writes about gurus and monasteries, the
Blue Lake, oracle-priests, mystery-plays, sacred music
and a score of other aspects of Tibetan religious life.

736   Guenther, H. V.   The Life and Teaching of Naropa.
         London: Oxford University Press, 1963.   292 p.
      Naropa's six doctrines are most characteristic of
Tibetan spirituality.   This is the second volume of Dr.
Guenther's previous work, "The Jewel Ornament of Liberation," and he has covered here, "Oral Tradition," both in
the theoretical and methodic realms.   The main text is
excellently rendered into English; anyone will be able to
understand and enjoy it.

737   _____ .   Tibetan Buddhism Without Mystification.
         Leiden: E. J. Brill, 1966.   156 p.
      The work is divided into two parts, the first called
the "Buddhist Way," in which the author discusses fundamental knowledge of Buddhism with special reference to
Tibetan Buddhism.   The second, the "Tibetan Sources," is
about the dge-lugs-pa school of Tibetan Buddhism.   The
author says, "I wanted to bring out the specific merits of
the dge-lugs-pa writers: the clear distinction between the
various philosophical trends that were developed by the
four major schools of thought in India and continued in Tibet."

738   _____ .   Treasure on the Tibetan Middle Way.
         London: Shambala Publications, 1971.   149 p.

This present work is a revised edition of Tibetan
Buddhism Without Mystification, which emerged from discussions held between the author and His Holiness the Dalai
Lama during 1961, who prompted him to counteract the
misinterpretation and "mystery-mongering" often associated
with the Tantras, and to emphasize their deep inner meaning
and development.   The relation between sutras and tantras
is elucidated by the author's translations of four texts
chosen from the dge-lugs-pa school.   The frequent lengthy
and detailed annotations to the texts give a clear interpretation of Tibetan terms.

739   Gyatsho, T., the XIV Dalai Lama of Tibet.   The
        Opening of the Wisdom-Eye.   Bangkok: Social
        Science Assoc., 1968.   131 p.
        The various Buddhist schools of thought in Tibet
are seen as ways of skillful means and any differences that
appear to exist are superficial.   Methods of practice imply
the threefold training in virtue, collectedness and wisdom
with the four seals of Impermanence, Unsatisfactoriness,
all Dharmas with self and Nirvana.   Excellent photographs
illustrate the practice of the Dharma in Tibet.

740   Hoffman, H.   Religions of Tibet.   Translated by E.
        Fitzgerald.   New York: Macmillan, 1960.   199 p.
        This work presents primarily Tibetan sources for
Buddhist history and gives a detailed exposition of religious
doctrine, ritual and way of life.   It is written for scholars
rather than for the general public interested in Buddhism.

741   Jivaka, L.   Imji Getsul: An English Buddhist in a
        Tibetan Monastery.   London: Routledge and Kegan
        Paul, 1962.   201 p.
        This is a story of extraordinary devotion to a cause
at first undefined even to himself, which led an English doc-
tor to abandon a promising career in order to seek ordination among the Hinayana monks at Sarnath.   He had come
slowly to Buddhism by way of Western philosophy at Oxford
and the teaching of Gourdjieff, but he found that renunciation
of the world fitted his sense of values.

742   Lang-Sims, L.   The Presence of Tibet.   London:
        Cresset Press, 1963.   240 p.
        This work describes the adventures, observations
and views of a lover of India and Tibet.   The author, though
a member of the Buddhist Society and a founding member of
the Tibet Society, writes under limitations, for she visited

for only a few weeks. Yet her word-portraits of many of
the people she met are shrewd and valuable, whether of the
great, as Mr. Nehru, or of humbler workers in the Tibetan
field, as Gyalo Thondup, Freda Bedi, and others.

743   Migot, A. Tibetan Marches. London: Hart-Davis,
         1955. 288 p.
      This book is written by a French doctor, who is
determined to try to find reality and not be misled by the
transient or superficial. The author's initiation in a monk's
cell high above the Yangste is related most strikingly. It
is a good companion book for Seven Years in Tibet, but
where author Thubten portrays the exterior of a people, Dr.
Migot seeks to find the inner truth within a people whose
sometimes uninviting exteriors belie their inner natures.
Maps and photographs are included.

744   Newark Museum Assoc. Catalogue of the Tibetan Col-
         lection and Other Lamaist Material in the Newark
         Museum. See entry no. 43.

745   Pallis, M. Peaks and Lamas. New York: Knopf,
         1940. 428 p.
      This book of travel in Tibet includes three interests:
the adventures of mountain climbing, a study of Buddhism,
and an account of Tibetan art and ways of life. The book
covers chronologically two trips made by the author in 1933
and 1936.

746   _____ . The Way and the Mountain. London: Peter
         Owen, 1960. 216 p.
      The Buddhism of the Himalayas and the application
of its teaching to daily life is a main theme. There are
two most valuable essays on "The Active Life," and there
are three on Tibet, including one on the function and process of rebirth of the Dalai Lama.

747   Richardson, H. E. Tibet and Its History. London:
         Oxford University Press, 1962. 297 p.
      The author lived in Tibet about fourteen years,
knows the language and its people, and knows most of the
surviving figures. His work gives an early history told in
an easy style with the character of the people, their religion and what it means to them and their form of government in some detail, clearly and well explained.

748   Sgam-po-pa, the Jewel Ornament of Liberation. See
         entry no. 1045.

749 Shen, T. L. Tibet and the Tibetans. Stanford, Cal.:
        Stanford University Press, 1953. 192 p.
        Mr. Shen was the resident Chinese Commissioner in
Tibet until 1947. The reader will be interested in the author's
detailed account of the organization of the three leading lama-
series which give instruction in esoteric studies. There is
also a short historical account of the introduction of Buddhism
to Tibet. He comes to the conclusion that Tibetan theocracy
is the peculiar product of the centuries of overlordship by
China.

750 Snellgrove, D. L. Buddhist Himalaya. See entry no.
        1064.

751 _____. Himalayan Pilgrimage. See entry no. 694.

752 Stein, R. A. Tibetan Civilization. Translated by J.
        E. S. Driver. London: Faber and Faber, 1972.
        334 p.
        The author gives background information on the
country's geographical characteristics and population, as he
narrates Tibet's complex story from the seventh century
A.D. to the present day. A detailed analysis of the main
elements of Tibetan society is then followed by an important
section on religion, describing the Tibetan forms of Buddhism and the earlier Bon and folk religions.

753 Thomas, L., Jr. The Silent War in Tibet. London:
        Secker and Warburg, 1959. 284 p.
        This work brings into sharp relief the distinction be-
tween materialist aggression and spiritual resistance. This
book makes clear that the holy war, in the Buddhist sense of
the resistance of the forces of spirit to those of matter,
will never cease until the last Tibetan is exterminated.

754 Thubten, J. N., as told to Heinrich Harrer. Tibet Is
        My Country. Translated from German by E. Fitz-
        gerald. New York: Dutton, 1961. 264 p.
        This work relates the personal story of "the brother
of the Dalai Lama, the spiritual head of the Himalayan Buddhists and today one of the leading figures in opposition to
the Chinese Communist overlordship in Tibet." For the most
part, it deals with Norbu's childhood and his early training
in a Tibetan Buddhist monastery.

755 Trungpa, C. Born in Tibet. See entry no. 278.

756 Tucci, G. Tibet: Land of Snows. Translated by
       J. E. Stapleton Driver, photography by W. Swaan,
       E. Smith and others, with 40 color plates and 60
       plates in all. London: Elek Books, 1967. 216 p.
     Professor Tucci, who has spent so much time in
Tibet, has produced one of the most comprehensive and
interesting books on Tibet. Systematically he gives details
of the history, religion, art, daily life, birth, marriage,
sickness, and death of the people. The book is illustrated,
both in color and monochrome, with high quality.

757 Waddell, A. Buddhism of Tibet; or Lamaism, with Its
       Mystic Cults, Symbolism and Mythology, and in Its
       Relation to Indian Buddhism. New York: Tudor,
       1969. 598 p.
     This book gives a vivid, brief account of the changes
through which Buddhism has passed on the way to its late
Tantric phase; it is by an authority on Tibetan Buddhism.

758 Willis, J. D. The Diamond Light of the Eastern Dawn;
       Collection of Tibetan Buddhist Meditations. See
       entry no. 479.

759 Yamada, K. R. A Catalogue of the Tohoku University
       Collection of Tibetan Works on Buddhism. Sendai
       (Japan): Seminary of Indology, Tohoku University,
       1953. 531 p.
     This work contains the Tibetan titles and summaries
of contents in English of 2083 block-printed Tibetan books,
written by Buston (1290-1364), Tsongkhapa (1358-1419), the
Dalai Lamas, the first Pan-chen Lama, and other great Buddhists. It also gives an index classified according to the
various schools, sects, rites, and cults, and a good Lamaist
bibliography.

UNITED STATES OF AMERICA

760 Ames, V. M. Zen and American Thought. Honolulu:
       University of Hawaii, 1962. 293 p.
     This work is on American philosophy in relation to
Zen. The arrangement is chronological, beginning with a
brilliant summary of the influence of Zen in America today
and of its lessons for human happiness. Then follow chapters
on Hume and Paine, Jefferson, Emerson, Thoreau, Whitman,
the elder Henry James, William James, Pierce, Royce,

Santayana, Dewey and Mead. The author has read all their
works and meditated profoundly upon them with his Zen experience in mind.

761   The Buddhist Church of America. Buddhism and Jodo
         Shinshu. San Francisco: Commission of Buddhist
         Research and Publication, 1955. 130 p.
         This is the work of three Japanese priests. Ad-
dressed to young people, it tries to simplify Buddhism for
the beginner and to introduce the Jodo Shinshu doctrines.
The biggest part of the work is a survey of Buddhism in
general. This is not authoritative and historical accuracy
is not always observed.

762   Donath, D. C. Buddhism for the West. New York:
         Julian Press, 1971. 146 p.
         Containing four chapters covering the founder and
the three great branches of Buddhism, Theravada, Mahayana,
and Vajrayana, plus a personal account of the author's own
Buddhist experiences, the work is written from a fresh view-
point--that of a Western student who has experienced and
felt deeply the need for a workable philosophy and a fulfilling
way of life. It is simply presented and applicable to the
problems of today.

763   Hunter, L. H. Buddhism in Hawaii: Its Impact on a
         Yankee Community. Honolulu: University of Hawaii
         Press, 1971. 266 p.
         This book can be recommended not only as a history
of Hawaii, where 57 percent of the whole population are
Orientals, its Buddhists and its religious and racial strife
from 1850 to the present, but also as a story of the attempt
to adapt Japanese Buddhism with its central focus on filial
piety and traditionalism to American Buddhism which attempts
to find the teachings and values within the rich tradition of
Buddhism most applicable to the contemporary needs of
Western man.

764   Jacobson, N. P. Buddhism: The Religion of Analysis.
         See entry no. 894.

765   Kerouac, J. The Dharma Bums. London: Andre
         Deutsch, 1959. 244 p.
         The Dharma Bums of the title are the young Ameri-
cans, intellectuals, artists, and poets, of the West coast
who were (in the 50's) in revolt against the material standards
of their civilization, and who were then becoming popularly

known as the Beat Generation. The author clearly writes
from personal experience and a genuine enthusiasm for Zen.

766 Matsunami, K. Introducing Buddhism; Jodo Mission
        Handbook. Honolulu: Jodo Mission, 1964. 150 p.
        This is a sound and well-produced handbook of the
Jodo sect of Japanese Buddhism, with a history of Buddhism
in Hawaii, a description of services, some illustrations and
a brief bibliography.

MONASTICISM

767 Dutt, S. Buddhist Monks and Monasteries of India.
        London: Allen and Unwin, 1962; Atlantic Highlands,
        N.J.: Hillary House, 1963. 397 p.
        This work supersedes the author's book, Early Bud-
dhist Monachism, published in 1924, and adds to his evidence
bearing on the monastic life in India. In it, the first connected history of the Buddhist monks of ancient India, the
author traces the growth of the Sangha from its origins in the
tradition of the wandering sannyasins of India. He includes
in his survey the rise and fall of the great Indian Buddhist
monastic universities and briefly sketches the teaching at that
period.

768 no entry

769 The Entrance to the Vinaya. Bangkok: Somdetch Phra
        Maha Samana Chao Mahamakutarajavidyalaya Founda-
        tion, 1972.
        This is a commentary on 227 fundamental rules of
training for monks by a son of King Mongkut, himself a great
reformer. This is the first of three volumes concerned with
the monastic discipline. The author has a nice sense of
humor and there is a difference and reasonableness in his approach to this subject, which makes it quite enjoyable reading.

770 Jivaka, L. Imji Getsui; An English Buddhist in a Ti-
        betan Monastery. See entry no. 741.

771 Kaestner, E. Mount Athos. Translated by Barry Sulli-
        van. London: Faber and Faber, 1961. 192 p.

This is a story of the author's two journeys to the Holy Mountain, written in beautiful prose. His experiences in the various monasteries he visited left a deep impression on him, and a Christian should find inspiration in his interpretation of Greek thought.

772   The Patimokkha with Introduction, Pali Text, Translation and Notes. Bangkok: Social Science Assoc. of Thailand, 1972.
This book gives a straightforward translation of the 227 rules of training for monks in the Theravada Sangha. There is also an interesting introduction by Phra Sasana Sobhana.

773   Prip-Moller, J. Chinese Buddhist Monasteries. 2nd ed. London: Oxford University Press, 1969. 396 p.
This work is on the plan of Chinese Buddhist monasteries and their function as a setting for Buddhist monastic life. All the material for this book was gathered from 1921 to 1926 while Buddhism was a powerful force in mainland China. Originally published in 1937, it gives several hundred photographs, maps, graphs, sketches, and floor plans.

774   Suzuki, D. T. Training of the Zen Buddhist Monk. See entry no. 665.

775   Welch, H. H. The Practice of Chinese Buddhism, 1900-1950. Cambridge, Mass.: Harvard University Press, 1967. 568 p.
Professor Welch uses oral sources in his research for this volume. "His transcription of these interviews with elderly practitioners has added immeasurably to the sparse literature of this subject"--Library Journal. The author discusses the China monastic institutions, their rules and education, but does not offer full information about the life of monks. The second half of the book deals with individual biographical sketches of Buddhists.

MYTHOLOGY

776   Boehme, J. Six Theosophic Points and Other Writing. Ann Arbor: University of Michigan, 1958. 208 p.

Boehme's mysticism has a highly dynamic quality, suggesting the arising of powerful forces and images from the unconscious. From the Buddhist point of view it is most interesting to see here the fundamental role of will, rising out of the depths of "nothingness," will as an impersonal autonomous factor, as Berdyaev put it, "the passionate desire of nothing to become something."

777 Campbell, J. The Masks of God; Oriental Mythology.
      London: Secker and Warburg, 1963. 561 p.
      This is Volume Two of the trilogy by the author and it takes one from the primitive mythology of the first volume into the Orient. The author tries to give some distinctions between Eastern and Western religious views.

778 Glasena, H. von. Buddhism: A Non-Theistic Religion.
      Translated by Irmgard Schloegl. London: George
      Allen and Unwin, 1972. 208 p.
      This is not a survey of Buddha-dhamma, but more in the nature of a long essay on the place of gods and the supernatural in Buddhism. The author's thesis is set out in the title, a non-theistic religion. This would once have been paradoxical and attempts were made to play down the Buddha's atheism and so make him respectable. There is an interesting chapter on the similar legends that surround religious heroes, a lucid résumé of the essentials of Buddhism and a selection of relevant Pali texts.

779 Govinda, A. B. Foundations of Tibetan Mysticism
      According to the Esoteric Teachings of the Great
      Mantra. New York: Dutton, 1960. 310 p.
      The esoteric principles of Mantra are explained, with descriptions of the terrible deities evoked by certain practices. The differences between Hindu and Tibetan Yoga are clarified. A bibliography is included.

780 Levy, P. Buddhism: A "Mystery Religion?" London:
      Oxford, 1957; New York: Schocken, 1968. 111 p.
      "This book is based on the Jordan Lectures in Comparative Religion given at the School of Oriental and African Studies, University of London in 1953 by Mr. Levy. It penetrates Buddhism through the back door of rituals, analyzing the initiation rites of present day monasteries, deducing from them what primitive Buddhism may have been.... This book contributes to the demythologizing of Buddhism and is a highly provocative, important contribution"--Library Journal.

781   Mukerjee, R.   The Theory and Art of Mysticism.
      New York: Asia Publishing House, 1960.   352 p.

782   Noble, M. E.   Myths of the Hindus and Buddhists.
      New York: Holt, Rinehart, 1914 (repr. New York:
      Dover, 1967; 399 p.).
      This is a collection of the best known Indian myths,
those most commonly illustrated in Indian sculpture and
painting, which not only reveal national ideals and religious
faith, but also many universal truths that reach out to the
ends of the earth; 32 illustrations of Indian artists under
the supervision of Abanindro Nath Tagore are included.

783   Reynolds, C.   An Anthology of Sinhalese Literature
      up to 1815.   See entry no. 427.

784   Spencer, H. S.   The Mysteries of God in the Universe.
      Bombay: Spencer, 1965.   175 p.
      This work treats of the doctrines of Karma and
Rebirth in the scriptures of the world.   The author also
discusses the dictrines in Hinduism, Buddhism, Judaism,
and Koran.   The author seems thoroughly explored in each
Bible.

785   Suzuki, D. T.   Mysticism: Christian and Buddhist.
      See entry no. 829.

                              NIRVANA

786   Evans-Wentz, W. Y.   The Tibetan Book of the Great
      Liberation.   See entry no. 730.

787   La Vallée Poussin, L. de.   The Way to Nirvana: Six
      Lectures on Ancient Buddhism as a Discipline of
      Salvation.   Cambridge, England: Cambridge Uni-
      versity Press, 1917.   172 p.
      This is a series of six lectures on the method of
attaining Nirvana.   The teaching of the Buddha is presented
as a discipline of salvation.

788   Matsunaga, D.   The Buddhist Concept of Hell.   New
      York: Philosophical Library, 1972.   152 p.

This book is a philosophical insight into the Buddhist understanding of the nature of the human mind and its unique capability to transform the hells of its own creation into enlightenment. The first half of the book studies the development of hell as a philosophical concept from early Buddhism through the Madhyamika and Vijnanavada schools. The second half presents an analysis of the light, symbolic Buddhist hells as a journey into self-reflection.

789 Reichelt, K. L. Meditation and Piety in the Far-East; Religious and Psychological Study. See entry no. 459.

790 Slater, R. H. L. Paradox and Nirvana. See entry no. 508.

791 Tripitaka. The Road to Nirvana; A Selection of the Buddhist Scripture. Translated from Pali by E. J. Thomas. London: Murray; New York: Grove, 1950. 95 p.
This is a translation of selected Buddhist texts from the Pali sources. Those passages tracing the life of the Buddha, his ministry, parables and sermons, his last meal and death are included. Several stories from the Jataka tales are also included.

792 Warren, H. C. Buddhism in Translations; Passages Selected from the Buddhist Sacred Books. See entry no. 1220.

793 Welbon, G. R. Buddhist Nirvana and Its Western Interpreters. Chicago: University of Chicago, 1968. 320 p.
This is a highly specialized treatise primarily to those who have already taken introductory studies in Buddhist thought. It includes a good bibliography. The author commences with a concise outline of Western Europe's contacts with and impressions of Buddhism up to the end of the 18th century. Then he leads into a detailed discussion of the period from the early 1800s to the start of World War II.

PARABLES

794   Burlingame, E. W. (translator). Buddhist Parables
         Translated from the Original Pali. New Haven:
         Yale University Press, 1922. 348 p.
      This is an especially fine anthology of Buddhist para-
bles and basic doctrines translated from the Pali sources.
Some later texts, Sanskrit and otherwise, along with European parallels, are included.

795   Burtt, E. A. (ed.). The Teaching of the Compassionate
         Buddha. See entry no. 1225.

796   Tripitaka. The Quest of Enlightenment; A Selection of
         the Buddhist Scriptures. See entry no. 1212.

797   _____ . The Road to Nirvana; A Selection of the
         Buddhist Scripture. See entry no. 791.

PHILOSOPHY

798   Allen, G. F. Buddha's Philosophy. New York: Mac-
         millan, 1959. 194 p.
      This work includes the atheistic philosophy of the
Theravada Buddhism of Ceylon and Southeast Asia, the Pan-
theism of Mahayana, the simple theism of the Japanese
Amidist sects, and the black magic of the Tantricists.
Basically this is for the European or American reader.

799   Bahm, A. J. Philosophy of the Buddha. New York:
         Harper, 1959. 175 p.
      This work states the philosophy of Buddha the man
by means of quotations from the Pitakas. It is a conscien-
tiously documented analysis of what the founder of Buddhism
said, according to the earliest Pali and Sanskrit scriptures.

800   Beck, L. A. The Story of Oriental Philosophy. New
         York: Cosmopolitan Book Corporation, 1928. 429 p.
      This work brings within understanding and readable
limits a knowledge of the thought of Asia. The smaller
philosophies are not detailed but the thought of the great men
who were the sources of the main philosophic systems of the

East is clarified for the general reader. The book is devoted about equally to Indian and Chinese philosophy, with a
chapter each on Tibet, Persia and Japan.

801   Blackie, J. S.   The Natural History of Atheism.
         London: Daldy, Isbister and Company, 1877.   247 p.
         The author tries to explain the historical and philo-
sophical background of Buddhism in terms of Far Eastern
atheism.

802   Bryson, L. and others.   Symbols and Values: An
         Initial Study.   New York: Harper, 1954.   827 p.
         This is the 13th symposium of the Conference on
Science, Philosophy, and Religion in the Relation to the
Democratic Way of Life held in New York City in 1952.
Dr. D. T. Suzuki gives a brief contribution on "Buddhist
Symbolism" (p. 149-154).

803   Cairns, G. E.   Philosophies of History; Meeting of
         East and West in Cycle-Pattern Theory of History.
         New York: Philosophical Library, 1962.   496 p.
         This book is about what is normally understood as
history and about cosmic processes spanning innumerable
world cycles.   The author has found three main groups of
human conceptions on the forms and meaning of time and
has described them under: Recurrent Cosmic Cycles, One-
Grand-Cycle Pattern of Cosmic and Human History, Culture
Cycles, Twentieth Century Views.   At least three chapters
will be of particular interest to the Buddhist reader.   The
author covers an enormous field of Eastern and Western
philosophy.

804   Chari, S. M. S.   Advaita and Visistadvaita.   London:
         Asia Publishing House, 1961.   204 p.
         This work is not only a sound study but also a
labor of love.   Samkara was the great exponent of Advaita,
the philosophy of non-duality, of the identity of the supreme
in man and the individual in man, of spirit and matter.   It
also brings out fully the philosophical implications of the
basic theories.   A useful appendix lists the topics dealt with
in the Satadusani and a very useful glossary and index are
included.

805   Chennakesavan, S.   The Concept of Mind in Indian
         Philosophy.   London: Asia Publishing House, 1960.
         164 p.
         The author performs a service by flashing her lamp

on the mind-cap as it is being drawn today. We may cite
her handling of the Advaitin theory of the mechanism of
knowledge as contrasted with a purely neuro-physiological
explanation. The author presents her comparative estimate
of the Indian and the modern Western concept of mind.

806 Conze, E. Buddhism, Its Essence and Development.
       See entry no. 375.

807 _____ . Buddhist Thought in India. Ann Arbor:
       University of Michigan, 1967. 302 p.
       Including three phases of Buddhist philosophy, this
book sets out to discuss and interpret the main themes of
Buddhist thought in India. The emphasis is everywhere on
those aspects of the doctrine which appear to be indubitably
true or significant.

808 Evans, C. O. The Subject of Consciousness. London:
       George Allen and Unwin, 1971. 240 p.
       This philosophical and psychological work is of con-
siderable interest to students of Buddhism. It is devoted to
solving the mystery of the self, and the author's arguments
and conclusions are productive parallels to traditional Buddhist thought. The greater part of the book is devoted to
his attempt to identify and communicate the self as experienced. His exposition relies upon an analysis of consciousness and attention.

809 Guenther, H. V. Philosophy and Psychology in the
       Abhidharma. Lucknow: Buddha Vihara, 1957.
       405 p.
       The author first surveys the mind and its states,
next deals with some aspects of meditation, then interprets
the world we live in, and finally explains the path.

810 Hiriyanna, M. Outlines of Indian Philosophy. See
       entry no. 593.

811 Horner, I. B. The Early Buddhist Theory of Man
       Perfected: A Study of the Arahan. London:
       Williams and Norgate, 1936. 328 p.
       This is a study of the Buddhist concept of the way
of perfection as this had been conceived by the Buddha and
his followers and recorded in the sacred literature.

812 Humphreys, C. Studies in the Middle Way. See entry
       no. 570.

813 Japanese National Commission for UNESCO. Philo-
        sophical Studies of Japan. Tokyo: Japan Society
        for the Promotion of Science, 1961. 151 p.
     Of the five essays in this book, the one entitled
"The Characteristics of Oriental Nothingness" is most interesting, subject to the Western Buddhist. The author re-
minds us that this nothingness is the basis of Oriental culture, the core of Buddhism, and the essence of Zen.

814 Jayasuriya, W. F. The Psychology and Philosophy of
        Buddhism; An Introduction to the Abhidhamma. See
        entry no. 872.

815 Jayatilleke, K. N. Early Buddhist Theory of Knowledge.
        London: Allen and Unwin, 1963. 519 p.
     Dr. Jayatilleke's work begins with a thorough review
and discussion of the state of Indian thought in the time of
the Buddha: Vedic thinkers, materialists, Sceptics, Ajivikas
and Jains. Further chapters deal with the attitude to authority, the attitude to reason, analysis and meaning, logic
and truth. Probably only scholars and those seriously interested in philosophical questions will read this book through.

816 Keith, A. B. Buddhist Philosophy in India and Ceylon.
        London: Oxford University Press, 1963. 339 p.
     Buddhism in the Pali Canon, developments in Hina-
yana Buddhism, philosophy of Mahayana and Buddhist logic
are included in this thorough-going treatment by a noted
Sanskrit scholar, which presupposes considerable knowledge
of the literature. This compact survey is based on references to original sources which are appropriately indicated
in footnotes. Detailed English and Sanskrit indices are included.

817 _____ . The Samkhya System; A History of the
        Samkhya Philosophy. London and New York: Ox-
        ford, 1918. 109 p.
     This is a standard survey of the history of the
Samkhya form of classical Hindu philosophy, discussing its
manifestation in the Upanishads, Buddhism, and the epics,
its relation to Greek philosophy. The basic texts and their
later developments are critically discussed.

818 Lankavatara-Sutra: A Mahayana Text. Translated
        from the original Sanskrit by D. T. Suzuki. See
        entry no. 1195.

819   Milindaponha. The Questions of King Milinda.   See
       entry no. 1013.

820   Muller, F. M.   The Six Systems of Indian Philosophy.
       New York: Longmans, Green and Co., 1899.
       478 p.
       This work concerns the philosophy of Hindu and
Buddhism.

821   Murti, T. R. V.   Central Philosophy of Buddhism.
       2nd ed. London: Allen and Unwin, 1960.   372 p.
       This work presents Buddhism, its philosophy and
religion, from the standpoint of Nagarjuna's Sunyata, the
"Silence of the Middle Way." It is a critical, philosophical
study of the Mahayana system of philosophy, its dialectics
and relation to other systems, both Buddhist and Hindu.   A
glossary of Sanskrit terms and an index are included.

822   Purucker, G. de.   Man in Evolution.   Covina: Theo-
       sophical University Press, 1957.   450 p.
       This one volume is a condensed version of the late
Dr. de Purucker's two volumes of Theosophy and Modern
Science.   He was a Buddhist who studied theosophy as pre-
sented by H. P. Blavatsky.   The chapters on Karma and
Rebirth are of great interest in themselves.

823   Radhakrishnan, S.   The Concept of Man: A Study in
       Comparative Philosophy.   London: Allen and Unwin,
       1960.   383 p.
       The book is divided into four great world traditions:
Greek, Jewish, Indian and Chinese.   The contributor in each
area is a member of the tradition he writes about as well
as being an expert on his subject.   Indian and Chinese
writers also deal with Buddhism.

824   _____. Indian Philosophy. New York: Macmillan,
       1923-1927.   2 vols. [also see entry no. 605].
       This is an interesting treatment by an Indian author
who freely uses Western parallels and interpretations.

825   Reyna, R.   The Concept of Maya from the Vedas to the
       Twentieth Century.   London: Asia Publishing House,
       1962.   120 p.
       This work, a Ph.D. thesis, will be difficult reading
for most, but it is of value for those interested in Indian
philosophy.   Maya is a key term in Indian thought, and the
author seeks to show the inadequacy of the usual rendering.

826 Sarkar, A. K. Changing Phases of Buddhist Thought.
        Patna: Bharati Bhawan, 1968. 147 p.
        The author concentrates on the four schools of Bud-
dhism in order to demonstrate ideological continuity between
them. This work is a collection of articles, most of which
have previously appeared in other journals and volumes.
His purpose is to clarify the unlimited, yet empirical thought-
process of the principal Buddhist schools.

827 Sharma, C. A Critical Survey of Indian Philosophy.
        London: Rider, 1959. 415 p.
        This work gives a clear, comprehensive and critical
account of the various systems of Indian philosophy. Jainism,
Buddhism, Yoga, the various schools of Vedanta, and the
Shaiva and Shakti schools are all dealt with in the same
critical way, each belief logically examined. There is also
a comparative study of the Hinayana and the Mahayana
schools.

828 Sinnett, A. P. Esoteric Buddhism. London: Theo-
        sophical Publishing House, 1972.
        This is a classic book of the theosophical movement
that deals with the constitution of man, the vast theory of
planetary and human evolution, and the great wisdom tradition.

829 Suzuki, D. T. Mysticism: Christian and Buddhist.
        New York: Harper, 1957. 214 p.
        In this lucid and highly readable study of the essence
of mysticism, D. T. Suzuki, perhaps the greatest modern
authority on the mystical aspects of both Oriental and Christian religions, compares the Zen and Shin Buddhism of the
East with the writings of the German philosopher Meister
Eckhart. With a wealth of illustration and explanation Suzuki
examines the underlying relationship between these three
great schools of mysticism, stressing the deep affinities between them. To illustrate his theme, Suzuki gathers together as the third part of this book a selection from the
writings of Japanese mystics, which gives a unique impression of the depth and beauty of Japanese mystical thought.

830 Takakusu, J. Essentials of Buddhist Philosophy.
        Honolulu: University of Hawaii Press, 1960. 221 p.
        This work contains brief analyses of the principal
Buddhist philosophical schools. It is a comprehensive, systematic exposition of the essentials of Buddhist philosophy by
a veteran Far Eastern scholar, which comes as a great aid
to the philosophic public.

831   Thomas, E. J.   History of Buddhist Thought.   2nd ed.
         See entry no. 405.

832   Upanishads.   Translated by Swami Nikhilananda.   New
         York: Harper, 1949- . Vol. 1.
      This work is translated from the Sanskrit with intro-
ductions embodying a general survey, the metaphysics and
the psychology of the Upanishads, with notes and explanations
based on the commentary of Sri Sankaracharya, the great
19th-century philosopher and saint of India.   This book provides the Buddhist with a handy means of comparing and dis-
tinguishing between Buddhism and Vedantism.

833   Van der Leeuw, G.   Religion in Its Essence and
         Manifestation: A Study of Phenomenology.   Trans-
         lated by J. E. Turner.   London: Allen and Unwin,
         1938.   709 p.
      This is a most comprehensive monograph of the
phenomenology of religion with references to all the relevant
works on each aspect of the material brought under review.

                              POETRY

834   Arnold, E.   The Light of Asia.   New York: Doubleday,
         1894.   238 p.
      This is a poetical presentation of Buddha and his
teachings by an imaginary Buddhist priest based on the Lali-
tavistara.

835   Ashvagosha.   The Awakening of Faith.   See entry no.
         1024.

836   Blyth, R. H.   A History of Haiku.   Tokyo: Hokuseido,
         1963.   427 p.
      This work is a vast collection of miniature poems of
17 syllables.   The author, a great authority on this subject,
gives many examples by the famous poets and arranges them
chronologically with some reference to the influence of one
on another.

837   Chang, C. C.   The Hundred Thousand Songs of Milarepa.
         New York: University Books, Inc., 1962.   730 p.
         2 vols.

Milarepa, the great Tibetan Yogin, was first introduced in Europe to the general public by W. Y. Evans-
Wentz, when in 1928 he published at the Oxford University
Press a translation of Milarepa's biography. This book has
translated 61 chapters, a formidable task and a very considerable achievement. There are many delightful glimpses
of Tibetan life in the 11th century.

838 _____. Sixty Songs of Milarepa. Ceylon: Wheel
         Publications, 1967. 101 p.
    This work, containing 60 of the poems of Milarepa,
selected and introduced by Bhikkhu Khantipalo, gives us the
flavor of Milarepa's teaching. These songs chosen from the
Tibetan writings show the wisdom behind the teachings of
Buddhism.

839 Clark, H. The Message of Milarepa. London: John
         Murray, 1959. 106 p.
    This is a work of Milarepa's songs in which he ex-
presses in ecstasy his deepest discoveries. Mr. Clark has
selected all the poetical phrases. Milarepa, one of the
greatest poets of Tibet of whom we have knowledge, is here
compared with St. Francis.

840 Dhammapada. Hymns of the Faith. See entry no. 205.

841 Gordon, A. K. The Hundred Thousand Songs Selected
         from Milarepa, Poet-Saint of Tibet. Rutland, Vt.:
         Tuttle, 1960. 122 p.
    This work contains an admirable selection from
Milarepa's collected poems and a precious addition to the
Tibetan Buddhist texts in English. The translation itself is
faithful both in style and content.

842 Horner, I. B. Early Buddhist Poetry; An Anthology.
         Ceylon: Semage, 1963. 84 p.
    The anthology which is addressed to the lay people
rather than to monks is confined to poems existing in the
Pali Canon which have already appeared in English translation. But these translations of the original Pali texts are
not easily accessible to the general reader. Miss Horner
analyzes the contents of these poems as embodying the
ethical principles and spiritual values taught by the Buddha
leading up to the final goal Nibbana.

843 Humphreys, C. Buddhist Poems; a Selection, 1920-
         1970. London: Allen and Unwin, 1971. 98 p.

The present volume is mainly inspired by Buddhist themes and thoughts, but also it includes a variety of poems on subjects such as nature, love and war. Selected from Humphreys' finest writing over a period of fifty years, it will add considerably to his standing in the field of literature. It is infused with a quality of spiritual calm rarely found in contemporary poetry.

844 _____ . Poems I Remember. London: Michael Joseph, 1960. 200 p.
This work contains an excellent preface and good provision of interesting introductory comments at the head of each group of poems. It seems to have been written with young people chiefly in mind.

845 _____ . Studies in the Middle Way. See entry no. 138.

846 Hyun, P. Voices of the Dawn; A Selection of Korean Poetry. London: John Murray, 1959. 120 p.
This latest edition to the Wisdom of the East series serves to remind us of the most unfortunate Buddhist land of Korea, and the author's introduction tells us something of its history and culture, particularly as pertaining to Buddhism.

847 Li, S. C. Popular Buddhism in China. See entry no. 550.

848 Rinpoche, C. T. Mudra. London: Shambhala, 1972. 107 p.
This work contains songs, poems, original translations of Zog-Chen texts, a commentary on the famous Ox Herding pictures, an article called "The Way of the Buddha," and a glossary of Buddhist terms, but, most momentous of all, it contains the Dharma.

849 Sangharashita, B. Messengers from Tibet and Other Poems. Bombay: Hind Kitabs, 1954. 50 p.
This little book of verse has a quality of peace, yet as though the author were compelled to write the poems as they overflowed from his consciousness made keen by insight.

850 Santideva. Entering the Path of Enlightenment; The Bodhicaryavatara of the Buddhist Poet Santideva. See entry no. 1043.

851   Stewart, H. A Net of Fireflies. Rutland, Vt.: Tuttle,
        1960. 180 p.
      This collection of miniature poems translated with
rare skill into English rhymed couplets is not only a charac-
teristic expression of Japanese artistic genius, but a precious document of Buddhist spirituality. Its 320 examples of
haiku provide almost as many themes of meditation for those
who will discern the underlying meaning. It is as if each
tiny poem had represented, for its author, a momentary experience of enlightenment.

852   Stryk, L. and Ikenoto, T. (eds.). Zen: Poems,
        Prayers, Sermons, Anecdotes, Interviews. See
        entry no. 1122.

853   no entry

854   Waley, A. The Life and Times of Po Chu-i. See
        entry no. 279.

855   Yasuda, K. The Japanese Haiku. Rutland, Vt.:
        Tuttle, 1969. 232 p.
      The author gives a fine chapter on the essential
nature of haiku, then deals with its history and the possibility of haiku in English, with special emphasis on rhyme,
which is unknown to Japanese writers. He gives many
examples, including poems of his own, but does not include
any English haiku.

              POLITICS and GOVERNMENT

856   Benz, E. Buddhism or Communism; Which Holds the
        Future of Asia? New York: Doubleday, 1965.
        234 p.
      Translated from the German by Richard and Clara
Winston, this work discusses the role played by present-day
Buddhism in shaping the political and social ideas of the
Buddhist nations.

857   Gard, R. A. Buddhist Influences on the Political
        Thought and Institutions of India and Japan. Los
        Angeles: California Society for Oriental Studies,
        1949. 50 p.

These Phoenix Papers were presented to the Society
for Oriental Studies at Claremont. It attempts to outline the
nature of Buddhist influences on the political ideas and traditions of India and Japan as typical contrasting cases.

858 Schecter, J. The New Face of Buddha: Buddhism and
        Political Power in Southeast Asia. New York:
        Coward-McCann, 1967. 300 p.
        This work discusses the new political role of Bud-
dhism in Communist China, Cambodia, Thailand, Burma,
Ceylon, Vietnam, and Japan. Mr. Schecter is a foreign
bureau chief in Tokyo for Time. His analysis of the tough,
politically astute Vietnamese Buddhists is particularly appropriate and balanced.

859 Smith, D. E. Religion and Politics in Burma. See
        entry no. 509.

860 _____ (ed.). South Asian Politics and Religion.
        Princeton, N.J.: Princeton University Press, 1966.
        563 p.
        The comparative analysis contained in 24 papers
shows how in South Asia the relationship between religion
and politics has evolved in an altogether different manner
than was the case with the countries of Western Europe.

PRAYER

861 Stryk, L. and Ikenoto, T. (eds.). Zen: Poems,
        Prayers, Sermons, Anecdotes, Interviews. See
        entry no. 1122.

PSYCHOLOGY

862 Benoit, H. The Supreme Doctrine: Psychological
        Studies in Zen Thought. Translated by Terence
        Gray. Foreword by Aldous Huxley. New York:
        Pantheon Books, 1955. 248 p.
        The theme bears upon diverse alleged psychological

states and moves from the mysterious to the incomprehensible. The theme of the book has little to do with Zen as customarily understood and little to do with Western psychologies. The author seems to have the idea that almost every man is capable, through insight, of attaining to a state of complete happiness and free creativity.

863 Davids, C. A. F. Rhys. A Buddhist Manual of Psychological Ethics of the Fourth Century B.C. London: Royal Asiatic Society, 1900. 393 p. [also see entry no. 865.]
A translation, made for the first time, from the original Pali language entitled Dhamma-Sangani (compendium of states or phenomena) discusses the history of psychology. The genesis of thoughts (cittuppada-kandam), form (rupa-kandam), and the division entitled "Elimination" (nikkhepa-kandam) are the main topics of discussion.

864 _____. Buddhist Psychology: An Inquiry into the Analysis and Theory of Mind in Pali Literature. New York: Macmillan, 1914. 212 p.
Habits of thought, psychology of the Nikayas, considering mind in term and concept, consciousness and the external world, feeling and ideation are the major topics. Here is seen clearly how a sound knowledge of Buddhist psychology is essential to the study of Buddhism.

865 Dhammasangani. A Buddhist Manual of Psychological Ethics. London: Royal Asiatic Society, 1923. 364 p. [also see entry no. 863.]
This is a translation made for the first time from the original Pali of the first book in the Abhidhamma Pitaka, entitled Dhamma-Sangani (compendium of states or phenomena), with introductory essay and notes by C. A. F. Rhys Davids.

866 Evans, C. O. The Subject of Consciousness. See entry no. 808.

867 Fromm, E., D. T. Suzuki, et al. Zen Buddhism and Psychoanalysis. New York: Harper, 1960. 180 p.
This work is a comparing of notes between Zen and psychotherapy: it contains six short papers by Erich Fromm and five by Suzuki, and one long paper by Richard DeMartino. A new introduction to Zen as a whole, it gives special attention to the unconscious and the concept of the self in Zen

philosophy. It discusses the really important question of the
differing social and cultural premises upon which Zen and
psychoanalysis are based.

868 Guenther, H. V. Philosophy and Psychology in the
     Abhidharma. See entry no. 809.

869 Hall, M. P. Buddhism and Psychotherapy. Los Ange-
        les: Philosophical Research Society, 1967. 324 p.
     The author is the president-founder of the Philosophi-
cal Research Society based in Los Angeles. He describes
here many of the sacred temples, gardens and places of pilgrimage which, in Japan, act as a focus for those people
who, in a simple and natural way, wish to pay homage to the
universal verities of different aspects of Buddhism. The
title of the book seems misleading.

870 Huber, J. Psychotherapy and Meditation. London:
        Victor Gollancz, 1965. 132 p.
     This is a very brief account of the comparison made
by the author between the meditation methods of Zen Buddhism in Japan and the Theravada Buddhism in Burma. The
author visited both countries for only a few days and seems
to give too brief an opinion.

871 Humphreys, C. Studies in the Middle Way. See entry
        no. 570.

872 Jayasuriya, W. F. The Psychology and Philosophy of
        Buddhism: An Introduction to the Abhidhamma.
     Colombo, Ceylon: YMBA Press, 1963. 254 p.
     This work gives a general introduction to Buddhism
and then a psycho-physical analysis of reality. Most instruc-
tive are the portions dealing with Nibbana, Karma, death and
rebirth and with the law of causation. Also there are brief
expositions of the Four Noble Truths and a useful glossary of
Buddhist te ns.

873 Jung, C. G. Synchronicity: An Acausal Connecting
        Principle. London: Kegan Paul, 1972. 150 p.
     What Jung means by his concept of synchronicity is
a meaningful coincidence, an acausal orderedness. This is
actually the principle whereon much of Eastern thinking is
based. Buddhism as an Eastern system of thought is based
on the same principle. It follows that it is essential for an
understanding of Buddhism. The work is not easy reading,
because it forces the mind to open and to forge a new way
of thinking.

874 Kelsey, D. and Grant, J. Many Lifetimes. London:
      Victor Gollancz, 1968. 275 p.
        The author, a psychiatrist, wrote this work with his
wife, Joan Grant. While he has only the vaguest feelings regarding his own previous lives, Joan Grant can remember
some forty-five of her previous existences. This work entitled "Reincarnation and Psychotherapy" offers as evidence
for reincarnation detailed accounts of how the psychological
ailments of many of his patients can be traced to experiences in earlier lives.

875 Krishnamurti, J. The Urgency of Change. See entry
      no. 333.

876 Naranjo, C. On the Psychology of Meditation. London:
      Allen and Unwin, 1973. 248 p.
        The author sees the recent popular rediscovery of
Eastern meditation as one concrete indication of a new
spiritual awakening in the technologically soaked culture of
the West. From Zen, Yoga, the Sufis, and Shamanism
have come the roots of the book's synthesis of the multiple
manifestations of meditative techniques, and from current
experimental work has come a new insight into the nature of
consciousness.

877 Neumann, E. The Great Mother. London: Routledge,
      1955. 380 p. 185 plates.
        This is a great book for anyone who is at all
interested in the psychology of religion. It also should go
far to open the eyes of Buddhists who want to find their way
through the variety of teachings which have been propounded
as Buddhist at different times and in different places.

878 Reichelt, K. L. Meditation and Piety in the Far East:
      A Religious-Psychological Study. Translated from
      the Norwegian by Sverre Holth. New York: Harper
      and Brothers, 1954. 171 p.
        The author was a Norwegian Lutheran missionary in
China for many years. He made a serious study of Buddhism, Taoism, and Confucianism, especially the religious
and mystical aspects of those systems. The first part of his
work contributes to the comparative study between "general
revelation" and "special revelation" in both Eastern and
Western systems. The second part is devoted to an analysis
of meditation which the author considered to be the heart of
the Eastern system.

879 Rogers, C. R. On Becoming a Person. Austin:
         Univ. of Texas, Constable Press, 1971. 400 p.
     With words of Kierkegaard, Carl Rogers pictures
the dilemma of the individual and, with inspired perception,
he takes us through many interviews with "clients" as they
search for the reality of self. This modern psychotherapy
movement comes very close to the doors of Buddhism.

880 Sarathchandra, E. R. Buddhist Psychology of Percep-
         tion. Colombo: Ceylon University Press, 1958.
         110 p.
     The purpose of this book, which is the author's
Ph.D. thesis, is to interpret, in terms intelligible to those
familiar with Western philosophy, the view of mind expressed
in the Nikayas and the Abhidhamma.

881 Suzuki, D. T.; Fromm, E.; and de Martino, R. Zen
         Buddhism and Psychoanalysis. See entry no. 1135.

882 Tucci, G. The Theory and Practice of the Mandala.
         Translated by A. H. Broderick. London: Rider,
         1961. 146 p.
     The mandala and its symbolism have a peculiar
universality of appeal in that such symbols are not arbitrary
constructs, but intuitive apprehensions of spiritual reality.
Professor Tucci wisely confines his attention to Indo-Tibetan
Buddhism and to those schools of Hinduism whose Yantra
diagrams he thinks of as embodying similar truths, though
their construction must seem alien to anyone accustomed to
Buddhist mandalas.

883 Wood, E. E. Mind and Memory Training. London:
         Theosophical Publishing House, 1961. 188 p.
     This work surveys and improves on various well-
known and lesser-known memotechnic systems, and even
spares some room at the end for some elementary advice
on concentration and meditation. Its special value lies in
the way in which it reveals the unconscious mechanics of
memorizing.

                RELATIONS WITH OTHER RELIGIONS

884 Anderson, J. N. D. The World's Religions. London:
         Inter-varsity Fellowship, 1950. 208 p.

This book gives a summary of Animism, Judaism, Islam, Hinduism, Buddhism, Shinto and Confucianism by distinguished scholars. It is one of the most concise summaries, if that is what one is seeking.

885   no entry

886   Browne, L. (ed.).   The World's Great Scriptures.
      See entry no. 1157.

887   Bunce, W. K.   Religions in Japan: Buddhism, Shinto, Christianity.   Rutland, Vt.: Tuttle, 1955.   194 p.
      This is a brief summary of Buddhism, Shinto and Christianity, giving the historical background and the present situation in Japan.   Originally it was a 1948 report for the Allied occupational authorities.   It contains statistics of religious sects and a glossary of religious terms.

888   Cave, S.   An Introduction to the Study of Some Living Religions of the East.   London: Duckworth, 1921. 225 p.
      This is an introduction to Hinduism, Buddhism, Taoism, Confucianism, Zoroastrianism and Islam.

889   Champion, S. G.   The Eleven Religions and Their Proverbial Lore; A Comparative Study.   New York: Dutton, 1945.   340 p.
      This is a reference book to the 11 surviving major religions of the world, with introductions by 13 leading authorities.   It contains quotations arranged under religion by key words, with a subject-matter index and alternative chief word index.   It also contains a useful bibliography on pp. 336-360.

890   Eaton, G.   The Richest Vein: Eastern Tradition and Modern Thought.   London: Faber and Faber, 1949. 229 p.
      The author of this book seems to go a very long way round and has many wise things to say on the journey only to come back to wrong conclusions in the end.   He examines the Vedas, the Upanishads, Buddhism, Taoism, the works of Rene Guenon, Coomaraswamy and others.

891   Finegan, J.   The Archeology of World Religions.
      See entry no. 15.

892   Harding, D. E.   Religions of the World.   London:

Heinemann Educational Books, 1966.   128 p.
The author has studied comparative religion for
many years and here describes the world's chief religions:
Hinduism, Buddhism, Confucianism, Taoism, Zen, Judaism,
Christianity, and Islam.   His concentration is on basic mysticism, the thread which runs through every chapter of the
book and binds it together.

893   Haydon, A. E.   Modern Trends in World Religions.
      New York: Books for Libraries, 1968.   255 p.
      In 1933 the Haskell Foundation was formed in order
to study the nature of the adjustments of six of the great
religions--Hinduism, Confucianism, Buddhism, Judaism,
Islam, and Christianity--to the crucial factors of change.

894   Jacobson, N. P.   Buddhism: The Religion of Analysis.
      London: Allen and Unwin, 1966; Carbondale:
      Southern Illinois University Press, 1970.   199/202 p.
      The author has spent a year at the New International
Institute for Advanced Buddhistic Studies in Rangoon, and
here he makes a brave attempt to facilitate understanding of
Buddhism through modern intellectual concepts.   A more
accurate title would be "The Teachings of the Buddha Compared and Contrasted with Those of Various Western Philosophers."   The author shows that the main difficulty with a
wide acceptance in the west of Buddhism is that it stresses
inner freedom before social freedom, and its techniques seem
to be devoted mainly toward the former.

895   Kapleau, P.   The Wheel of Death; Writing from Zen
      Buddhists and Other Sources.   London: Allen and
      Unwin, 1973.   110 p.
      This work is an anthology of statements by Buddhist,
Taoist, Hindu, and Western masters on death, Karma and
rebirth.   This work was inspired by a mounting concern in
America with the perfunctory treatment of the dying and the
widespread attitude of disguising or ignoring the fact of death.

896   Kitagawa, J. M.   Modern Trends in World Religions.
      La Salle, Ill.:   Open Court, 1959.   286 p.
      This work is compiled largely from papers pre-
sented at a 1957 symposium in memory of Paul Carus, who
pioneered in introducing Oriental thought to the English
speaking world.   All the participants of the symposium were
subject specialists.   The topics discussed are Islam, Judaism,
Christianity, Indian spirituality, Chinese philosophy and religion, Theravada Buddhism, and Zen Buddhism.

897 Ling, T. Buddha, Marx and God. New York: St.
     Martin's Press, 1966. 227 p.
     This work is prepared for "those who are in any
way interested in the subject of religion in the modern
world." The author's main goals are: "to present Buddhism as a religious tradition; to show its relationship to
secularism and Marxism; to demonstrate the inadvisability
of regarding Marxism as a religion; and to make clear the
ways in which Buddhism corrects those notions of religion
which are only based on its Western manifestations."

898 Melamed, S. M. Spinoza and Buddha: Visions of a
     Dead God. Chicago: University of Chicago Press,
     1933. 391 p.
     The author's main thesis is that the philosophy of
Spinoza derives not from Western but from Oriental thought,
and especially from Buddhism. It first deals with Spinoza's
influence on modern culture, second with his theory of God
and the world, third with the backgrounds of Spinozism. He
develops a new philosophy of history.

899 Parker, E. H. Studies in Chinese Religion. London:
     Chapman, 1910. 308 p.
     The contents of this book may be described in the
main as the original studies from which a summary was
made and a popular work published in 1905 called China and
Religion. The present study is republished with alterations
almost necessitated for clearness' sake.

900 Parrinder, G. Man and His God, an Encyclopedia of
     the World's Religions. London: Hamlyn, 1972.
     440 p.
     This book brings together all the important religions
of the world, both past and present. It is a work which will
appeal to the newcomer to the subject of comparative religion as well as to the scholar. The article on Buddhism
was written by Trevor Ling.

901 _____. Worship in the World's Religion. London:
     Faber and Faber, 1960. 239 p.
     The author has produced a very readable and com-
pact, comparative study of the religions of the world, from
the point of view of the worship of the laity. Only the main
living religions are included, and three quarters of the book
is concerned with the religions of Asia.

902 Reischauer, A. K. The Nature and Truth of the Great

Religions: A Scholarly Study of the Great Religions.
Rutland, Vt.:   Tuttle, 1966.   340 p.
The author emphasizes Christianity and the remaining
religions are discussed for comparative study with Christianity. As far as Buddhism is concerned the author places
all the emphasis on the Mahayana schools, as these can
more easily be forced into the theistic mold he is using than
can the Theravada ideals.

903 Smart, N. A Dialogue of Religions. London: S. C.
      M. Press, 1960. 142 p.
The book is cast in the form of a classical dialogue;
but there are so many protagonists (a Christian, a Jew, a
Moslem, a Hindu, a Sinhalese and a Japanese Buddhist),
their views are expressed, owing to the form, in such a
forced didactic manner and there are so many qualifying
parentheses that it soon becomes tiresome and confusing
reading.

904 Smith, H. The Religions of Man. New York: Harper
      and Brothers, 1958. 328 p.
The author treats seven popular world religions:
Buddhism, Hinduism, Confucianism, Taoism, Islam, Judaism,
and Christianity. He gives short introductions of the development of each, and pertinent historical information is provided to clarify the modifications of doctrine inherent. This
work is written for the general reader and further study is
provided for by selected reading lists at the end of each
religion's section.

905 Smith, W. C. The Faith of Other Men. New York:
      Mentor Books, 1963. 128 p.
This study of Hinduism, Buddhism, Islam, and
Chinese philosophy differs impressively from all other
studies of comparative religion. The author shows how we
can understand the aims, motivations, and values of different peoples through a clearer comprehension of their deepest
personal beliefs.

906 Spiegelberg, F. Living Religions of the World. Lon-
      don: Thames and Hudson, 1957. 511 p.
This is probably the best work of its kind on the
market; the general student and the expert alike will find
something to reward their reading. The author examines
20 religions of mankind. On Buddhism he divides the topic
into three parts: Buddhism, Zen Buddhism and Tibet. The

chapter on Zen Buddhism is a real addition to the scanty
literature about the subject produced by Western minds.

907 Stroup, H. Four Religions of Asia. See entry no. 28.

908 Walker, K. So Great a Mystery. London: Victor
  Gollancz, 1958. 224 p.
  This work gives a résumé of the outstanding world
religions beginning with Vedanta, and following with Buddhism, Christianity, Confucianism, Taoism, and Islam. His
contention is that the transcendental experience is the same
in all these religions, but that enlightenment is a far greater
achievement than the transcendental experience that can be
obtained through certain religious observations and practices.

909 Yatiswarananda, S. Adventures in Vedanta. London:
  Rider, 1960. 224 p.
  The author is one of the readers of the Ramakrishna
Order. Various aspects of the spiritual life are dealt with
both theoretically and practically on the basis of comparative
religion. There are many quotations from and references to
all the great religions which infer the similarity in aims
and experiences of the devotees of each. Such subjects as
salvation, happiness, meditation, grace and God are reviewed in the light of Taoism, Zoroastrianism, Judaism,
Christianity, Islam and Buddhism.

910 Zaehner, R. C. At Sundry Times; An Essay in the
  Comparison of Religions. London: Faber and
  Faber, 1958. 230 p.
  This is a study of the religions of Asia with the
object of showing that in them may be found a preparation
for the Christian revelation.

CHRISTIANITY AND BUDDHISM

911 Anesaki, M. History of Japanese Religion. See entry
  no. 620.

912 Appleton, G. The Christian Approach to the Buddhist.
  London: Edinburgh House, 1960. 63 p.
  This short description of the main ideas in Theravada and Mahayana Buddhism and their application, particularly in the popular Buddhism of Burma with which the
author is acquainted, having lived there, preserves on the

whole a courteous and sympathetic tone, though it naturally
stresses the points where Christians and Buddhists disagree.

913 Appleton, G. On the Eightfold Path. See entry no.
       286.

914 Baptist, E. C. Nibbana or the Kingdom. London:
       Richard and Company, 1953. 364 p.
       The author is a former British Catholic who was
born in and is a resident of Ceylon, now practicing Buddhism. The earlier chapters deal with the fact that Jesus,
like Buddha, taught the doctrines of Karma and Rebirth.
The essential thesis of the book is the usual Theravada view
of a lower "Path of the Gods." Jesus is seen as a great
Bodhisattva who, with perfect unselfishness, deliberately
sacrificed in order to save the people he loved.

915 Barlaam and Joasaph. Baralam and Yewasef. Cam-
       bridge: The University Press, 1923. 2 volumes.
       This is the Ethiopic version of a Christianized re-
cension of the Buddhist legend of the Buddha and the Bodhisattva. The Ethiopic text is edited for the first time with
an English translation.

916 Barlaam and Josaphat: The Balavariani; A Tale from
       the Christian East. See entry no. 345.

917 Boedeker, H. E. Thus Have I Proved; or, "Knight's
       Move." Oakley (Beds.), England: Robin Olney,
       1966. 116 p.
       This is an account of a testing of the teachings of
Jesus and Buddha in a 40-year experiment. It asserts to
be "an answer to atomic-age anxiety and a message of
assistance to those many people who feel confused in this
age of winds-of-change with a brief historical survey of the
possible causes thereof."

918 Brown, W. N. The Indian and Christian Miracles of
       Walking on the Water. Chicago: Open Court Pub.
       Co., 1897. 316 p.
       This contribution to comparative religion is ad-
dressed mainly to those Christians who are anxious to ac-
quire an insight into the significance of Buddhist thought at
its best.

919 Dechanet, D. J. M. Christian Yoga. London: Burns
       and Oates, 1959. 196 p.

    This relates an attempt by Father Dechanet, a
Benedictine monk, to apply Hatha Yoga to Catholic practices.

920   Graham, A. Conversations; Christian and Buddhist:
         Encounters in Japan. New York: Harcourt, 1968.
         206 p.
      The author, an American, is an early Zen student.
This book is the first fruit of his journey in Asia, and it
consists of 13 discussions held with representatives of the
Buddhist faith in Japan.

921   Graham, D. A. The End of Religion. See entry no.
         704.

922   _____. Zen Catholicism. London: Collins, 1963.
         218 p.
      This book is about the meeting of two religions and
how one might affect the other. That such meetings and
adaptations are to take place, that people bent on this busi-
ness should entertain a lively and charitable view of one
another's methods, ways and insights is desirable, and this
work must be welcomed for this reason.

923   Guirdham, A. The Cathars and the Reincarnation.
         London: Neville Spearmen, 1971. 208 p.
      The book provides a valuable introduction to the
Cathar religion and way of life. Dr. Guirdham justifiably
compares it with Buddhism. Although there are important
differences at the philosophical level, the Cathars seem,
within the European tradition, to resemble most closely the
Buddhists.

924   Hilliard, F. H. The Buddha, the Prophet and the
         Christ. New York: Macmillan, 1956. 169 p.
      The main purpose of this work is to bring together
from the canonical writings of all these three great religions
the most important of the passages in which the views of
the founder are reflected.

925   Hunter, L. H. Buddhism in Hawaii: Its Impact on a
         Yankee Community. See entry no. 763.

926   Johnston, W. Christian Zen. New York: Harper,
         1972. 109 p.
      An Irish Catholic priest shares the insights into the
Oriental method of contemplative prayer that he gained from
his Buddhist friends during a 20-year stay in Japan. He

tells how Zen meditation and dialogue with his Buddhist
friends have enriched and deepened his Christian faith.
Johnston believes with Arnold Toynbee that the most significant development in the 20th century is that Christianity
and Buddhism have begun to respond to and to learn from
one another.

927   King, W. L.   Buddhism and Christianity.   Philadelphia:
         Westminster, 1962.   240 p.
         This work explains the similarities and differences
in the religious concepts of Christianity and Buddhism.   The
author starts with a reminiscence of discussions in Burma
with the Venerable U Thittila and points out the difficulty of
communication which repeatedly showed itself despite strenu-
ous efforts at mutual understanding--efforts which he feels
are too rarely made on either side.

928   Lang, D. M.   The Balavariani: A Buddhist Story from
         the Christian East.   London: George Allen and Un-
         win, 1966.   187 p.
         Balavariani is the Georgian name for the story of
Barlaam and Josaphat.   The story is an adaptation of the
legendary biography of Gautama Buddha.   The author, who
is professor of Caucasian Studies at the University of London,
seeks to discover why the Christian story, "The Life of
Baarlam and Joasaph," resembles that of the life of the
Gautama Buddha.

929   Lin, Y.   From Pagan to Christian.   London: William
         Heinemans, 1960.   251 p.
         The author rebelled against Christian theological
dogma and set out on a search for truth which led him to a
study of Confucianism, Buddhism and Taoism.   He gives an
excellent section on Taoism.   The teachings of the Buddha
appear to him as a somewhat dry intellectual analysis and
he is happiest with Zen, though he also gives a very fair
selection from the Surangama Sutra.

930   Linssen, R.   Living Zen.   See entry no. 1096.

931   Lubac, H. de.   Aspects of Buddhism.   Translated by
         George Lamb.   Atlantic Highlands, N.J.:   Hillary,
         1954.   192 p.

932   Matsutani, F.   A Comparative Study of Buddhism and
         Christianity.   Tokyo: Young East Assoc., 1957.
         184 p.

The aim of this book is to compare Buddhism and Christianity, not in regard to their doctrines and theology, but in regard to their aims and methods, and their evaluation of the human situation. The book is divided into four parts under the questions: (1) What is the nature of man? (2) What should I hope to be? (3) Upon what should I rely? (4) What should I do?

933   Richard, T.   New Testament of Higher Buddhism.
        New York: Scribner, 1911.
        This volume contains the translation of two Buddhist treatises, "The Awakening of Faith" and "The Lotus Scripture," and a very significant introduction by the translator.

934   Saunders, K. J.   Buddhist Ideals.   Madras: Christian
        Literature Society, 1912.   179 p.
        This is a study in comparative religion.

935   Slater, R. H. L.   Paradox and Nirvana.   See entry
        no. 508.

936   Streeter, B. H.   The Buddha and the Christ.   New
        York: Kennikat Press, 1970.   336 p.
        An exploration of the meaning of the universe and of the purpose of human life, this work describes the contrast and the similarity between Buddhism and Christianity in origin, history, and development.

937   Suzuki, D. T.   Mysticism: Christian and Buddhist.
        See entry no. 829.

938   Walker, K.   Diagnosis of Man.   Los Angeles: Pelican
        Books, 1962.   259 p.
        The author's diagnosis is that of a consulting surgeon with a broad culture and interest in Eastern philosophy, including Buddhism. He notes that it is necessary to develop a higher cognitive faculty in order to come to a greater awareness of the truth. The book includes chapters on Vedanta, Yoga, Buddhism, and Christianity.

939   Watts, A. W.   Myth and Ritual in Christianity.   Lon-
        don: Thames and Hudson, 1953.   262 p.
        The author presents what he terms the Christian myths and rituals in the light of philosophy. His theme is basically Christian, yet the interest to the practicing Buddhist is great, for it is the author of The Spirit of Zen who writes on every page.

940 _____. The Way of Zen. See entry no. 1144.

COMMUNISM AND BUDDHISM

941 Benz, E. Buddhism or Communism: Which Holds the
      Future in Asia? Garden City, N.Y.: Doubleday
      Anchor Books, 1965. 234 p.
      Dr. Benz, professor of Church and Dogmatic History
at the University of Marburg, Germany, gives an evaluation
of the impact of contemporary Buddhism on the political and
social ideas in India, Ceylon, Burma, and Japan.

942 Ling, T. O. Buddha, Marx, and God: Some Aspects
      of Religion in the Modern World. See entry no. 897.

CONFUCIANISM AND BUDDHISM

943 Anesaki, M. History of Japanese Religion. See
      entry no. 620.

944 Reichelt, K. C. Meditation and Piety in the Far East;
      Religious Psychological Study. See entry no. 459.

945 Soothill, W. E. The Three Religions of China. 3rd
      ed. See entry no. 558.

HINDUISM AND BUDDHISM

946 Coomaraswamy, A. K. Hinduism and Buddhism. New
      York: Philosophical Library, 1943. 86 p.
      This work states the fundamentals from a strictly
orthodox point of view, both as to principles and their application. It contains elaborate notes, textual references, and
cross-cultural concepts. Interpretation is highly subjective
and is based on selected texts.

947 Dasgapta, S. N. A History of Indian Philosophy. See
      entry no. 583.

948 Eliot, C. N. E. Hinduism and Buddhism. See entry
      no. 381.

949 Fausset, H. I. The Flame and the Light. See entry
      no. 96.

950 Hiriyanna, M. The Essentials of Indian Philosophy.
     See entry no. 592.

951 _____ . Outlines of Indian Philosophy. See entry
     no. 593.

952 Joshi, L. M. Brahmanism, Buddhism and Hinduism.
     Kandy: Buddhist Publication Society, 1970. 75 p.
     The aim of this work is "to review and restate the
origins of Buddhism, its relation with early Brahmanism and
with the medieval form of the latter, called Hinduism."

953 Keith, A. B. The Samkhya System; A History of the
     Samkhya Philosophy. See entry no. 817.

954 Noble, M. E. Myths of the Hindus and Buddhists.
     See entry no. 782.

955 no entry

956 Radhakrishnan, Sir S. A Source Book in Indian
     Philosophy. See entry no. 606.

957 Renou, L. Religions of Ancient India. See entry no.
     608.

958 Ross, F. H. The Meaning of Life in Hinduism and
     Buddhism. London: Routledge, 1952. 167 p.
     The author seems convinced that Christianity must
embrace values from other cultures if it is to survive. He
outlines the basic teachings of Hindu and Buddhist metaphysics for the general reader. It includes a bibliography.

959 Ross, N. W. Hinduism, Buddhism, Zen. London:
     Faber and Faber, 1967. 222 p.
     The work is done by an author well known for her
intuitive understanding of the "isness" of life. The first two
sections of her book treat Hinduism and Buddhism in every
orthodox way, the way the two religions have developed,
their doctrine, myths, and poems. The last section is devoted to discussion of Zen history and how it has influenced
Western teaching.

960 The Sacred Books of the Hindus. Allahabad: Panini
     Office, 1909-1937. 32 volumes.
     In this valuable collection, as in Muller's Sacred
Books of the East, the most notable Hindu scriptures appear

as complete documents. Some thirty extensive works have
been translated and published in the two collections.

961 Singh, G. The Religion of the Sikhs. See entry no.
       985.

962 Weber, M. The Religion of India: The Sociology of
       Hinduism and Buddhism. See entry no. 615.

963 Zimmer, H. R. Philosophies of India. See entry no.
       619.

JAINISM AND BUDDHISM

964 Dasgupta, S. N. A History of Indian Philosophy. See
       entry no. 583.

965 Farquhar, J. N. An Outline of the Religious Literature
       of India. See entry no. 589.

966 Gaina Sutras. Translated from Prakrit by H. G.
       Jacobi. Oxford: Clarendon, 1884-1895. 2 vols.
       (Sacred Books of the East XXII and XLV.)
       As translations from the Prakrit of fundamental
Jain religious scriptures, these volumes constitute the basic
sources for our knowledge of early Jain religion, including
discussions on the doctrine, religious practice, and behavior
of the true monk.

967 Hiriyanna, M. The Essentials of Indian Philosophy.
       See entry no. 592.

968 _____. Outlines of Indian Philosophy. See entry
       no. 593.

969 Jaini, J. Outline of Jainism. London: Cambridge
       University, 1940. 159 p.
       This work is a concise summary account of Jain
theology, metaphysics, ethics, ritual, logic, cosmogony, and
literature. Part two includes texts translated to illustrate
major points in the religion.

970 Radhakrishnan, Sir S. A Source Book in Indian
       Philosophy. See entry no. 606.

971 Renou, L. Religions of Ancient India. See entry no.
       608.

972 Stevenson, S. The Heart of Jainism. London: Oxford,
      1915. 336 p.
      One of the best single-volume studies of the Jain
religion in English, this work includes a summary of the
life of Mahavira, his predecessors and disciples, the Jain
community, Jain philosophy, asceticism, methodology, and
practical religious practices of one of the major indigenous
religions of India. An excellent index and an appendix summarizing categories of Jain philosophy and the 24 "saviors"
are included.

973 Zimmer, H. R. Philosophies of India. See entry
      no. 619.

ISLAM [Muslims] AND BUDDHISM

974 Farquhar, J. N. An Outline of the Religious Literature
      of India. See entry no. 589.

975 Singh, G. The Religion of the Sikhs. See entry no.
      985.

SHAMANISM AND BUDDHISM

976 Eliade, M. Shamanism: Archaic Techniques of Ec-
          stasy. Translated from French by W. R. Trask.
      London: Routledge and Kegan Paul, 1964. 610 p.
          Professor Eliade shows that the Shaman was not
the sorcerer hitherto popularly envisaged, but the surviving
practitioner of an important archaic form of mysticism.
The close connection between Shamanism and Tibetan Buddhism needs no underlining, but the author points out hitherto
unsuspected links. The basic structure of the Bardo Thodol
is clearly Shamanic, and Shamanic in origin are many well-
known Buddhist meditations directed to another end than
ecstasy.

SHINTOISM [or Shin, or Jodo-Shin] AND BUDDHISM

977 Anesaki, M. History of Japanese Religion. See entry
      no. 620.

978 The Buddhist Church of America. Buddhism and Jodo
      Shinshu. See entry no. 761.

979 Eliot, Sir C. N. E. Japanese Buddhism. See entry
     no. 631.

980 Fujiswa, C. Zen and Shinto. New York: Philosophi-
     cal Library, 1959. 92 p.
       This work is not much as a comparative study be-
tween Zen and Shintoism. The author concentrates on Shinto
and presents Zen as able to reach the culminating point of
its development only under the overwhelming influence of
Shintoism. Zen is treated by side remarks, so readers who
expect much from the title of this book will be disappointed.

981 Matsunaga, A. The Buddhist Philosophy of Assimila-
     tion. Rutland, Vt.: Tuttle, 1969. 310 p.
       This work gives the historical development of the
Honji-Suijaku theory.

982 Suzuki, D. T. Shin Buddhism. London: Allen and
     Unwin, 1971. 92 p.
       Shin Buddhism is Japan's major religious contribu-
tion to the West. Suzuki emphasizes that Europeans did not
understand Shin Buddhism which at its highest could be described as a complement to Zen.

983 Yamamoto, K. The Other Power: The Final Answer
     Arrived at in Shin Buddhism. Ube, Japan: The
     Karinbunko, 1966. 146 p.
       Jodo Shin-shu or the True Pure Land Sect was
founded by Honen Shonin, and it is today the largest and
most powerful sect in Japan. Professor Yamamoto has
here written extensively on the peculiarly Japanese phenomenon of the Shin sect and its version of Buddhism.

SIKHS AND BUDDHISM

984 Archer, J. C. The Sikhs in Relation to Hindus,
     Moslems, Christians, and Ahamadiyyas. Prince-
     ton, N.J.: Princeton University Press, 1946.
     353 p.
       This is a useful single-volume survey of the Sikhs,
their religion and community, from the standpoint of comparative religion, with special relevance to Buddhists, Moslems, Christians, and Ahamadiyyas. A glossary of Indic
terms is given.

985 Singh, G. The Religion of the Sikhs. London: Asia

Publishing House, 1972. 191 p.

This is a most interesting book for the student of
comparative religion. The founder of the Sikhs was the
famous Guru Nanak who was born in the Punjob in 1419.
He came under the influence of the Hindus and Muslims,
though he stated that he was neither a Nindu nor a Muslim.
For he neither approved of the idol-worship of the Hindus,
nor would he accept the Koran with its worship of Allah.
On one hand he attacked the Hindus' caste system, but on
another he condemned Muslim dogmatism. He cut down
dogma and doctrine to a minimum and taught that the mystical path of self-surrender through prayer and meditation was
the only way to God.

TAOISM AND BUDDHISM

986 Blofeld, J. The Secret and the Sublime. London:
        George Allen, 1973. 217 p.
        Perhaps for the first time, all aspects of Taoism
are brought within the covers of one book: popular Taoism
with its lavish ceremonies, demon exorcism, oracles,
ghosts, and adepts with strange powers; Yogic Taoism with
its emphasis on rejuvenation; and mystical Taoism. The
author provides some comparative aspects between Buddhism
and Taoism.

987 Chang, C. Y. Creativity and Taoism: A Study of
        Chinese Philosophy, Art and Poetry. New York:
        Julian Press Inc., 1966. 241 p.
        Particular attention is paid to the relationship be-
tween Taoism and Buddhism. It is clarified in numerous
ways, both in the section dealing with philosophy and also
those dealing with the arts of poetry, painting and calligraphy.

988 Graham, A. C. The Book of Lieh-tzu [Lao-Tzu].
        London: John Murray, 1960. 183 p. (Wisdom of
        the East Series.)
        This is the first complete translation into English
of the collection of Taoist teachings and fables known as
"The Book of Lao-Tzu." Dr. Graham's introduction and explanations are excellent.

989 Merton, T. The Way of Chuang Tzu. London: Unwin
        Books, 1972. 160 p.
        This work is an anthology of the thought, the humor,
the gossip, and the irony current in Taoist circles in the

fourth and third centuries B.C.   Thomas Merton, with the
aid of John Wu, has selected interpretation of them based
on the four best English translations.

990   Reichelt, K. L.   Meditation and Piety in the Far East;
         Religious Psychological Study.   See entry no. 459.

991   Soothill, W. E.   The Three Religions of China.   3rd
         ed.   See entry no. 558.

992   Wei, S.   Treatise on Buddhism and Taoism.   See entry
         no. 563.

RITUALS

993   I-Ching.   A Record of the Buddhist Religion as
         Practiced in India and the Malay Archipelago, A.D.
         671-695.   Translated by J. Takakusu.   See entry
         no. 389.

994   Levy, P.   Buddhism: A "Mystery Religion?"   See
         entry no. 780.

995   Spiro, M. E.   Buddhism and Society: A Great Tradi-
         tion and Its Burmese Vicissitudes.   New York:
         Harper, 1971; London: Allen and Unwin, 1972.
         510/524 p.
         This is the second of a projected three-volume
study of Burma.   The author, an anthropologist at the University of California, examines the Burmese interpretations
and uses of Theravada Buddhism.   He discusses and compares the ideas expressed in the Buddhist Canon with the
Burmese practices.   The book gives a comprehensive account of the ritual system of the Buddhist monastic structure.
It explores the intricate connections between religion and
social integration, economic development, and political organization.   Spiro discusses three interlocking types of Buddhism, which he calls: (1) Normative or Nibbanic, aspiring
to a goal and characterized by inwardness and meditation,
(2) Non-normative or Kammatic, (3) Apotropaic or protective.   A good comprehensive bibliography on Burmese Buddhism is included.

996   Tambiah, S. J. Buddhism and the Spirit Cults in
        Northeast Thailand. See entry no. 1238.

997   Vidyarth, L. P. The Sacred Complex in Hindu Gaya.
        London: Asia Publishing House, 1960. 238 p.
        This pioneer piece of Hindu anthropology was
written as a thesis on the author's native town of Gaya,
which is near Buddha Gaya, the place of the Buddha's enlightenment. The core of the book is a study of the Gaya-
wal, a priestly community which traditionally lives off the
pilgrim and tourist traffic to the religious centers in Gaya.
The author's analysis of the sacred rites performed will be
of considerable interest to the anthropologist.

998   Visser, M. W. de. The Arhats in China and Japan.
        Berlin: Oesterheld and Company, 1923. 215 p.
        This is a full description of a particular ceremony
performed in honor of the sixteen arhats.

999   Welch, H. H. The Practice of Chinese Buddhism
        1900-1950. See entry no. 775.

1000 Wirz, P. Exorcism and the Art of Healing in Ceylon.
        See entry no. 528.

                    SCHOOLS OF BUDDHISM

HINAYANA or THERAVADA

1001 Baptist E. C. Nibbana or the Kingdom. See entry
        no. 914.

1002 Buddhaghosa. The Path of Purification. See entry
        no. 1158.

1003 Conze, E. Buddhist Scripture. See entry no. 1165.

1004 Conze, E. Buddhist Texts through the Ages. See
        entry no. 1166.

1005 Davids, T. W. R. Buddhist Suttas. Translated from
        Pali. Oxford: Clarendon Press, 1900. (Sacred
        Books of the East, XI.)

This is the translation from the Pali of seven of the
basic discourses or Suttas of Theravada Buddhism. The all-
important first sermon of the Buddha, discussing the "foundation of the kingdom of righteousness," is included. Each
of these fundamental sermons is preceded by a short critical
introduction by the translator.

1006   Dhammapada. The Dhammapada; A Collection of
       Verse. See entry no. 1175.

1007   Digha-nikaya. Dialogues of Buddha. See entry no.
       1183.

1008   Donath, D. C. Buddhism for the West. See entry
       no. 762.

1009   Keith, A. B. Buddhist Philosophy in India and Ceylon.
       See entry no. 816.

1010   King, W. L. A Thousand Lives Away. London:
       Bruno Cassirer, 1964. 238 p.
       This is a valuable addition to the world's knowledge
of Theravada Buddhism. The author's analysis is scientific,
and he concludes that such comparison, though facile to a
point, is profitable. The real value of the book is its
analysis of meditation, its place in Buddhist practice as a
whole and its manifold methods in Burma. The author concludes with a discussion on the comparative merits of meditation and doctrine, and the place of inner experience in the
use of both.

1011   Landon, K. P. Southeast Asia: Crossroad of Re-
       ligions. Chicago: University of Chicago, 1949.
       215 p.
       This work consists of the Haskell Lectures in
Comparative Religion, delivered at the University of Chicago
in 1947, on Malay peninsular religion.

1012   Ling, T. O. Buddhism and the Mythology of Evil;
       A Study in Theravada Buddhism. London: Allen
       and Unwin, 1963. 179 p.
       Dr. Ling has given a survey of various popular
beliefs about demonology in ancient India and draws his material from this source in the introductory chapter. With
the advent of the Buddhist teaching the approach to evil and
the image of evil both changed. It places the Mara legend,
which it treats with a sound critical judgment, in the context

of the Pali Canon.   This work gives judicious annotations, a
scholarly appendix and very adequate bibliography and indexes.

1013 Milindapanha. The Questions of King Milinda.   Trans-
          lated from Pali by T. W. R. Davids.   Oxford:
          Clarendon Press, 1890-1894.   2 vols.   (Sacred Books
          of the East, XXXV-XXXVI.)
     This is one of the most important prose philosophi-
cal works of Theravada Buddhism, translated from the text
of discussions of the Greek king, Milinda, and the Buddhist
monk, Nagasena.

1014 Nanananda, B.   Concept and Reality in Early Buddhist
          Thought.   Kandy, Ceylon: Buddhist Publication
          Society, 1971.   143 p.
     The author attempts to explain the two important
terms "papanca" and "papanca-sanna-sankha," which occur
so often in the basic sutta literature.   This study will be a
great help to students interested in studying Hinayana theory
and practice.

1015 Pachow, W.   A Comparative Study of the Pratimoska.
          New Delhi: Indian Cultural Society, 1959.   219 p.
     This book contains a scholarly study of the laws of
Vinaya as contained in the scriptures of various schools that
sprang up during the centuries prior to the advent of Mahayana Buddhism.   The author collected from Chinese sources
the Pratimoksa rules of the six major Hinayana schools and
has compared them with Pali Patimokkha.   This book is a
valuable source for the students of Vinaya and also students
of early Buddhism, with special reference to the authenticity
of the Councils and the origin of the traditional 18 schools of
Hinayana Buddhism.

1016 Ray, N. R.   An Introduction to the Study of Theravada
          Buddhism in Burma.   Calcutta: University of Cal-
          cutta, 1946.   306 p.
     This work is a study in Indo-Burmese historical and
cultural relations from the earliest times to the Britist conquest.

1017 Slater, R. H. L.   Paradox and Nirvana.   New York:
          Columbia University Press, 1950.   145 p.
     This is a study of religious ultimates with special
reference to Theravada Buddhism.   See also entry no. 508.

1018   Snellgrove, D.   Buddhist Himalaya.   New York:
            Philosophical Library, 1957.   324 p.
       The author gives attention to Tibetan history and
religion.   He also investigates Buddhism in Nepal, Tantric
Buddhism, and Tibetan Buddhism.   This work also has many
translated materials including an invocation, the order of
ceremony in a monastery, a prayer, a portion from a Tantric
text, and excerpts from historical annals.

1019   Ward, C. H. S.   Buddhism, Vol. One: Hinayana.
            London: Epworth Press, 1947.   143 p.
       This is a revision of a book first published as
Outlines of Buddhism in 1934.   The first part of the work
contains the Pali sources and the life of Gotama.   The
second part gives early Buddhist doctrines, and the last
part is a brief sketch of the Buddha's disciples and the historical development of Buddhism.   The author also gives a
selected bibliography and an index of names and subjects.

1020   Yu, L. K.   Practical Buddhism.   London: Rider,
            1971.   192 p.
       The author gives Chinese historical background of
Hinayana and Mahayana Buddhism as practiced.   The author
adds some personal accounts.

MADHYAMIKA

1021   Prajnaparamita Selections; Selected Sayings from the
            Perfection of Wisdom, chosen, arranged, and trans-
            lated by E. Conze.   London: The Buddhist Society,
            1955.   125 p.
       This anthology, containing original translations
from the Prajnaparamita literature of Mahayana Buddhism,
is devoted primarily to the Madhyamika System.   Along with
T. R. V. Murti's The Central Philosophy of Buddhism,
which treats the same subject, it now places the Western
world in a much better position to become acquainted with
the total thrust of the Prajnaparamita development.   The
selections are classified under the three main headings of
the sangha (order), the dharma (doctrine), and the Buddha.

1022   Ramanan, K. V.   Nagarjuna's Philosophy as Presented
            in the Maha-prajnaparamita-Sastra.   Rutland, Vt.:
            Tuttle, 1968.   409 p.
       This work provides much useful information about
the early and later developments of the Mahayana Madhyamika

philosophy in India and China. Arrangement of works is
very well done. Following a preface containing its purpose
as well as a general outline, a long introduction is devoted
to the problems of the life and work of Nagarjuna, and the
basic conceptions of his philosophy.

1023   Robinson, R. H.   Early Madhyamika in India and
         China. Madison: University of Wisconsin, 1967.
         The author is professor of Indian studies at the Uni-
versity of Wisconsin, and the book is his doctoral thesis
submitted to London University. The title is highly significant and is an important system of Buddhist thought. In
China it became known as the Three Treatise School, or
San-lun in Japan; it is based on the Sutras of the Perfection
of Wisdom and the doctrine of emptiness. The author describes the early Indian phase of the school, its literature
and teachings, and the early exponents of the Madhyamika
in China. He gives some interesting documents relevant to
the subject matter of this study.

MAHAYANA

1024   Ashvagosha.   The Awakening of Faith.   Translated
         with commentary by Yoshita S. Hakeda. New York:
         Columbia University Press, 1967. Also: transla-
         ted by Timothy Richard, edited with introduction by
         Alan Hull Walton, foreword by Aldous Huxley (1907).
         University Books Reprint, 1967. 128 p.
         Originally written in Sanskrit about 600 years after
the death of the Buddha, the work was later translated into
Chinese in A.D. 550. It contains the fundamental doctrines
of the Mahayana school of Buddhism by an Indian poet of
the first or second century A.D. The translator of the University Books edition is a British scholar who spent most of
his life in China. The author Hakeda has based his translation on the old text by Daramartha. His intent "is to present as accurate as possible a translation of the text as it
is interpreted in the light of the traditional commentaries, at
the same time taking into consideration the results of
modern critical scholarship on the text and the history of
Buddhist thought in general...." This work will contribute
to the further study of the Mahayana text.

1025   Barnett, L. D.   The Path of Light.   See entry no.
         1044.

1026   Buddhist Mahayana Texts.   Translated by E. B.
       Cowell, F. M. Muller, and J. Takakusu.   London:
       Oxford, 1894.   2 vols. in 1.   (Sacred Books of the
       East, XLIX.)
       This contains translations of the basic Mahayana
Buddhist texts.   The first part is the eloquent life of Buddha
of Asvaghosa, and the second part includes texts dealing with
the pure land, the Diamond Sutra, and larger and smaller
texts of the "Prajnaparamitahrdaya."   A text from the
Japanese devotional school "Amitayurdhyana Sutra" is also
included.

1027   Burtt, E. A.   The Teaching of the Compassionate
       Buddha.   See entry no. 1225.

1028   Conze, E.   Buddhist Scripture.   See entry no. 1165.

1029   _____.   Buddhist Texts Through the Ages.   See
       entry no. 1166.

1030   Coomaraswamy, A. K.   Buddha and the Gospel of
       Buddhism.   See entry no. 1227.

1031   Donath, D. C.   Buddhism for the West.   See entry
       no. 762.

1032   Keith, A. B.   Buddhist Philosophy in India and Ceylon.
       See entry no. 816.

1033   Lankavatara-Sutra; A Mahayana Text.   See entry no.
       1195.

1034   Madiyanse, N.   Mahayana Monuments in Ceylon.
       Colombo: M. D. Gunasena, 1967.   135 p.

1035   Mahayanasutras.   The Perfection of Wisdom.   The
       Career of the Predestined Buddha.   A Selection of
       Mahayana Scriptures.   Translated from Sanskrit by
       E. J. Thomas.   London: Murray, 1952.   90 p.
       This work contains a selection of Mahayana Buddhist
texts competently translated from the original Sanskrit.   It
includes a parable indicating the superiority of the Mahayana
Buddhism to the other forms and the nature of the Bodhisattva
(savior).   His training, confession, duties, and worship are
indicated by these selections.

1036   McGovern, W. M.   An Introduction to Mahayana

Buddhism. New York: Dutton, 1922. 233 p.
This work is intended to serve as a guide to the
general reader and to lead up to a more detailed study of
the subject. It points out the difference between Mahayana
and Hinayana Buddhism and in the conclusion gives a short
history of Buddhism and the principal Buddhist sects.

1037 Murti, T. R. V. Central Philosophy of Buddhism;
A Study of the Madhyamika. 2nd ed. See entry
no. 821.

1038 Pachow, W. A Comparative Study of the Pratimoksa.
See entry no. 1015.

1039 Prajnaparamita Selections. Selected Sayings from the
Perfection of Wisdom.... See entry no. 1204.

1040 Reichelt, K. L. Truth and Tradition in Chinese Buddhism. See entry no. 555.

1041 Saddharmapundarika. The Saddharma-pundarika; or,
The Lotus of the True Law. See entry no. 1206.

1042 Sangharakshita, B. A Survey of Buddhism. See
entry no. 122.

1043 Santideva. Entering the Path of Enlightenment; The
Bodhicaryavatara of the Buddhist Poet Santideva.
Translated with a guide by Marion L. Matics. New
York: Macmillan, 1972. 318 p.
This is the first complete English translation of the
Bodhicaryavatara. Santideva, an eighth-century poet and
monk at the Buddhist University of Nalanda, describes and
explains the various steps one must take in order to become
a Bodhisattva. This work offers practical explanations and
methods for realizing the Prajna-Paramita vision of Maha-
yana Buddhism. There is another translation by L. D.
Barnett published in 1947 by Murray of London.

1044 Santideva. The Path of Light; Rendered for the First
Time into English from the Bodhicharyavatara of
Santa-devi; A Manual of Mahayana Buddhism. Trans-
lated by L. D. Barnett. London: Murray, 1947;
New York: Grove, 1909. 111 p.
This is a partial translation from the Sanskrit text
of Santideva's Bodhicharyavatara. It is a basic manual of
Mahayana Buddhism, treating the nature of enlightenment and
those who pursue it.

1045   Sgam-po-pa; The Jewel Ornament of Liberation.
       Translated by H. V. Guenther. London: Rider
       and Company, 1959. 333 p.
       This work should be in the hands of all serious
students of the Dharma. It belongs to the class of literature known in Tibet as Lamrim (the successive stages of
the path), which describes one by one all the things we have
to do, feel, and think in order to win Buddhahood. Most of
the book's contents would commend themselves to almost any
follower of the Mahayana, and a large portion of it is made
up of quotations from the Sutras and Shastras.

1046   Sharma, C. Dialectic in Buddhism and Vedanta. New
       York: Hafner Pub. Co., 1952. 272 p.
       This work is a doctoral dissertation approved by the
University of Allahabad. The first half of the dissertation
is devoted to an exposition of the philosophy of the Mahayana,
to Asvaghosa, and to other Buddhist themes. The second
half deals with the attitude toward Buddhism in the writings
of the sixth century Vedanta philosopher Gaudapada.

1047   Shcherbatskoi, F. I. The Central Conception of Bud-
       dhism and the Meaning of the Word "Dharma." 2nd
       ed. See entry no. 313.

1048   Slater, R. H. L. Paradox and Nirvana. See entry
       no. 508.

1049   Suzuki, B. L. Mahayana Buddhism. With an intro-
       duction by D. T. Suzuki and a foreword by C.
       Humphreys. New York: Collier, 1959. 146 p.
       This work is written in a manner which does not
assume previous knowledge on the part of the reader and it
includes Mahayana scriptures and other writings from the
Japanese not readily available elsewhere.

1050   _____. Mahayana Buddhism; A Brief Outline. New
       York: Macmillan, 1971. 158 p.
       This paperback is an abridged version of a book that
has already seen three editions. The present edition is
minus the introduction by the late Dr. D. T. Suzuki and
minus the foreword by C. Humphreys. The author adds
more information on historical development, philosophy,
sutras, and the relationship between the Hinayana and the
Mahayana and particularly Mahayana practices. An excellent
bibliography and a glossary are given along with the twelve
principles of Buddhism.

1051   Suzuki, D. T.   The Lankavatara Sutra.   See entries
       no. 1055, 1195.

1052   _____ .   Manual of Zen Buddhism.   Rev. ed., 1950.
       See entry no. 1128.

1053   _____ .   On Indian Mahayana Buddhism.   New York:
       Harper and Row, 1968.   284 p.
          This work gives an historical development of Maha-
       yana Buddhism which originates from Indian Buddhist Sutras
       and then moves to China, to Korea and to Japan.   Biblio-
       graphical notes, a glossary of Sanskrit terms, and an intro-
       duction are also given.

1054   _____ .   Outlines of Mahayana Buddhism.   New York:
       Schocken Books, 1963.   383 p.
          This is a reprint from Bailey Brothers of London
       in 1907.   Although the author has great knowledge on this
       subject, he disregards some new developments and fails to
       supplement his old edition.   As a pioneer work, this is still
       magnificent as a textbook on its subject.   Alan Watts pro-
       vides a "Prefatory Essay."   This is an excellent, though
       limited survey of trends of current philosophic thought in the
       light of Mahayana Buddhism.

1055   _____ .   Studies in the Lankavatara Sutra.   2nd ed.
       London: Routledge, 1956.   300 p.
          This is one of the most important texts of Mahayana
       Buddhism, in which almost all its principal tenets are pre-
       sented, including the teaching of Zen.   It is a useful com-
       panion book to the author's translation of the Lankavatara
       Sutra (see entry no. 1195), one of the most important re-
       ligious texts of Mahayana Buddhism.   The text is regarded
       and interpreted primarily from the standpoint of Zen teachings,
       a subject on which the author is a specialist.

1056   Thomas, E. J.   The History of Buddhist Thought.   2nd
       ed.   See entry no. 405.

1057   Tripitaka.   The Quest of Enlightenment; A Selection
       of the Buddhist Scriptures.   See entry no. 1212.

1058   Vajrachchedika.   Buddhist Wisdom Books.   See entry
       no. 1266.

1059   Vajrachchedika Prajnaparamita.   Edited and translated
       with an introduction and glossary by E. Conze.

Rome: Istituto Estremo Oriente, 1957. 112 p.
This text, best known to most as the Diamond
Sutra, is an event of some importance. For the study of
Mahayana Buddhism the Diamond Sutra is essential. The
glossary explains the principal Sanskrit terms. In the introduction the author discusses the state of the text, its historical context and its basic ideas, as well as the principles
which have guided the translation.

1060 Ward, C. H. S. Buddhism. Vol. Two: Mahayana.
       London: Epworth Press, 1952. 222 p.
The first part of the book gives a brief history and
the characteristics of Mahayana texts. In the second part
the developing concepts of the Buddha and bodhisattva are
traced from the early Pali Pitakas and Mahayana scriptures.
And the last part gives a comparative study between Hinayana and Mahayana doctrines.

1061 Yu, L. K. Practical Buddhism. London: Rider,
       1971. 192 p.
The historical background of Hinayana and Mahayana
Buddhism as practiced in China is presented. The author
adds some personal accounts.

TANTRIC BUDDHISM

1062 Guenther, H. V. Treasure on the Tibetan Middle
       Way. See entry no. 738.

1063 Rawson, P. The Art of Tantra. See entry no. 179.

1064 Snellgrove, D. L. Buddhist Himalaya. London:
       Oxford, 1957. 324 p.
In India the Abhidharma, Mahayana, and Tantra, in
China the Chan school, and in Japan the Zen give the most
creative efforts to recapture the Buddha's original experience
and insight. Among these the Tantra is so far the least
known. After a sketch of Indian Buddhism up to about A. D.
500, the author outlines the principles of Tantric Buddhism,
follows it through its developments in Nepal and Tibet, describes Tibetan ceremonies and then concludes with a few
reflections.

ZEN

1065 Aitken, R. Zen Training: A Personal Account.

Honolulu: Old Island Books, 1960. 26 p.
This is a small pamphlet of great interest to all in
the West interested in Zen. It is the factual account by a
young man who spent a substantial period in Zen monasteries
as an accepted pupil. All aspects of the training are described, and a typical day is examined in detail.

1066 Ames, V. M. Zen and American Thought. See
      entry no. 760.

1067 Benoit, H. Let Go! Theory and Practice of Detach-
      ment According to Zen. Translated by A. W. Low.
      London: Allen and Unwin, 1962. 336 p.
In the preface the author states the purpose of his
book. He says that his previous work, The Supreme Doctrine, does not reach a solution to the question of an effective technique for letting go. The third part of the present
work is entirely devoted to this exercise, to the analysis
of language on which this exercise is based, and necessary
conclusions for it to be effective.

1068 _____. The Supreme Doctrine: Psychological
      Studies in Zen Thought. See entry no. 862.

1069 Blyth, R. H. Zen and Zen Classics. London: Hef-
      fer's, 1960- . Vol. 1- .
So far of eight volumes planned, five have appeared,
covering the history of Zen in China, Korea (where Mr.
Blyth spent 16 years in Zen monasteries), and Japan, and
containing various essays on Zen subjects. Each book is
concise and sets forth the unusual combination of scholarship, practical experience, and basically Zen humor which
characterize and make a classic work of the author's Zen
English literature.

1070 Briggs, W. Anthology of Zen. Introduction by W.
      Barrett. New York: Grove Press, 1961. 300 p.
The selection is excellent, for though many of the
35 items come from books long out of print, it is well to
preserve the best of this early material, and the net result
of the editor's choice is a well-balanced arrangement of an
immense variety of approaches to the same experience.

1071 Chang, C. C. Practice of Zen. New York: Harper,
      1959. 199 p.
A Chinese Buddhist scholar has selected and translated a number of short autobiographies and discourses of the

great Zen masters, from ancient and modern sources. In
addition, he includes his own comments on Zen practice and
a survey of the essential aspects of Zen Buddhism. The
work also contains a bibliography.

1072 Dogen. A Primer of Soto Zen. See entry no. 443.

1073 Dumoulin, H. The Development of Chinese Zen After
        the Sixth Patriarch in the Light of Mumonkan. See
        entry no. 539.

1074 _____. A History of Zen Buddhism. New York:
        Pantheon Books, 1963. 335 p.
        The author who is a Roman Catholic priest has very
extensive experience and study on Zen Buddhism. He has
tried to investigate Zen history from the evolution of the
early Buddhism through the present practice of Zen Buddhism.
Zen development in China, the transplanting of Zen to Japan,
the work of Dogen and other developers in Japan, the en-
counter of Zen with Christianity, and contemporary Zen are
the main topics which the author has here discussed.

1075 The Eastern Buddhist, Memorial Issue to Dr. D. T.
        Suzuki. Kyoto: Eastern Buddhist, 1967. 232 p.
        For the 97th birthday of Dr. Suzuki, The Eastern
Buddhist issued a memorial book which contains some twenty
articles and as many reminiscences by a distinguished set
of writers. Throughout this remarkable volume there are
flashes of insight into the teacher's views on all manner of
subjects. There is much true understanding of Zen to be had
from this issue.

1076 Fontein, J. Zen Painting and Calligraphy. See entry
        no. 213.

1077 Genro, F. The Iron Flute: 100 Zen Koans with
        Commentary. See entry no. 1116.

1078 Hai, H. The Path to Sudden Attainment; A Treatise
        of the Chen (Zen) School of Chinese Buddhism.
        Translated by John Blofeld. London: Buddhist So-
        ciety of London, 1948. 51 p.
        The author philosophizes that, as concepts, neither
path nor attainment exists, that there is nothing in the universe that is static, save in the mind of man. If you think
you are practicing non-attachment, read this little work.

1079   Hasumi, T.   Zen in Japanese Art, a Way of Spiritual
       Experience.   See entry no. 167.

1080   Hayakawa, S.   Zen Showed Me the Way; To Peace,
       Happiness and Tranquility.   Edited by Croswell
       Bowen.   New York: Bobbs, 1960.   256 p.
       This is Mr. Hayakawa's autobiographical version of
Zen which seems little more than a method of mind control
and concentration with the goal of cultivating serenity and
will power.

1081   Herrigel, A. L.   Zen in the Art of Flower Arrange-
            ment.   Foreword by D. T. Suzuki.   Translated
            from the German by R. F. C. Hull.   London:
            Branford, 1958; Routledge and Kegan Paul, 1957.
            124 p.
       This serves as an introduction to the spirit of the
Japanese art of flower arrangement.   The author gives her
own experience in Japan working with one of the great of
the Japanese flower arrangers.   The importance of the work
stems from her comparison of the flower arrangements with
the inner attitudes.

1082   Herrigel, E.   The Method of Zen.   Translated by
            R. F. C. Hull.   London: Routledge; New York:
            Pantheon Books, 1959.   124 p.
       The book consists of material drawn from the many
papers on Zen Buddhism found after the author's death in
1955.   These notes range over a wide field and describe,
among other things, the techniques used in Zen training.

1083   _____ .   Zen in the Art of Archery.   Translated
            by R. F. C. Hull, with an introduction by D. T.
            Suzuki.   New York: Pantheon Books, Inc., 1953.
            109 p.
       This work gives an autobiographical account of a
six-year course in archery with Master Kenzo Awa, a cele-
brated Japanese archer.   The author is more concerned
with an approach to the nature of Zen training and to the
Zen experience.   Dr. Suzuki recommends the book very
highly.

1084   no entry

1085   Hisamatsu, S.   Zen and the Fine Arts.   Tokyo:
            Kodansha International, 1971.   400 p.

This is the first book to disclose the spiritual relationship between Zen and the fine arts and to show its in-
trinsic meaning. The author, former professor of Religion
and Buddhism at Kyoto University, is one of the foremost
scholars in both the fields of Zen and art in Japan. 293
art plates and explanatory notes are given.

1086 Huang-Po. Zen Teaching. Translated by John Blo-
         feld. New York: Grove, 1959. 135 p.
      This is a translation of a 19th-century Chinese
Buddhist text. It is a concise account of the teachings of
a great master of the Dhyana Sect.

1087 Humphreys, C. A Western Approach to Zen. London:
         Allen and Unwin, 1972. 210 p.
      The characteristics of Buddhism represented by Zen
allows the author the opportunity to use his talents of poetry
and humor. This work forms an anthology of memorable,
helpful phrases. The author first gives an exposition of the
basic principles of Buddhism, clearly explaining the role of
Buddha and his most important teachings.

1088 _____. Zen: A Way of Life. New York: Emer-
         son Books, 1965. 196 p.
      In the introduction of this book the author considers
the qualities necessary to a Zen follower. Part One is
devoted to basic principles, the Three Signs of Being, the
Four Noble Truths, the Eightfold Path, Karma, Rebirth,
concentration, and meditation, which are essential to the
understanding of Zen. Part Two considers the expansion of
the Mahayana and is followed by selections from the Mahayana scriptures. Part Three looks at Zen from all its
aspects.

1089 _____. Zen Buddhism. London: Heinemann,
         1949. 241 p.
      This work concerns that form of Buddhism that is
unique in the history of religious philosophy. Of the schools
of religious experience it alone has no reliance on scriptures
or sermons, on services or prayer, or on ritual of any kind.

1090 _____. Zen Comes West; The Present and Future
         of Zen Buddhism in Britain. New York: Mac-
         millan, 1960. 207 p.
      This is a collection of letters pro and con, on the
successes and failures of Humphreys' group to reach an

answer to the 20th-century koan. Eight sets of notes from
various talks to the Zen class are represented.

1091 Kapleau, P. The Three Pillars of Zen. Tokyo:
      John Weatherhill, 1965. 350 p.
      Professor Huston Smith writes in his foreword, "a
remarkable book that is certain to assume a permanent place
in the library of Zen literature in the Western languages, "
as his recommendation for this work. Part I discusses
Zazen, Zen mind-body training; Part II consists of eight re-
ports on experiences of enlightenment; Part III has four
sections on Dogen, the Zen master, the ten ox-herding
pictures, illustrations of Zazen postures, and notes on Zen
vocabulary and Buddhist doctrines.

1092 Koestler, A. The Lotus and the Robot. London:
      Hutchinson, 1960; New York: Macmillan, 1961.
      296 p.
      The book starts with the description of four con-
temporary Indian saints and goes on to the physical and
mystical aspects of Yoga and to recent research into its
supernatural claims. The second part of the book contains
impressions of the contradictory trends in modern Japan.
The author gets Taoism and Zen somewhat mixed up, com-
plicating further a complicated subject.

1093 Lassalle, H. M. Zen, Way to Enlightenment. Lon-
      don: Burns and Oates, 1968. 126 p.
      Father Lassalle lived in Japan for about thirty years.
This book is an account of his study and practice of Zen
meditation, leading to the view that, practiced in the right
way, Zen could be useful to anyone regardless of his religious convictions and denomination.

1094 Leggett, T. A First Zen Reader. Rutland, Vt.:
      Tuttle, 1960. 236 p.
      The author, who is now in charge of the Japanese
section of the BBC, is better known as the leading English
exponent of Judo and as a lecturer on Zen Buddhism. In
this work he has collated and translated extracts from the
writings of Zen masters, old and new, "to form an approach
to Zen for the Western reader." His book certainly gives
the general idea of Zen theory and practice.

1095 _____. The Tiger's Cave. London: Rider, 1964.
      191 p.

This is a translation of Japanese Zen texts. The
book includes a commentary on the Heart Sutra by Abbot
Obora of the Soto Sect, a translation of Hakuin's Yasenkanna,
an article comprised of two sermons by Rosen Takashina,
primate of the Soto Sect, and several interesting short
pieces, including a study of the physical reactions accom-
panying different meditation methods as indicated on an
electroencephalograph.

1096 Linssen, R. Living Zen. Foreward by Christmas
        Humphreys. New York: Macmillan, 1960. 348 p.
        This work serves as an introduction to the discipline
and technique of Zen Buddhism as a way of life seeking
liberation from self-centered thought and feeling, drawing
upon Western science for the light it throws on the process.
There is a comparative study of the Zen experience with that
of Christianity.

1097 Luk, C. Chan and Zen Teaching. London: Rider,
        1962. 306 p.
        This work includes three important texts, namely:
the Sutra of the Sixth Patriarch, Yung Chia's Song of Enlightenment, and the Sutra of Complete Enlightenment. The
first two are well known to the West and have been translated before. The author's new translation has definitely
made a considerable improvement both in accuracy and in
interpretation. The third text is new to the West; in China
it is regarded as one of the most important sutras of the
Hua Yen School.

1098 Lu K'uan Yu. Ch'an and Zen Teaching. London:
        Rider, 1960. 255 p.
        The book falls into four parts. The first gives
Master Hsu Yun's discourses about Ch'an training, delivered
around 1930. The second six stories describe the concurrent
causes producing the awakening of six masters whose inner
potentialities had been activated to the full, ready for in-
stantaneous union with the absolute. Parts three and four
consist of Han-Shan's commentaries to the Diamond Sutra.

1099 Masunaga, R. The Soto Approach to Zen. Tokyo:
        Layman Buddhist Society Press, 1958. 215 p.
        The author who is Professor of Buddhist Philosophy
and History of Zen Buddhism at Komazawa University at
Tokyo, presents a very important account of the Soto Sect
of Zen in Japan. It will be interesting to compare it with
D. T. Suzuki's, who represents the Rinzai Sect. The author

discusses Buddhism, Zen and Dogen, who brought Soto from China to Japan in 1228. This work is for general readers who do not have much background in Buddhism.

1100   Merton, T.   The Zen Revival.   New York: Farrar,
         Straus and Giroux, 1967.   35 p.
         In this small pamphlet the author considers Zen in relation to the criticisms on Buddhism by Zaehner, Teilhard de Chardin and Thomas Dumoulin, contemporary Roman Catholics.

1101   Mitchell, E. P.   Sun Buddhas, Moon Buddhas; A Zen
         Quest.   New York: Weatherhill, 1973.   214 p.
         This work is the chronicle of one woman's continuing quest for her true nature.   With compassion, humor and a great talent for anecdote, the author recounts the many ways in which people of widely different backgrounds and beliefs experience the quest for the true self.   It is also a dialogue between East and West, between Buddhism and Christianity, that should broaden the perspectives of any on either side.

1102   Miura, I.   Zen Dust; The History of the Koan in
         Rinzai.   New York: Harcourt, Brace and World,
         Inc., 1966.   547 p.
         The book is about the koan, which has proved to be a powerful medium of communication.   The first part of the book is devoted to the koan from the historical perspective. Part two discusses a hierarchical classification of the various types of koans.   Part three is a selection from the anthology of phrases used in koan study.   The author provides a very extensive bibliography.

1103   _____.   The Zen Koan.   Kyoto: First Zen Institute
         of America in Japan, 1965.   145 p.
         According to the author the Zen koan "concerns the course of Koan study, which was originated by the eighteenth-century Japanese Zen master Hakuin Ekaku which is now used in all Rinzai Zen monasteries in Japan."   Part I discusses koan and a history of its use in Chinese and Japanese. Part II is a study of koan by M. I. Roshi.   Part III is a Zen anthology.

1104   Ogata, S.   Zen for the West: For the Buddhist So-
         ciety of London.   New York: Dial Press, 1959.
         182 p.
         A Japanese Zen monk and teacher explains the doctrines and experiences of Zen Buddhism.

1105   Original Teaching of Chan Buddhism: Selected from
         the Transmission of the Lamp.   Translated with
         introduction by Chang Chung-Yuan.   New York:
         Pantheon Books, 1970.   333 p.
         This study is a very valuable contribution to the
study of Chan ("Zen," in Japan) Buddhism.   The author
gives the basic characteristics of the teaching of Chan and
its pedagogic informality which has been exemplified in the
dialogues between the Chan masters and their disciples.
The records of these dialogues have contributed significantly
to the treasures of Buddhist literature.

1106   Pirsig, R. M.   Zen and the Art of Motorcycle
         Maintenance.   New York: William Morrow, 1974.
         412 p.
         An autobiography of the mind and body, this is the
story of a summer month's motorcycle trip taken by the
narrator and his 11-year-old son, from their home in Minne-
sota to California.   Despite the title, its relevance to Buddhism (i.e., to Zen) is by analogy only.

1107   The Platform Sutra of the Sixth Patriarch: The Text
         of the Tun-huang Manuscript.   See entry no. 1260.

1108   Powell, R.   Zen and Reality: An Approach to Sanity
         and Happiness on a Non-sectarian Basis.   London:
         Allen and Unwin, 1960.   140 p.
         This work contains 30 short essays originally given
as lectures to the London Buddhist Society.   Mainly they
are on the philosophical basis of non-duality and non-exis-
tence of the "I" as propounded by Buddhism.

1109   no entry

1110   The Recorded Sayings of Layman P'ang; A Ninth
         Century Zen Classic.   New York: Weatherhill,
         1972.   109 p.
         Translated from the Chinese by Ruth Fuller Sasaki,
Yoshitaka Iriya and Dana Fraser, the book consists of
revealing incidents about P'ang and his family, followed by
a representative selection of his verses and a portion of
verse praising him by later Zen followers.   The book is
well known in China and Japan and some of the anecdotes
are used as subjects for Zen meditation.

1111   Reps, P.   Zen Flesh, Zen Bones.   Rutland, Vt.:
         Tuttle, 1957.   211 p.

The first section is "101 Zen Stories" from the 13th-century teacher Muju and from anecdotes of masters well into modern times. The second part, the famous Mumonkan, with its 48 koans, each with a commentary by Mumon in prose and another in verse, is a source-book for study. The third section is "Ten Bulls," first published as a pamphlet in 1935 under that name, but better known to the West as the "Tex Ox-herding Pictures."

1112   Ross, N. W.   The World of Zen; An East-West
        Anthology.   See entry no. 149.

1113   Sasaki, R. F.   Rinzai Zen Study for Foreigners in
        Japan.   Kyoto: First Zen Institute of America in
        Japan, 1960.   104 p.
        This is a valuable booklet for the study by any who are interested in Zen. Here is a candid description of the hardships and expense of that life.

1114   Sato, K.   The Zen Life.   Photographs by Sosei
        Kuzunishi.   London: Weatherhill, 1972.   190 p.
        The first half of the book pictures life in a Rinzai Zen monastery, Empuku-ji. It gives everyday discipline and activity in the life of a monastery and its training methods. The author is a psychologist and so is mainly interested in the conversion psychology of the Harada Zen.

1115   Senzaki, N. and McCandless, R. S. (ed. & trans-
        lator).   Buddhism and Zen.   New York: Philosophi-
        cal Library, 1953.   91 p.
        This work contains the questions most frequently asked by non-Buddhists along with the appropriate answers, notes on meditation, a long section on Sho-do-ka by Yoka-Daishi, mainly sermonettes on Zen with comments by Senzaki, and fragmentary notes attributed to Bodhidharma's disciples from the Aurel Stein in Peking.

1116   _____ and _____. (translator & ed.).   The
        Iron Flute: 100 Zen Koan; With Commentary by
        Genro, Fugai, and Nyogen.   Illustrated by Toriichi
        Murashima.   Rutland, Vt.:   Tuttle, 1960.   91 p.
        Koan are mental exercises which are designed to facilitate a student's intuitive understanding of Zen Buddhism. This is a good translation of the classical koan, together with the comments of masters from the 18th-century Zen master Genro and his pupil Fugai to a 20th-century master, one of the authors, Senzaki. The illustrations, painted especially for this volume by a Zen artist, are very good.

1117   Shaw, R. D. M.   The Blue Cliff Records.   Translated
       and edited with commentary by Dr. Shaw.   London:
       Michael Joseph, 1961.   299 p.
       This is the first attempt to translate into English the
central part of the most famous collection of Zen history.
The Blue Cliff Records were compiled in the 11th century by
the abbot of a Chan temple and include his cryptic words and
also the introductory words of a later abbot.   The true
strength and character of Zen are fully revealed by the author's own explanatory notes.

1118   Shibayama, A. Z.   A Flower Does Not Talk.   See
       entry no. 469.

1119   _____.   Zen Comments on the Mumonkan.   New
       York: Harper and Row, 1974.   361 p.
       This is an outstanding source of practical Zen
teaching and an authoritative translation with commentary of
a basic Zen text.   The basis of the book is the Mumonkan,
a classic collection of 48 cryptic sayings or koan commonly
used in monastic teaching.   A glossary is included which
identifies names, places, and writings, and clarifies the Zen
meaning of terms.

1120   Spiegelberg, F.   Zen, Rocks and Waters.   See entry
       no. 232.

1121   Stryk, L.   World of the Buddha: A Reader....   See
       entry no. 125.

1122   _____ and Ikenoto, T. (eds.).   Zen: Poems,
       Prayers, Sermons, Anecdotes, Interviews.   New
       York: Doubleday Anchor Books, 1965.   160 p.
       This work is accounted a worthy contribution to the
understanding of Zen.   The selections are revealing, and the
translations very good.   It is highly recommended.

1123   Suzuki, D. T.   Essays in Zen Buddhism.   New York:
       Harper, 1953.   383 p.
       This is the first American edition of this interpre-
tation of Zen Buddhism, the branch of Buddhism developed
by Chinese scholars.   This is an easily read, but comprehensive exposition of the philosophy of spiritual development
known as "sudden enlightenment."

1124   _____.   The Essentials of Zen Buddhism: An
       Anthology of the Writings of Daisetz T. Suzuki.

Introduction by Bernard Phillips. New York:
Dutton, 1961. 544 p.
This convenient and authoritative work is recommended for anyone who does not need Suzuki's complete
works, but who is interested in a good volume on Zen.

1125 _____. The Field of Zen. Edited with a Foreword
by Christmas Humphreys. New York: Harper and
Row, 1969. 105 p.
This collection covers such a broad scope and is so
complete that its title is apt. It is mainly a collection of
talks and answers to questions given by Dr. Suzuki upon
various aspects of Zen Buddhism's training.

1126 _____. Introduction to Zen Buddhism. New York:
Grove, 1961. 136 p.
This work gives an interpretation of Zen by a
Japanese professor of Buddhist philosophy. It discloses the
system of the school of spiritual development known as Zen,
a special branch of Buddhism which claims to transmit the
quietness of that philosophy.

1127 _____. Living by Zen. New York: Rider, 1950.
187 p.
Dr. Suzuki is here describing a system which seeks
to free the mind from slavery to logical words and philosophical reason. The goal of Zen is the personal experience
of the flash of direct illumination, called satori, which
transcends the mind and its functioning.

1128 _____ (ed.). Manual of Zen Buddhism. Rev. ed.,
1950. Nottingham: Grove Evergreen Books, 1960.
232 p.
This work is an anthology from original sources,
containing reproductions of Buddhist paintings, drawings, and
religious statues. The object of the manual is to provide
information connected with Zen monastery life.

1129 _____. Sengai, the Zen Master. See entry no. 218.

1130 _____. Studies in the Lankavatara Sutra. See
entry no. 1055.

1131 _____. Studies in Zen. Edited by Christmas
Humphreys. New York: Philosophical Library,
1955. 212 p.
This work consists of seven articles and lectures by

the author as he was professor of Buddhist philosophy at the
Otani University at Kyoto.   The first essay covers concisely
the history of Zen.   The second study is a Zen teaching.
Also included are the papers read by Dr. Suzuki at the 1939
and the 1951 East-West Philosophers' Conferences.

1132 _____ . The Training of the Zen Buddhist Monk.
See entry no. 665.

1133 _____ . Zen and Japanese Culture. See entry no.
667.

1134 _____ . Zen Buddhism and Its Influences on
Japanese Culture. Kyoto: Eastern Buddhist Society, 1938. 288 p.
In these printed lectures the role of Zen in traditional Japanese arts, such as swordsmanship, the tea ceremony, and flower arrangement, is explained and interpreted
in relation to the love of nature.

1135 _____ , E. Fromm, et al. Zen Buddhism and
Psychoanalysis. See entry no. 867.

1136 _____ . Zen Buddhism, Selected Writings. Edited
by William Barrett. Garden City: Doubleday, 1956.
298 p.
The editor has selected seven of the best known of
Suzuki's essays on Zen Buddhism and studies in Zen.   The
following subject headings are listed: "The Meaning of Zen
Buddhism, " "The Historical Background of Zen Buddhism, "
"The Heart of Zen, " "Techniques of Zen, " "Zen and Philosophy, " and "Zen and Japanese Culture. "

1137 _____ . The Zen Doctrine of No-Mind; Significance
of the Sutra of Hui-neng. London: Buddhist Society, 1949. 155 p.
A leading exponent of Zen evaluates the meaningful-
ness of the writings of Hui-neng, who, along with his immediate disciples, developed Zen thought in China in the
seventh and eighth centuries.

1138 _____ . Zen Mind, Beginner's Mind. See entry
no. 471.

1139 Swann, J. Toehold on Zen. London: George Allen,
1962. 103 p.
The title is the key to the author's approach to Zen--

not at all pretentious and very engaging. The author is
trying to account a living Zen experience and begins with the
four faces of Zen. There is a pleasant chapter on the author's impressions of the famous exponents of Zen, including
Professor Ogata and Dr. Suzuki.

1140 Walker, K. Life's Long Journey. London: Gollancz,
        1960. 191 p.
        This is an illuminating book portraying some phases
of Zen Buddhism, written in biological, evolutionary and
psychological terms. The author has produced a philosophical account of life's long journey in evolving to man's present
state, looking towards his future enlightenment, which de-
pends upon individual and personal effort.

1141 Watts, A. W. The Book: On the Taboo Against
        Knowing Who You Are. New York: Pantheon, 1966.
        146 p.
        Certain aspects of Zen are presented here as a guide
to young people in particular. It offers a philosophy for the
"alienated." The individual is urged to consider himself not
as an "ego" but as a part of a great cosmic, harmonious
design, needing his cooperation rather than his continual
striving to better it as a world "outside" him. Watts says
we are our world, and we must accept it and fall in with its
rhythm and change it in spirit, becoming loving instruments
of something greater than ourselves.

1142 _____ . "This Is It," and Other Essays on Zen and
        Spiritual Experience. New York: Pantheon Books,
        1960. 158 p.
        This work is a series of essays written over the last
several years concerning the relation of spiritual or mystical
experience to ordinary material life.

1143 _____ . The Way of Liberation in Zen Buddhism.
        Los Angeles: American Academy of Asian Studies,
        1955. 24 p.
        The author, who heads his first page with a sketch
of a bamboo worthy of a great Japanese artist, is excellent
at epigrammatic form. He surveys the usual solutions to the
average mind's unhappy tensions and produces the Zen answer
to all problems, which is that the solution to any question
lies in the questioner.

1144 _____ . The Way of Zen. New York: Pantheon
        Books, 1957. 236 p.

This work is, for the general reader and the more serious student, a comprehensive, orderly and scholarly account of Zen including its historical background and its relation to Chinese and Indian ways of thought. It would make an excellent text for a general course on Zen and its philosophical and religious background.

1145   Wei, W. W. Why Lazarus Laughed. London: Routledge and Kegan Paul, 1960. 302 p.
The title is deliberately absurd and serves as a reminder that words may be radically different from the things they stand for. This book is a series of observations on the quasikoans provided by the section-headings, of which there are 133 in 294 pages. Sometimes the author seems to be pulling the reader's leg, but in Zen one must expect it.

1146   Wienpahl, P. Matter of Zen; A Brief Account of Zen. New York: New York University Press, 1964. 162 p.
This is a book of a young American's experience of Zen training in Japan. The author's main thesis is that Zen is Zazen, or Zen is sitting in meditation. He implies that true Zen training is only possible under a Japanese roshi. He dismisses all else, including the works of Dr. Suzuki, because such writers do not sufficiently emphasize the supreme importance of Zen sitting.

1147   _____ . Zen Diary. New York: Harper and Row, 1970. 244 p.
The author spent several months in Japan where he practiced both Zazen and Sawzen. This work is an account of his journey and is a record of a Western philosopher's own experience with Japanese Zen. It represents Zen as traditionally practiced in Japan.

1148   Woodworth, H. Zen, the Turn Towards Life. La Crosse, Wis.: Sumac Press, 1960. 40 p.
The author contends that the move towards Zen is what is important. He takes it to mean that he can safely ignore the history of Zen, the development of Zen, and its schools and authorities.

1149   Zen Buddhism. New York: Peter Pauper, 1959. 61 p.
This pocket size book is full of Zen parables and stories. It is good as the first reader for the Zen student.

1150   The Zen Master Hakuin: Selected Writings. See entry no. 284.

1151   The Zen Teaching of Hui Hai on Sudden Illumination.
          Translated by J. Blofeld. London: Rider and
          Company, 1962. 150 p.
          The translator's introduction is very good. This
work is complementary to the Society's previous work, The
Zen Teaching of Huang Po, in that it relates its doctrine to
the background principle of Mahayana as a whole.

SCRIPTURE

1152   Allen, G. F. Buddha's Words of Wisdom. London:
          Allen and Unwin, 1959. 88 p.
          The Buddhists' companion book, containing 365
maxims and utterances attributed to Gotama Buddha, contains a suitable Buddhist quotation for each day of the year,
most of which would make admirable themes for meditation.

1153   Beal, S. Buddhism in China. See entry no. 531.

1154   _____ . Buddhist Records of the Western World.
          Translated from Chinese. London: Trubner, 1884.
          2 vols.
          This work contains the accounts of the travels and
observations of Fa-Shien, Sung Yün, and Hsüan Chwang, who
made special journeys to India to secure Buddhist books.

1155   _____ . A Catena of Buddhist Scripture from the
          Chinese. See entry no. 34.

1156   _____ . Texts from the Buddhist Canon Commonly
          Known as Dhammapada. London: Trubner, 1878.
          176 p.
          Among the great body of books comprising the
Chinese Buddhist Canon, presented by the Japanese Government to the Library of the India Office, Mr. Beal discovered
a work bearing the title of "Law Verses, or Scriptural
Texts," which on examination was seen to resemble the Pali
version of Dhammapada in many particulars. The original
recension of the Pali text found its way into China in the
third century where the work of translation was finished, and
afterwards thirteen editorial sections added. The Dhammapada,
as hitherto known by the Pali Text Edition, as edited by Faus-
boll, Max Muller's English and A. Weber's German translations,

consists of only 26 chapters, but this book contains 39 sections. Mr. Beal has added to the great service he has already rendered to the comparative study of religious history.

1157   Browne, L. (ed.).   The World's Great Scriptures.
         New York: Macmillan, 1961.   554 p.
         All the classical religions are represented in this book with the addition of extracts from Babylonian and Egyptian works. Buddhism is squeezed into 73 pages. Theravada preponderates and Mahayana is covered in three short extracts. As an introduction this book has great merits. It is a reissue in paper covers of an original 1946 edition.

1158   Buddhaghosa.   The Path of Purification.   (Visuddhim-
         magga) Translated from the Pali by Bhikkhu Nana-
         moli.   Ceylon: R. Semage, 1956.   3 vols.   2nd
         edition published in 1964.   885 p.
         The name of Bhadantacariya Buddhaghosa is indissolubly linked with that of Ceylon. Circumstances leading to this connection, which gave rise to a revival of Pali Buddhism, are discussed in the brilliant introduction to this new translation of the venerable Buddhaghosa's great and sole surviving original work in a manner that meets all the requirements of modern historical investigation. His prime object was to study and master the complete body of Sinhalese commentary that had been built up during the nine centuries that separated him from the Buddha, and then to translate it into Pali.

1159   A Buddhist Bible.   Edited by D. Goddard.   2nd ed.
         See entry no. 9.

1160   Buddhist Mahayana Texts.   Translated by E. B.
         Cowell, F. Max Muller, and J. Takakusu. (Sacred
         Books of the East, XLIX.)   See entry no. 1026.

1161   Burlingame, E. W. (translator).   Buddhist Parables
         Translated from Original Pali.   See entry no. 794.

1162   Byles, M. B.   The Lotus and the Spinning Wheel.
         See entry no. 83.

1163   Chan, W. T.   The Platform Scripture.   Jamaica: St.
         John's University Press, 1963.   193 p.
         This is another complete English translation of the Tang-Ching of Hui-neng, known as the Sixth Patriarch of the Chan School of China. The original is one of the most

important documents of that school. It represents the
Chinese interpretation of the Indian concept of the Prajnaparamita (perfection of intuitional insight). The content of
this new translation differs greatly from others. It is
based on the version from the Tun-huang manuscripts.

1164   Conze, E. Abhisamayalankara; Introduction and Trans-
         lation from Original Text, with Sanskrit-Tibetan
         Index. Rome: Instituto Estremo Oriente, 1954.
         223 p.
         The Abhisamayalankara is the key to the Prajnapara-
mita Sutra. The text here published is a summary, in 273
memorial verses, of the Prajnaparamita, made about the
fourth century A.D. It is well provided with the necessary
explanations by the editor who gives scholarly terminology
and includes Sanskrit-Tibetan-English and Tibetan-Sanskrit
glossaries.

1165   _____ . Buddhist Scripture. Baltimore: Penguin
         Books, 1959. 250 p.
         This is an anthology of Buddhist texts, many newly
translated by the author. Major concepts represented are the
Buddha's former lives, the historical Buddha (Sakyamuni),
doctrines of morality and ethics, meditation, wisdom, and
points of controversy in Mahayana and Hinayana forms of
Buddhism. Ideas of Buddhist eschatology and the future
Buddha (maitreya) are presented. A short glossary of technical terms and a list of source citations are included.

1166   _____ . Buddhist Texts Through the Ages. New
         York: Philosophical Library, 1954. 300 p.
         This work is essentially a source book arranged in
four parts. The first part, I. B. Horner's translated selections from Pali scriptures, represents the teaching of
the Elders (Theravadina). The second part contains Conze's
translations from Sanskrit texts, setting forth basic Mahayana
notions in teachings of the New Wisdom (Prajnaparamita)
School, the Buddhism of faith, and doctrines of the Yoga-
carins. In part three David Snellgrove offers translations
from Tibetan Tantric literature. In part four Arthur Waley
furnishes extracts from texts on China and Japan. A bibliography, an index to sources and a glossary are also included.

1167   _____ et al. Buddhist Texts Through the Ages.
         New York: Harper, 1964. 322 p.

This work is newly translated from the original
Pali, Sanskrit, Chinese, Tibetan, Japanese and Apabhramsa.
The collection includes the widest possible range of materials, Hinayana and Mahayana, canonical and post canonical, through many centuries.   It gives a bibliography also.

1168 _____ . Buddhist Wisdom Books.   See entry no.
          1266.

1169 _____ . The Prajnaparamita Literature.   London:
          The Hague, 1960.   123 p.
This work presents a valuable, concise survey of
the Prajnaparamita literature in Sanskrit, Chinese and
Tibetan, together with the theories scholars have evolved
about it, and an annotated bibliography.   The author says in
the preface that this field, though vital to an understanding
of the Mahayana, has been somewhat neglected by European
scholars.

1170 Davids, C. A. F. R.   The Minor Anthologies of the
          Pali Canon.   London: Humphrey Milford, 1931.
          165 p.
The last of the five collections of Nikayas of the
Sutta-Pitaka in the Pali Canon is called Khuddaka, and of
its contents, which are mainly anthologies, the first two are
Khuddaka-Patha and Dhammapada.   Thus the present volume,
in taking the Dhammapada first, inverts the canonical order.
It is re-edited and translated by Mrs. Rhys Davids.

1171 Dayal, H.   The Bodhisattva Doctrine in Buddhist
          Sanskrit Literature.   See entry no. 300.

1172 Dhammapada.   The Buddha's Path of Virtues.   Madras,
          India: Theosophical House, 1929.   105 p.
This is a translation of the Dhammapada by F. L.
Woodward with a foreword by Sir Ponnambalm Arunachalam.
Dhammapada is a part of the Khuddaka Nikaya of the Buddhistic Canon and consists of about 420 stanzas in the sloka
meter.   It seems to be an anthology, prepared for Buddhists, of verses believed to be the real words of Buddha.

1173 _____ . The Dhammapada.   London: Luzac, 1900.
          94 p.
This is a collection of moral verses in Pali, edited
a second time, with a literal Latin translation and notes for
the use of the Pali student by V. Fausball.

1174 _____ . The Dhammapada. London: Murray, 1954.
         88 p.
      This is a lucid translation by Narada Thera from the
devout Buddhist point of view of one of the best-loved books
of Buddhism. This moral and ethical classic has been
rendered by Western scholars from a philological point of
view. Numerous explanatory footnotes are included, along
with an essay on the work by the eminent scholar, E. J.
Thomas.

1175 _____ . The Dhammapada; A Collection of Verse.
         Oxford: Clarendon Press, 1881. 99 p.
      One of the canonical books of the Buddhists, trans-
lated by F. Max Muller from the Pali, this is a scholarly
translation of the two most important Theravada Buddhist
texts, the Dhammapada and Sutta-Nipata. Footnotes and a
critical introduction are included.

1176 _____ . The Dhammapada; Translated from the
         Pali. See entry no. 288.

1177 _____ . The Dhammapada with Introductory Essays,
         Pali Text, English Translation and Notes by S.
         Radhakrishnan. London: Oxford University Press,
         1950. 194 p.
      With its introductions, explanatory notes and the
citation of many relevant and comparable passages from the
literature of other traditions, such as the Upanishads, the
Mahabharata, the Bhagavadgita and the Bible, Pali Buddhism
emerges as a teaching unmistakably belonging to the philo-
sophia perennis. In this practical and scholarly work we
have a presentation of the Dhammapada that is based on the
Indian outlook of the time.

1178 _____ . English Dhammapada. Boston: C. F.
         Libbie, 1889.
      This work presents the system of ethics law be-
queathed by Gautama Buddha, to which is appended some
account of the psychical experience of one who gained tem-
porarily the condition of Nirvana.

1179 _____ . Hymns of the Faith. See entry no. 205.

1180 _____ . The Path of the Eternal Law. Washington,
         D.C.: Self-Realization Fellowship, 1942. 286 p.
      This work is translated from the Pali text into
English with the purpose of bringing out the spiritual and
mystical significance of Buddha's words.

1181 _____. Texts from the Buddhist Canon Commonly
        Known as Dhammapada. See entry no. 1156.

1182 The Diamond Sutra and Other Buddhist Scriptures.
        The oldest printed book in the world, published in
        China in A.D. 868.
        The Diamond Sutra, a Chinese version of a Buddhist
scripture, was discovered in 1900 and is now possessed by
the British Museum. Printed from wooden blocks, this copy
of the Sutra is a roll 16 feet long and a foot wide and is made
up of seven sheets of paper pasted end to end. Six sheets
contain the text and one the woodcut frontispiece. It is a
picture of Buddhist monks listening to a religious discourse
by Buddha. At the end of the roll is the clear statement
that it was printed on May 11, 868, by Wang Chieh, for free
distribution, in order to perpetuate the memory of his parents.
Although this is the earliest known dated, printed book, and
Wang Chieh is the name of the first known printer, it is ob-
vious that this production was not the result of a sudden
miraculous discovery but could only have been made after a
long line of others had pioneered the printing of both pictures
and words.

1183 Digha-nikaya. Dialogues of Buddha. Translated from
        the Pali by T. W. R. Davids. London: Luzac,
        1956. 3 vols.
        This is an accurate translation of various basic sut-
tas (dialogues) of the Dighanikaya section of the Theravada
school of Buddhism. These scriptures may well represent
the oldest portions of the Buddhist Canon. A certain part is
entitled Sacred Books of the Buddhists.

1184 Dignaga, on Perception (The Pratyaksapariccheda of
        Dignaga's Pramanasamuccaya from the Sanskrit
        Fragments and the Tibetan Versions). Translated
        and annotated by Masaaki Hattori. Cambridge:
        Harvard University Press, 1968. 265 p.
        The Pratyaksapariccheda, as its name suggests,
deals with problems pertaining to perception. In the introduction the author gives the life and works of Dignaga.
Following are the main parts of the translation and notes to
the translation. There is a Sanskrit index of verses and
technical terms and a Tibetan index.

1185 Discourse on Elements (Dhatu-Katha). A translation
        with charts and explanation by U. Narada. London:
        Pali Text Society, 1963. 155 p.

The Dhatu-Katha is the third book of the Abhidhamma
Pitaka in Pali Canon, and the work under review is the first
translation of it to any Western language, undertaken by an
eminent Burmese scholar-monk known as Abhihamma. The
treatment of the subject in the original work is as laconic as
can be. The author says in his preface that the Dhatu-Katha
was expounded by the Buddha in order to dispel wrong views
of atta which is ego-entity, self, being.

1186 Dutt, N. Bauddhasangraha: An Anthology of Buddhist
      Sanskrit Texts. New Delhi: Sahitya Akademi, 1962.
      143 p.
      According to the preface to this work, the aim of
this anthology is two-fold: (i) primarily, to present a running account of Gautama Buddha's life with a brief survey
of his spiritual and philosophical teachings along with their
later developments and (ii) secondarily, to illustrate the
different types of Prakritic Sanskrit current at different
times among the Buddhist writers, mostly in the region of
Northwestern India, from the third century B.C. to the sixth
and seventh centuries A.D.

1187 Duyvandak, J. J. L. Tao Te Ching; The Book of the
      Way and Its Virtue. Translated and annotated by
      J. J. L. Duyvendak. London: John Murray, 1953.
      172 p.
      The Tao Te Ching ranks with the Bhagavad Gita and
The Voice of the Silence as one of the supreme scriptures of
mankind. In 1937 Mr. Chu Ta-Kao first translated it into
English. Now Professor Duyvendak of Leyden tries again
from the Western point of view and brings to his task the
wealth of scholarship and detailed analysis which he thinks
the subject demands.

1188 The Entrance to the Vinaya. See entry no. 769.

1189 Goddard, E. D. (ed.). A Buddhist Bible: The
      Favorite Scriptures of the Zen Sect. London:
      Theffold, 1956. 316 p.
      This gives a brief history of the Chan sect in China
(Zen in Japan). The Buddhist texts presented are the Lan-
kavatara Sutra, the Vajracehedika Sutra, part of the Maha-
Prajnaparamita Sutra, and the Sutra of the Sixth Chinese
Patriarch.

1190 _____. A Buddhist Bible [also see entry no. 9].
      Boston: Beacon Press, 1970. 677 p.

The basic contribution of this work is "its making conveniently available for general study a number of important Buddhists texts not easily accessible to general readers and students. The most notable of these texts are the Surangama Sutra, the Lankavatara Sutra, the awakening of faith in the Mahayana, the sutra spoken by the Sixth Patriarch, and the life and hymns of Milarepa. For the Theravada tradition the volume includes a summary of the life of Buddha, a compilation of Buddha's teaching drawn from a variety of sources, and two sutras emphasizing conduct and meditation."

1191 Growing the Bodhi Tree. The verses of the Dhammapada newly translated into English verse and rearranged in the order of the Buddhist way of training by Bhikkhu Khantipalo. Bangkok: Buddhist Association of Thailand, 1966. 93 p.

The idea of a rearrangement of the verses of the Dhammapada to show stages on the Path was suggested to the author by Mr. C. M. Chen. The stages, ten in number and preceded by "Prologue" and "The West Land," are well thought out, and such a presentation has the merit of making one look at this well known text with fresh eyes. For those who prefer the traditional order a concordance is provided, so there is no difficulty in finding any particular verse.

1192 Hamilton, C. H. Buddhism; A Religion of Infinite Compassion. New York: Liberal Arts, 1952. 189 p.

This is a good anthology of Buddhist texts translated from the Pali, Sanskrit, Chinese, Japanese, and Tibetan sources. Brief introductory comments are prefaced to the selections. An introduction to Buddhist literature, a glossary of technical terms, and a selective bibliography are given.

1193 Jaini, P. S. (ed.). Abhidharmadipa with Vibhashaprabhavtrti. Patna: Jayaswa Research Institute, 1959. 499 p. (Tibetan Sanskrit Works Series, 4.)

This work sheds great light on the discussion of Abhidharma topics in the fourth and fifth centuries. This is Sanskrit, but there is also an English introduction which explains a great deal that was so far obscure.

1194 Khuddakanikaya. Sayings of Buddha. New York: Columbia University, 1909.

A Pali work of the Buddhist Canon, this is translated for the first time with an introduction and notes by

J. H. Moore. The date and the author of the original are
unknown.

1195 Lankavatara-Sutra; A Mahayana Text. 2nd ed. Trans-
        lated from the original Sanskrit by D. T. Suzuki.
        London: Routledge, 1956. 300 p.
        This is a translation from the original Sanskrit of
one of the most important scriptures of Mahayana Buddhism.
The text treats numerous philosophical problems, such as
the doctrine of mind-only, dharmas, momentariness, nirvana,
the chain of causation, etc. The principal concepts are the
nature of consciousness and the impermanancy of the world.
The author's introduction discusses the roles of the Buddha
and Bodhisattva in a psychological and religious context.

1196 The Large Sutra on Perfect Wisdom, with Part 1 of
        the Abhisamayalankara.... See entry no. 1259.

1197 Mahayana Sutras. The Perfection of Wisdom: the
        Career of Predestined Scriptures. See entry no.
        1035.

1198 A Manual of Abhidhamma: Abhidammattha Sangaha,
        Vol. 1. Pali text, translation and explanatory notes
        by Narada Thera. Colombo, Ceylon: The Pali Text
        Society, 1956. 189 p.
        In 1884 the Pali Text Society published Abhidhammat-
tha-Sangaha; 26 years later, in 1910, appeared the very
notable joint translation into English by Shwe Zan Aung and
Mrs. Rhys Davids under the title of Compendium of Philosophy. In 1942 Indian author Bhikkhu J. Kashyap made a
second translation of this work and included the Pali original.
This work is the most recent work and the author's main
concern is to give a just and fair interpretation of the
Abhidhammattha-Sangaha so that it may be understood in the
sense intended by its author.

1199 Mindfulness of Breathing, Buddhist Texts from the
        Pali Canon and Extracts from the Pali Commen-
        taries. 2nd ed. See entry no. 456.

1200 Muller, F. M. Buddhist Texts from Japan. Oxford:
        Clarendon Press, 1881-1884. 3 vols.
        V1 The Diamond Cutter--1881; V2 The Land of
Bliss: part 1, text and translation of Sanghavarman's
Chinese version of the poetical portions of the Sukhavti-
vyuha; and part 2, Sanskrit text of the smaller Sukhavativyuha

--1883; V3 The Ancient Palm-leaves Containing the Prag-
naparamitahridaya-sutra--1884.

1201 Nikhilananda, S. The Upanishads: Translated from
        Sanskrit with Comprehensive Introduction Including
        Notes on the Commentary of Sri Sankarachrya.
        London: Phoenix House, 1943. V1 319 p.; V2
        389 p.
      The Upanishads may truly be described as the
foundation from which springs the spiritual insight of the
great Indian thinkers and sages. The Upanishads constitute
the background of the wisdom and teaching of the Sage of
the Sakyas, the Buddha. The reader will find in these
volumes a comprehensive account and translation of seven
principal Upanishads. These discussions range through
Svetasvatara, Prasna, Mandukya, Katha, Isa, Kena and
Mundaka.

1202 The Patimokkha with Introduction, Pali Text, Trans-
        lation and Notes. See entry no. 772.

1203 The Platform Sutra of the Sixth Patriarch: The Text
        of the Tun-huang Manuscript. See entry no. 1260.

1204 Prajnaparamita, Selections. Selected Sayings from
        the Perfection of Wisdom. See entry no. 1021.

1205 Ranasinghe, C. P. The Buddha's Explanation of the
        Universe. See entry no. 1248.

1206 The Saddharma-pundarika; or, the Lotus of the True
        Law. Translated by H. Kern. Oxford: Clarendon,
        1884. 454 p. (Sacred Books of the East, XXI.)
      This work is a translation from the Buddhist Sanskrit
original of the basic text of the Mahayana form of Buddhism.
The celestial qualities of the Buddha and the activities of the
Bodhisattvas (those destined to enlightenment) are given in
this somewhat heterogeneous scripture.

1207 Saddhatissa, H. The Buddha's Way. See entry no.
        1249.

1208 Santideva. The Path of Light; Rendered for the First
        Time into English.... See entry no. 1044.

1209 Snellgrove, D. L. The Hevajratanta: A Critical
        Study. London: Oxford University, 1959. 2 vols.
        (Oriental Series, v. 6.)

This critical study of an original Sanskrit text consists of two parts. Part one is a preface, an introduction and an English translation with commentary. Part two contains a side-by-side version of the Sanskrit and Tibetan texts as restored with the help of Tibetan commentaries, the chief commentary in Sanskrit which is called the Yogaratnamala, a Tibetan-Sanskrit-English vocabulary and a Sanskrit-Tibetan vocabulary.

1210 Stryk, L. (ed.). World of the Buddha: A Reader....
      See entry no. 125.

1211 Suttanipata. Buddha's Teachings; Being the Suttanipata,
      or, Discourse Collection. Translated from Pali by
      Lord Chalmers. Cambridge: Harvard; London:
      Oxford, 1932. 300 p. (Harvard Oriental Series,
      v. 37.)
      The Suttanipata (discourse collection) is a literary
translation of one of the oldest and most important Pali Buddhist scriptures. Many short texts are included, most of
which are still used in Buddhism today in Ceylon, Burma,
etc. The Pali text in Romanized transliteration appears
opposite the translation.

1212 Tripitaka. The Quest of Enlightenment; A Selection of
      the Buddhist Scriptures. Translated from Sanskrit
      by E. J. Thomas. London: Murray, 1950. 89 p.
      New York: Grove.
      This short anthology of Buddhist texts translated
from original Sanskrit sources attempts to bring out the
development of Mahayana Buddhism with its interpretation of
the events in the Buddha's life. The role of the Bodhisattva
and his vow as a savior and the Buddha as supramundane are
illustrated by selected passages. Several significant stories
and parables are also translated to indicate the role of the
Buddhist saint.

1213 _____. The Road to Nirvana: A Selection of the
      Buddhist Scripture. See entry no. 791.

1214 _____. The Vedantic Buddhism of the Buddha, a
      Collection of Historical Texts. Translated from
      Pali by J. G. Jennings. London: Oxford, 1948.
      679 p.
      This is an anthology of many texts belonging to
Theravada (Southern) Buddhism. The major topics include
the Buddha and his doctrine (dhamma) and order (sangha).

Numerous supplementary texts bearing on points of the
doctrine and organization of the order, extensive critical
notes, cross references, and source citations are also included. These historical texts are probably misrepresented
and their worth considerably diminished by the reference to
"Vedantic" in the title.

1215   Tucci, G. Minor Buddhist Texts. New York: Para-
          gon, 1956. 312 p.
      Six of the Sanskrit manuscripts which Professor
Tucci has found on his travels in Tibet and Nepal are here
edited together with their Tibetan and Chinese translations.
Asanga's 70 verses on the "Diamond Sutra," Nagarjuna's 20
verses on the "Mahayana," and Kambalapada's nine verses on
"Prajnaparamita" are three of the texts.

1216   Vajrachchedika. Buddhist Wisdom Books Containing the
          Diamond Sutra and the Heart Sutra. See entry no.
          1266.

1217   Vajrachchedika Prajnaparamita. See entry no. 1059.

1218   Visuddhimagga of Buddhaghosacariya. Edited by
          H. C. Warren. Cambridge: Harvard University
          Press, 1950. 617 p. (Harvard Oriental Series,
          v. 41.)
      This is the most useful text of one of the greatest
works of Pali Buddhism. It contains a brief treatment of
Buddhaghosa's life and work.

1219   Waley, A. Monkey Wucheng-en. Translated from
          the Chinese by A. Waley. Baltimore: Penguin,
          1961. 350 p.
      This is a delightful tale, in which, some 900 years
after the events, are recorded the legends arising from the
pilgrimage of Tripitaka to India in the seventh century A.D.
in order to obtain the Buddhist scripture.

1220   Warren, H. C. Buddhism in Translations; Passages
          Selected from the Buddhist Sacred Books. Trans-
          lated from Pali. Cambridge: Harvard, 1953.
          496 p.
      This is the best anthology of Pali Buddhist texts
translated by one of America's most competent scholars.
Representative texts are classified under such major
headings as the Buddha, Sentient Existence, Karma and
Re-birth, Meditation and Nirvana, and the Order.

1221 The Wisdom Gone Beyond. Translated from Tibetan,
        Sanskrit, and Pali by various ones. Bangkok:
        Social Science Association of Thailand, 1967. 135 p.
        This is an anthology of six works from Tibetan,
Sanskrit, and Pali sources. The aims of the book are to
make available to Theravada Buddhists something of other
traditions, and to show their similarities since the differences have been too much noticed. Of the book's six chapters, three are devoted to Prajnaparamita literature. The
book finishes with a short section on the Ten Perfections of
the Bodhisattva. Most of the illustrations are Tibetan and
this work is for those who practice the Dhamma.

1222 Won Buddhist Half-Centennial Commemoration Commis-
        sion, Buddhist Federation of Korea. The Canonical
        Textbook of Won Buddhism. See entry no. 682.

                              SERMONS

1223 Allen, G. F. Buddha's Words of Wisdom. See
        entry no. 1152.

1224 Buddhism: A Religion of Infinite Compassion, ed. by
        C. H. Hamilton. See entry no. 1192.

1225 Burtt, E. A. (ed.). The Teachings of the Compas-
        sionate Buddha. New York: New American Library,
        1955. 247 p.
        This is a useful and inexpensive anthology based on
existing translations of Buddhist religious and philosophical
writings. The fundamental sermons of the Buddha and his
parables are represented; Mahayana religious ideals, and
devotional Buddhism in China and Japan, are included.

1226 Carus, P. Gospel of Buddha. Chicago: Open Court
        Pub. Co., 1917 (reprinted 1969). 310 p.
        This work contains ideas for which prototypes can
be found somewhere among the traditions of Buddhism, and
which have been added as elucidations of its main principles.

1227 Coomaraswamy, A. K. Buddha and the Gospel of
        Buddhism. New York: Harper and Row, 1964.
        369 p.

The aim of this book is to set forth as simply as
possible the gospel of Buddhism, according to the Buddhist
scriptures, and to consider the Buddhist systems in relation.
One chapter discusses the contemporary philosophical environment of Buddha, and Buddhist art, literature, sculpture, and
painting. It gives a glossary of Pali and Sanskrit terms.

1228   Davids, C. A. F. R.   What Was the Original Gospel
       in Buddhism?   London: The Epworth Press, 1938.
       143 p.
       This work seeks to answer what is the original
Buddhism from which both Hinayana and Mahayana Buddhism
come.   Emphasis on ideas such as the time and place in
which Buddha's teaching took birth make the answer both
possible and plausible.

1229   Gautama Buddha.   Sayings of Buddha.   New York:
       Peter Pauper, 1957.   61 p.
       This work of Buddha's quotations is illustrated with
wood-engravings by Boyd Hanna.

1230   Hui-Neng.   The Sutra of Wei Lang.   See entry no. 547.

1231   Koros, A. C.   The Life and Teaching of Buddha.
       Calcutta: Susil Cupta, 1957.   143 p.
       This volume is made up of two papers which origi-
nally appeared in The Asiatic Researches.   The first paper,
"Notices on the Life of Shakya" is extracted from the Tibetan
authorities and the second is "Analysis of the Dulva," a
portion of the Tibetan work.

1232   Stryk, L. and Ikenoto, T. (eds.).   Zen; Poems,
       Prayers, Sermons, Anecdotes, Interviews.   See
       entry no. 1122.

1233   Tripitaka.   The Road to Nirvana; A Selection of the
       Buddhist Scripture.   See entry no. 791.

1234   Watts, A. W.   The Wisdom of Insecurity: A Message
       for an Age of Anxiety.   London: Rider, 1954.
       126 p.
       The author has been writing, more or less, the same
book right through a spiritual odyssey which has taken him
from Christianity to Zen, then back to a wider Christianity,
and ultimately to Zen again.   This is an important book
heavily laden with a rich cargo of spiritual news.   The
author maintains that insecurity is the result of seeking to

feel secure, and that greater insight and strength and satisfaction come from the awareness that our impermanence and
insecurity are inescapable in life.

1235 Wong, J. Buddha, His Life and Teaching. See entry
      no. 364.

SOCIOLOGY and ANTHROPOLOGY

1236 Malalasekera, G. P. Buddhism and the Race Question.
      Paris: UNESCO, 1958. 73 p.
      Two Ceylonese Buddhist scholars investigate their
Buddhistic view of distinctions between men on the basis of
skin color or other physical appearances. "This brief work
will serve to demonstrate the incompatibility of a doctrine of
sharply differentiated breeds of men with the discovery by
the penetrating observers of man in every generation of a
common humanity which transcends the accidents of birth or
station."

1237 Spiro, M. E. Buddhism and Society: A Great Tradi-
      tion and Its Burmese Vicissitudes. See entry no.
      995.

1238 Tambiah, S. J. Buddhism and the Spirit Cults in
      Northeast Thailand. London: Cambridge University,
      1971. 388 p.
      The author examines the relationship of the religious
practices of the villagers to the classical Buddhist tradition.
It is a detailed, penetrating account of selected aspects of
supernaturalism among the residents of a village in Northeast Thailand. An outstanding contribution to our knowledge
of Thai peasant religious activities, it demonstrates the value
of anthropology's concern with the present as a means of
better understanding the past.

1239 Weber, M. The Religion of India, the Sociology of
      Hinduism and Buddhism. See entry no. 615.

STUDY and TEACHING

1240   Csoma, S.   Life and Teachings of Buddha.   Calcutta:
          Gupta, 1957.   143 p.
          This work originally appeared in 1836.   It will be
useful for students of the history of European research into
Buddhism, but, viewed as an analysis of the Vinaya section
of the Kanjur, they are now, over a century later, inevitably
out of date.   To fill their volume, the publishers have added
an anonymous article on the literature of Tibet.

1241   Davids, C. A. F. R.   What Was the Original Gospel
          in Buddhism?   See entry no. 1228.

1242   Jivaka, S.   Growing Up into Buddhism.   See entry
          no. 414.

1243   Maurice, D.   The Lion's Roar; An Anthology of the
          Buddha's Teachings Selected from Pali Canon.
          London: Rider, 1962.   253 p.
          The author has chosen his material with great dis-
crimination and discernment.   He emphasizes that the Buddha's teaching must be based on the concept of God and on
an understanding of the philosophical teaching, which gives
access to the goal by means of mental discipline and mental
detachment.

1244   Nyanatiloka, B.   The Word of the Buddha.   13th rev.
          ed.   Kandy, Ceylon: Buddhist Publication Society,
          1959.   97 p.
          This is an outline of the teaching of the Buddha in
the words of the Pali Canon.

1245   Ouspensky, P. D.   The Fourth Way.   London: Rout-
          ledge and Kegan Paul, 1957.   446 p.
          Four ways are characterized by the predominance of
different centers of functions postulated by the author: the
instinctive and the moving center in the fakir, the emotional
center in the monk, the intellectual center in the Yogi and a
harmonious balance of all centers in the adept of the fourth
way.

1246   Rahula, W.   What the Buddha Taught.   With a foreword
          by P. Demieville.   Bedford, England: Gordon
          Fraser Dufour, 1967.   103 p.
          These are the essential teachings of the Buddha as

found in the Pali Canon. It is almost exclusively on these
that the author bases his work, constantly quoting them and
referring to them. Authoritative and clear, logical and
sober, and far more than a mere outline, this study is as
comprehensive as it is masterly in its grouping of the leading
concepts of the teachings. The Four Noble Truths and the
Eightfold Path are explained very clearly.

1247 Ram, N. S. Seeking Wisdom. See entry no. 140.

1248 Ranasinghe, C. P. The Buddha's Explanation of the
      Universe. Colombo, Ceylon: Colombo University
      Press, 1957. 414 p.
      The work attempts the difficult task of giving a
popular account of the contents of the Abhidhamma Pitaka.
At best it may be said that Abhidhamma forms only a very
general basis for the contents. A great deal of information
is taken from the Suttas and commentarial literature, together with the author's own interpretations.

1249 Saddhatissa, H. The Buddha's Way. London: Allen
      and Unwin, 1971. 139 p.
      This is the simplest and most understandable intro-
duction to the teachings of the Buddha. In addition to his
exposition of Buddhist principles and practices, Dr. Saddhatissa includes a selection from the Pali scriptures, a
chronological table of Buddhist history, and a glossary. The
book's value is greatly enhanced by translations of the Satipatthana, Sigalovada, Dhammika, Mangala, Parabhava and
Vyagghapajja Suttas, together with a selection from the
Dhammapada. The final chapter is devoted to bhavana
(meditation). Clear instructions are given both in Samatha
(tranquillity) and Vipassana (insight) practices which may
preclude the necessity of an actual guru.

1250 Thera, P. The Buddha's Ancient Path. See entry
      no. 338.

1251 Walker, K. The Making of Man. London: Routledge
      and Kegan Paul, 1963. 163 p.
      This book, which introduces the system of training
evolved by Gurdjieff after his many wanderings in the East,
is a very good interpretation of Eastern esoteric teachings
to the West and is well worth reading by those studying Buddhism. The author, discovered through Ouspensky, emphasizes the possibility of man's evolution towards self. And
also he stresses that man's personality must be rendered

more passive in order that the more real parts of himself,
the essence, should be given a better chance to grow.

1252   Watts, A.   The Deep in View.   London: Fifth Estate
           Press, 1971.   17 p.
           The author's answers to questions about faith,
responsibility, authority, and technology are rewarding to
read.

SUTRA

1253   Buddhist Mahayana Texts.   (Sacred Books of the East,
           XLIX.)   See entry no. 1026.

1254   The Diamond Sutra and Other Buddhist Scriptures; The
           Oldest Printed Book in the World (China, A.D. 868).
           See entry no. 1182.

1255   The Diamond Sutra and the Sutra of Hui Neng.   Trans-
           lated by A. F. Price and Wong Mou-Lam.   Berkeley,
           Cal.:   Shambhala Booksellers, 1969.   114 p.
           This paperback edition contains the translations of
two most important texts of the Mahayana school of Buddhism.
The first is the Diamond Sutra, an English translation of the
Vajracchedika Prajnaparamita Sutra by the editor.   The
second is the Sutra of Hui Neng translated by Wong Mou-Lam.

1256   Guenther, H. V.   Treasure on the Tibetan Middle Way.
           See entry no. 738.

1257   Hui-Neng.   The Sutra of Wei Lang.   See entry no. 547.

1258   Lankavatara-Sutra; A Mahayana Text.   See entry no.
           1195.

1259   The Large Sutra on Perfect Wisdom; With the
           Divisions of the Abhisamayalankara.   Part 1 trans-
           lated by E. Conze.   London: Luzac, 1961.   203 p.
           The Oriental Studies Foundation of London sponsored
this translation project.   It contains the first third of the
large Prajnaparamita.   The author says in his introduction
that this Sutra can be summed up in two sentences, with the
idea that one should become a Bodhisattva, someone content

with nothing less than all knowledge attained through the perfection of wisdom for the sake of all living beings.

1260   The Platform Sutra of the Sixth Patriarch: The Text
       of the Tun-huang Manuscript. Translated with in-
       troduction by P. B. Yampolsky. New York: Colum-
       bia University Press, 1967. 216 p. plus 30 p. of
       Chinese text.
       This is a basic text of Zen Buddhism, originating in
China in the ninth century. Dr. Yampolsky, a lecturer in
Japanese at Columbia, presents the history of the sutra,
varying versions, the biography of Hui-neng (founder of
Chan [Zen] Buddhism), and extensive critical comment. The
value in this work is that the author has collected and collated as much knowledge as possible about Hui-Neng himself
and the evolution of the Platform Sutra. This translation is
of the original Tun-huang manuscript, the earliest known
version of the text.

1261   Saddharmapundarika. The Saddharma-Pundarika; or
       the Lotus of the True Law. See entry no. 1206.

1262   The Surangama Sutra. Translated by Upasaka L. K.
       Yu. London: Rider, 1966. 262 p.
       This work reveals the law of causality relating to
both delusion and enlightenment. It aims at breaking up
alaya, the store of consciousness whose characteristics are
self-evidencing perception and form, by means of the three
meditative studies of noumenon which is immaterial, of
phenomenon which is unreal and of the mean which is inclu-
sive of both; and all this leads to the all-embracing Surangama Samadhi which is the gateway to Perfect Enlightenment and reveals the nature of the Tathagata Store of one
reality.

1263   Suzuki, D. T. The Lankavatara Sutra. See entries
       no. 1055, 1195.

1264   _____. Studies in Lankuvatava Sutra. See entry
       no. 1055.

1265   _____. The Zen Doctrine of No-Mind; Significance
       of the Sutra of Hui-neng. See entry no. 1137.

1266   Vajrachchedika. Buddhist Wisdom Books Containing
       Diamond Sutra and the Heart Sutra. Translated by
       E. Conze. Illustrated. London: Allen and Unwin,
       1958. 110 p.

From the large number of works which the Buddhists
have devoted to Prajnaparamita, or "The Perfection of
Wisdom, " Dr. Conze has selected two short texts which contain all the essential teachings and which for centuries have
enjoyed an immense popularity in China, Korea, and Japan,
as well as in Mongolia and Tibet. This is a translation from
the Buddhist Sanskrit original, interspersed with the author's
critical comments on various sections. The Romanized
Sanskrit of the Heart Sutra is included.

1267 _____ . The Diamond Sutra; or, The Jewel of
           Transcendental Wisdom. 2nd ed. See entry no.
           561.

1268 Vajrachchedika Prajnaparamita. See entry no. 1059.

1269 The Vimalakirti. Translated by Lu Kuan Yu. London:
           Kegan Paul, 1973. 157 p.
           Since 1960 Lu Kuan Yu has given Dharma students
in the West a series of translations of Mahayana Sutras and
commentaries from the Chinese. It is of particular relevance to Western Buddhists who are mostly laymen rather
than members of the Sangha, as it is the one Sutra that is
spoken by a layman.

1270 Yampolsky, P. B. The Platform Sutra of the Sixth
           Patriarch. See entry no. 1260.

                          THEOSOPHY

1271 Blavatsky, H. P. An Abridgement of the Secret
           Doctrine. London: Theosophical Publishing House,
           1907. 583 p. [also see entry no. 291].
           This work is a careful selection of the essential
material, in the author's own words, compiled from the
original 1888 edition by Elizabeth Preston and Christmas
Humphreys.

1272 _____ . H. P. Blavatsky, Collected Writings.
           V. 6 (1883-1885). Los Angeles: Blavatsky Writings
           Publications Fund, 1955. 480 p.
           The period under review covers three vital years in
the history of the theosophical movement, but the main

interest is to the Buddhist.   The remarks on the Buddha's possibly too full disclosure of the higher truths of the Buddha-Dhamma, the relationship of Sankaracharya to Gautama the Buddha, the causes of the expulsion of Buddhism from India are all included.

1273 _____. The Key to Theosophy.   London: Theo-
        sophical Publishing House, 1889.   310 p.
        This is a clear exposition in the form of question and answer of the ethics, science, and philosophy of theosophy, for the study of which the universal brotherhood and theosophical society has been founded.   It contains a huge glossary of general theosophical terms.

YOGA

1274 Aurobindo, Sri.   The Synthesis of Yoga; More Lights
        on Yoga.   London: Watkins, 1948.   5 vols.
        This work gives a recapitulation in everyday terms of the great scripture of Karma Yoga.   The method is called synthetic because it relates the three paths of knowledge, devotion and works into one process leading to that state which is the meaning of yoga.

1275 Chang, G. C. C.   Teachings of Tibetan Yoga.   New
        York: University Books, 1963.   128 p.
        The author is a Chinese Buddhist who trained under Tibetan instructors.   Here in his work he sets out to give the Western reader an idea of the workings of the Tantric methods under the double heading of Mahamudra and six yogas of Naropa.   The author's version is concrete and practical, rather than philosophical or psychological.   He gives useful notes that accompany each section of the text and an explanation of various Sanskrit names and other technical terms.

1276 Diang, U. T.   The Doctrines of Paticcasamuppada.
        Rangoon: Society for the Propagation of Vipassana,
        1968.   132 p.
        This work is an exposition and practical application of emancipation from Samsara and has been written specifically for the yogi to gain access to a path of deliverance from suffering and to acquaint English readers with its

methods and practices, without the necessity of learning
Pali.

1277 Danielou, A. Yoga; The Method of Reintegration.
        New York: University Books, 1955. 164 p.
        The author argues in his work that Buddhism is
fundamentally yogic. He warns that the student of yoga
must be critical and wary because the analysis of the human
body and mind is so penetrating in some of the Upanishads
that the uninstructed may easily do harm to themselves.
This work is based on extracts from Sanskrit treatises,
with a short introduction by the author.

1278 Eliade, M. Yoga: Immortality and Freedom.
        Translated by W. R. Trask from the French. Lon-
        don: Routledge and Kegan Paul, 1958. 529 p.
        A comprehensive survey of yoga, with its origins
and development described by the author who gives references to the texts involved, the work concerns yoga and
Hinduism, yoga and Buddhism, yoga and Tantrism, yoga and
alchemy, yoga and aboriginal India, all in the author's point
of view. The scope of the book makes it valuable but some
of the detail may be open to scholarly criticism.

1279 Haich, E. Sexual Energy and Yoga. Translated from
        German by D. Q. Stephenson. London: George
        Allen and Unwin, 1972. 158 p.
        The world-famed co-author of Yoga and Health here
turns her profound understanding of the human soul and yoga
to the nature of sexuality. She helps readers come to terms
with their own situation by liberation as they transmute it to
reach the higher levels of awareness.

1280 Iyengar, B. K. S. Light on Yoga. London: Allen
        and Unwin, 1971. 342 p.
        Over 200 postures, 14 breathing exercises and 600
illustrations are presented in this work. However, probably
most of the postures are impossible for the average practitioner to attain. But the choices are astounding.

1281 Krishna, G. Kundalini, the Evolutionary Energy in
        Man. See entry no. 451.

1282 Krishna Prem, Sri. The Yoga of the Bhagavad Gita.
        London: J. M. Watkins, 1938. 220 p.
        The Gita is based on direct knowledge of reality and
of the path that leads to that reality. In this book Gita is a

textbook of yoga, a guide to the treading of the path. By
yoga is here meant the path by which man unites his finite
self with infinite being.

1283 McCartney, J. Yoga: The Key to Life. London:
      Rider, 1968. 233 p.
      The author points out in this comprehensive survey
of the aims and practices of yoga teaching that the preparation is most important. He contends that yoga is designed
to unify physical, mental and spiritual planes of existence,
that one without the other would be incomplete. This work
gives place to all of the branches of Yoga such as: Hatha
Yoga, Bhakti Yoga, Karma Yoga, Raja Yoga, and Jnana
Yoga for the path of Enlightenment.

1284 Rutledge, D. D. In Search of a Yogi. London:
      Routledge and Kegan Paul, 1962. 321 p.
      The author is a Roman Catholic priest who went to
India in order to start a Benedictine monastery for Indian
monks. The work can be recommended as a travel book
giving vivid pictures of the everyday life and customs of
Indians in a range of different classes, and it gives some
knowledge of the spiritual teachings of India.

1285 Suzuki, S. Zen Mind, Beginner's Mind. See entry
      no. 471.

1286 Thomas, E. J. The History of Buddhist Thought. 2nd
      ed. See entry no. 405.

1287 Van Lysebeth, A. Yoga Self Taught. London: George
      Allen and Unwin, 1971. 190 p.
      Traditionalists say one must have a teacher, but
that brings back the question, "Who taught the first teacher?"
This book is excellent, but it seems that too much space is
devoted to only nine postures.

1288 Von Durckheim, K. G. Hara: The Vital Centre of
      Man. London: Allen and Unwin, 1962. 208 p.
      Professor Durckheim's book deals with a fascinating
theme--Hara, or "the belly" and its place in Japanese culture.
In most systems of Yoga the solar plexus is recognized to
be an important center of spiritual energy. In Japan Hara
is esteemed as the inner physical center of gravity, corres-
ponding to a state of psychological and spiritual unity. According to this idea the enlightenment comes to a man living
not from his conscious ego but in accordance to Hara.

1289 Walker, K. Diagnosis of Man. See entry no. 938.

1290 Wood, E. E. Practical Yoga, Ancient and Modern.
      London: Rider, 1955. 227 p.
      This work is a new translation from the Sanskrit of
the Aphorisms of Patanjali with a comprehensive commentary
by Professor Wood. Beginning with the three basic units of
matter, energy and law (Karma), the author shows the paral-
lel disciplines of body-conditioning, mind-conditioning and
attentiveness to God, thus presenting Patanjali's theory of
Yoga. The author lived in India for 38 years and is a
Sanskrit scholar, making him a highly suitable person to
offer this new translation.

1291 _____. Yoga. Baltimore: Penguin Books, 1959.
      271 p.
      This is an ideal introduction to the techniques and
philosophy of Yoga. It covers the entire scope of classical
literature on Yoga and is recommended by the author's own
experiences with advanced Hindu practitioners. He writes in
simple terms of the awakening of the higher mind, the self-
realization of the spirit and the discovery of God.

1292 Yesudian, S. and Haich, E. Raja Yoga. London:
      George Allen and Unwin, 1971. 100 p.
      This short work especially concerns meditation and
the study and practice of the Eight Limbs. The authors sum
it up shortly also with the advice to live moderately, a senti-
ment expected to appeal to followers of the Middle Way.

MISCELLANEOUS

1293 Beckett, L. C. Unbounded Worlds. London: Ark
      Press, 1959. 95 p.
      Deeply versed in the literature of modern astronomy,
the author boldly examines the present contending theories on
the origin of the universe, pointing out that this is based on,
of all documents, the Lankavatara Sutra.

1294 Brown, E. E. The Tasajara Bread Book. Berkeley,
      Cal.: Shambhala Publications, 1971.
      Here is a breadmaking guide that stands on profound
respect for simple, wholesome ingredients and a ripening,

maturing, blossoming process, that turns a glob of dough
into a fragrant food fit for any man's meal.   There are
recipes for breads yeasted and unyeasted, fruit-filled loaves,
sourdough, pancakes, pastries, muffins, and various favorite
snacks from the Tassajara kitchen.   This Zen cook knows
the true nature of bread.

1295 Coleman, J. E.   The Quiet Mind.   London: Rider,
        1971.   238 p.
        John Coleman was an espionage agent for the Ameri-
can Central Intelligence Agency for 12 years and it was
during this period while stationed in Bangkok that he experienced an incident that led to an almost world-wide investigation of occult philosophy and religion.   The book
gives account of how he reached the quiet and peaceful state
of Nirvana.

1296 Dahlke, P.   Buddhism and Science.   New York: Mac-
        millan, 1927.   256 p.
        Dr. Dahlke is one of the chief European exponents
of Buddhism as a living faith, and his exposition here of
the world-theory presented by Buddhism, of the relation of
that faith to physics, biology, the problem of thought, etc.
deserves the close attention of students of Buddhist thought.

1297 Frank, R. O.   The Buddhist Councils at Rajagaha and
        Vesali.   London: Journal of the Pali Text Society,
        1908.
        This is a very close examination of the sources on
the two first councils, with the conclusion that they never
happened, at least as Buddhists understood them.

1298 Gabb, J. W.   The Goose Is Out.   London: Buddhist
        Society, 1956.   120 p.
        This work is simply written and therein lies its
strength and beauty, for it touches close upon a moving,
active mind in all the freshness of its continuous re-birth.

1299 Hackman, H. F.   Buddhism as a Religion.   2nd ed.
        London: W. C. Probsthain and Co., 1910.   315 p.
        This is a description of the essentials and a criti-
cism of the character of Chinese monasticism.

1300 Horner, I. B.   Women Under Primitive Buddhism.
        London: Routledge and Sons; New York: Dutton,
        1930.   391 p.
        In this inquiry into the position of women prior to

Buddhism, and during the rise of the Buddhist religion, Miss
Horner proves that woman's status greatly improved with the
advance of Buddhist propaganda. In part one, she discusses
the mother, the daughter, the wife, the widow, and the woman
worker. Part two is concerned with the religious life of
women.

1301 Koestler, A. The Lotus and the Robot. See entry
      no. 1092.

1302 Mayhew, C. Men Seeking God. London: Allen and
      Unwin, 1955. 145 p.
      The author has given a summary of six religions.
Each exponent gives his conception of God, and the outcome
of this belief in his life of prayer and service. A personal
anthology of the scriptures and other literature has been
chosen for each one. There is also a short bibliography at
the end of the book to aid in further study. In the last
chapter the author discusses the psychological and scientific
findings with these religious beliefs.

1303 Northbourne, Lord. Looking Back on Progress.
      Bedfont: Perennial Books, 1971. 122 p.
      Buddhists will find interest in this book even if they
do not entirely accept all of his Lordship's theories, but
we all confirm the necessity to "look within" and his assertion that man's search is for freedom from bondage. These
bonds, he says, are self-created and therefore must be and
can be self-erased. Supposedly the Buddha taught how that
can be achieved.

1304 Radhakrishnan, S. Recovery of Faith. London: G.
      Allen, 1956. 205 p.
      Professor Radhakrishnan was Vice President of
India. This is a plea for a spiritual awakening and for
interreligious friendship. The book is filled to the brim
with unexceptionable sentiments, and many are the warnings
it contains against contempt for religions other than one's
own.

1305 Skutch, A. The Golden Core of Religion. London:
      George Allen and Unwin, 1971. 270 p.
      This book develops the view that religion's chief
contribution to humanity has been its capacity to care deeply
about things. The author describes religion as "Life's"
ceaseless effort to preserve and perfect itself, to become
at last self-conscious, foreseeing and in consequence fearful
amid the thousand perils that beset it.

1306   Spiritual Disciplines: Papers from the Eranos Year-
          books.   London: Routledge and Kegan Paul, 1960.
          506 p.
          This book contains 12 selected papers originally
published in German, which were delivered between 1933
and 1948 during the annual meetings of distinguished scholars
held at Ascona in Switzerland.

1307   Suzuki, D. T.   Shin Buddhism.   New York: Harper,
          1970.   93 p.
          This is a transcription of five Suzuki lectures taped
in 1958 at the New York Buddhist assembly.   Suzuki explores
the Pure Land Sect of Buddhism, which began in China and
reached its ultimate development with Shin thought in Japan.
The author develops the Shin Sect's focus upon Amida Buddha
and the joining of Amida with the individual in the expression
of oneness.

AUTHOR, EDITOR, TRANSLATOR INDEX

TITLE INDEX

235